# HOW THINGS WORK

**Editor:** Thomas Keegan
**Design:** David West Children's
Book Design
**Consultant:** Rowena Knox

The publishers would like to thank
the following artists for contributing
to this book:

Graham Austin (The Garden Studio)
pp. 124–129; Peter Bull pp. 14–17,
18–27, 32–35, 40–43, 52–61, 108–
123, 134–145; Neil Bulpitt pp. 44–47,
86–99; Peter Gregory (Introductory
illustrations) pp. 44, 48, 62, 68, 74,
78, 82, 86, 92, 96, 104, 106; Aziz Khan
pp. 62–65, 68–73, 100–107;
Ian Moores pp. 36–39, 48–51, 74–85,
92–95, 130–133; Alex Pang, cover;
Rob Shone (Introductory
illustrations) pp. 15, 18, 24, 28, 32,
36, 40, 52, 56, 58, 108, 114, 116, 120,
130, 134, 138, 142.

Kingfisher Books, Grisewood and Dempsey Ltd
Elsley House, 24–30 Great Titchfield Street,
London W1P 7AD

First published in 1990 by Kingfisher Books

6 8 10 9 7 5

© Grisewood & Dempsey Limited 1990

BRITISH LIBRARY CATALOGUING IN PUBLICATION DATA
Parker, Steve, 1952–
How things work.
1. Technology
I. Title
600

ISBN 0-86272-573-9

Phototypeset by Southern Positives and Negatives (SPAN),
Lingfield, Surrey
Printed in Italy

# THE KINGFISHER BOOK OF
# HOW THINGS WORK

## STEVE PARKER

Kingfisher Books

# CONTENTS

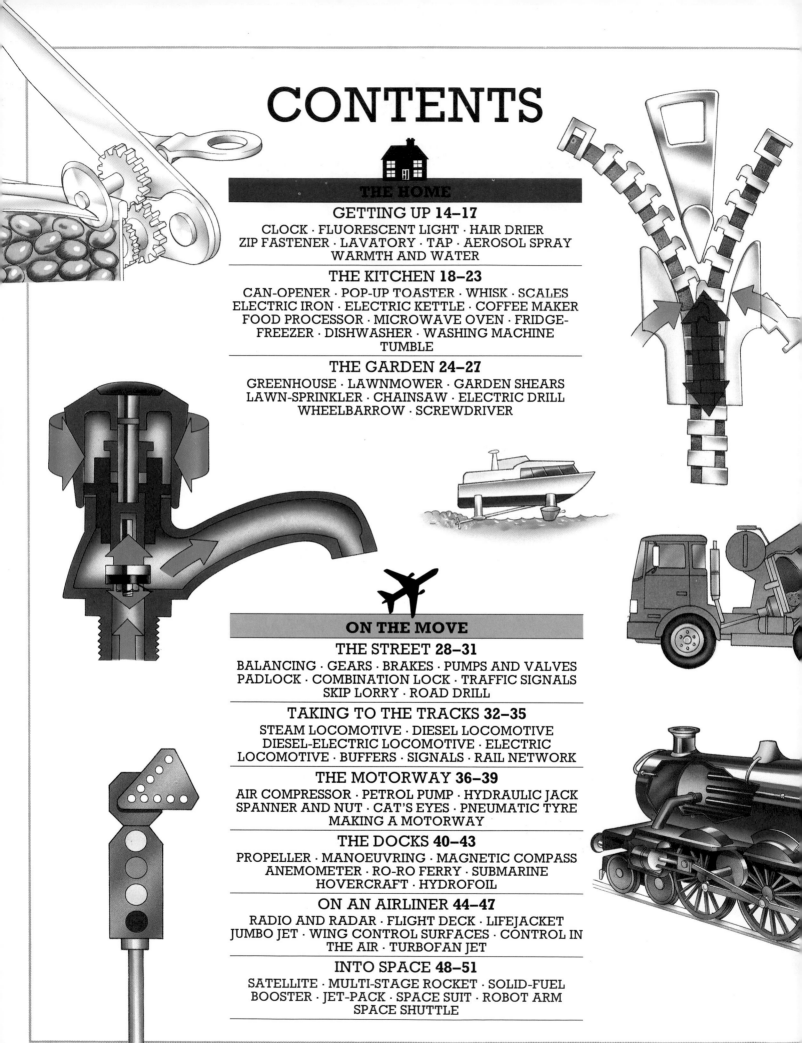

## BUILDING AND CONSTRUCTION

### ON THE BUILDING SITE 52–55

DIGGER · TOWER CRANE · UNDERGROUND SERVICES
DRILLING AND PILEDRIVING · RIVETS AND WELDS
CONCRETE MIXER · SPIRIT LEVEL · LIFT

### BRIDGES 56–57

TYPES OF BRIDGE · SPANNING THE RIVER
NUTS AND BOLTS · THEODOLITE

### TUNNELS 58–61

TUNNEL STRUCTURE · TUNNEL-BORING MACHINE
PISTON RELIEF DUCT · SUMP PUMP · FIRE DETECTOR
FIRE EXTINGUISHER · 'DO-DO' TRAIN

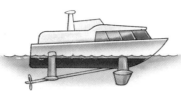

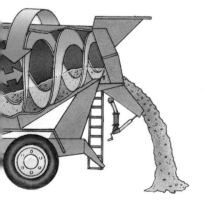

## POWER AND SERVICES

### OIL EXPLORATION 62–67

RIGS AND PLATFORMS · DRILLING · EXPLORATION RIG
PRODUCTION PLATFORM · DIVING EQUIPMENT
HELICOPTER

### POWER STATIONS 68–73

COAL-FIRED POWER STATION · ELECTRICITY
DISTRIBUTION · NUCLEAR POWER STATION · STEAM
TURBINES · GENERATOR · HYDROELECTRIC POWER
STATION · TIDAL POWER STATION

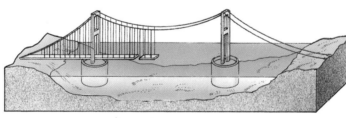

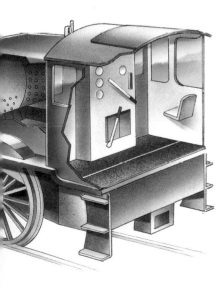

## COMMUNICATIONS

### THE NEWSROOM 74–77

TELEPHONE · OPTICAL FIBRE · MOBILE PHONE
BALLPOINT PEN · FAX MACHINE · COMPUTER
PRINTERS · BINOCULARS · SLR CAMERA

### PRINTING A BOOK 78–81

TYPESETTER · COLOUR SCANNER · PRINTING
METHODS · COLOUR PRINTING · PRINTING PRESS
PHOTOCOPIER

### THE TELEVISION STUDIO 82–85

AUTOCUE · TELEVISION CAMERA · RHEOSTAT
ANIMATION · SATELLITE TELEVISION

## SPORTS AND GAMES

### GRAND PRIX CIRCUIT 86–91
RACING CAR · SUSPENSION, STEERING AND BRAKES
PETROL ENGINE · CLUTCH AND GEARBOX · ENGINE
LAYOUTS · DIFFERENTIAL

### THE SPORTS CENTRE 92–95
LIGHT METER · TURNSTILE · BAR CODE
LCD STOPWATCH · SOCCER BALL · SAILS AND
SAILING · SHOOTING · BOUNCING

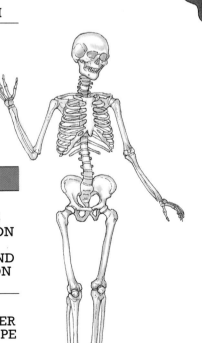

## FACTORY AND INDUSTRY

### PRODUCTION LINE 96–103
IRON · STEEL · SHAPING METALS · ALUMINIUM
ALLOYS · ELECTROPLATING · GLASS-MAKING
GLASS-BLOWING · SAFETY GLASS · GLASS
CONTAINERS · CAR PRODUCTION

### TEXTILES 104–105
NATURAL FIBRES · SPINNING · ARTIFICIAL FIBRES
WEAVING

### THE REFINERY 106–107
REFINING NATURAL GAS · REFINING PETROLEUM

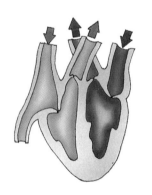

## THE HUMAN BODY

### INSIDE YOUR BODY 108–113
SKELETON AND JOINTS · MUSCLES AND MOVING
LUNGS AND BREATHING · HEART AND CIRCULATION
STOMACH AND DIGESTION · KIDNEYS AND
EXCRETION · TEETH AND EATING · SKIN · BRAIN AND
NERVES · SIGHT, HEARING, TASTE · REPRODUCTION
DEVELOPMENT

### THE DOCTOR'S SURGERY 114–115
BODY REFLEXES · BLOOD PRESSURE · THERMOMETER
HYPODERMIC NEEDLE AND SYRINGE · STETHOSCOPE
OTOSCOPE AND OPHTHALMOSCOPE

### THE OPERATING THEATRE 116–119
ANAESTHETICS · ENDOSCOPE · HEART-LUNG
MACHINE · LASER SCALPEL · X-RAYS · CAT SCANNER
ARTIFICIAL IMPLANTS

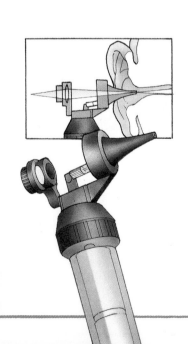

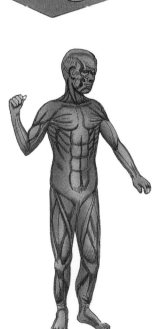

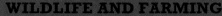

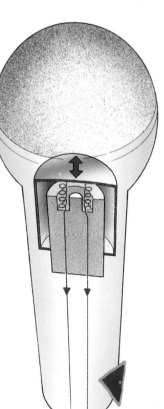

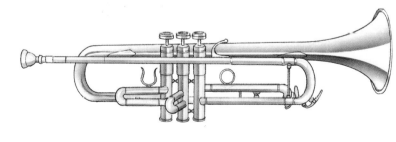

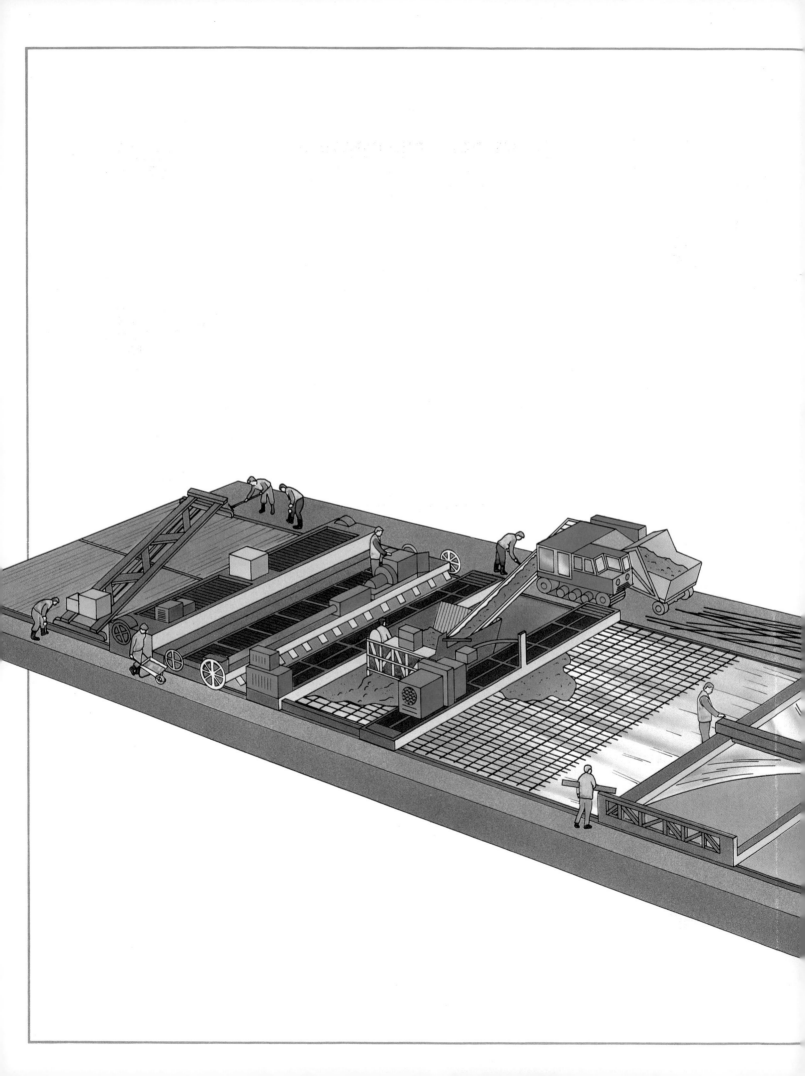

# INTRODUCTION

Look around you. Unless you are reading this book on a desert island, or deep in the jungle, you should be able to see at least one kind of machine. It might be quite a simple device, such as a pair of scissors, or a nut and bolt. Or it could be a complicated one, like a music hi-fi system, a motor car, or a jumbo jet flying overhead.

How does it work? Nearly all of us have an in-built curiosity about how things work – and especially about the workings of machines and bits of equipment designed by other humans. What happens inside the shiny white box of a dishwasher? Or in the great construction machines on a building site? Or even in an electric light bulb, when you flick on the switch?

*How Things Work* takes the lid off dozens of machines, devices, instruments and pieces of equipment. Clear diagrams show how the parts move, and what goes where. It shows that many machines rely on basic mechanical and electrical parts, such as levers, screws, springs and electromagnets. The trick is putting these simple parts together in the right way to do the job.

The book is divided into ten main sections, each based on a different aspect of our daily lives. See what happens when you wash your clothes, or turn on the lawn sprinkler in *The Home*. Find out what oil rigs do and how electricity is made in *Power and Services*. And see how your own body works, and how plants and animals live together in nature in *The Human Body* and *Wildlife and Farming*.

Many small devices, and the principles by which they work, are used again and again in different machines. These are explained in the *Glossary*, together with less familiar terms.

So, next time you pull on a new sweater, take the train to the next town, and watch a movie – think about the many processes and machines that have gone into making these things. They have been devised and constructed by people. Someone has to invent each machine, from a humble zip, to the printing press or the Space Shuttle. Great inventors started with their in-built curiosity and a desire to make things work. Could this be you?

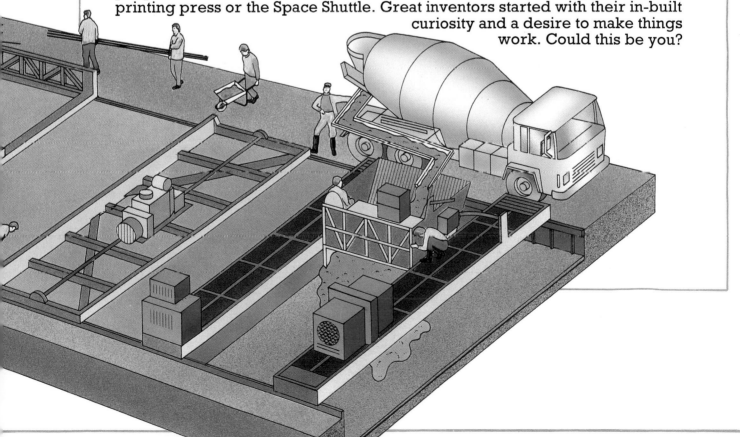

# GETTING UP

**FLUORESCENT LIGHT** 6

**ALARM CLOCK** 1

**HAIR DRIER** 4

**LAVATORY** 9

**TAP** 3

**AEROSOL SPRAY** 8

**ZIP FASTENER** 7

**WARMTH AND WATER** 2

## 1 CLOCK

The clock is one of the most familiar machines. In an escapement-type clock (as opposed to an electric one), energy for its mechanism comes from you, as you wind it up. The escape wheel clicks round slowly like a rotating ratchet, allowing the energy from the mainspring to unwind very slowly, and by regular amounts each time. The mechanism that measures out the small bursts of movement is the *escapement mechanism*. The energy from the mainspring keeps the balance wheel swinging back and forth. The pallets alternately catch and release the escape wheel. This breaks up the irregular unwinding of the mainspring into small measured bursts of time which are then transmitted via the train of connecting gears to the minute and the hour hands.

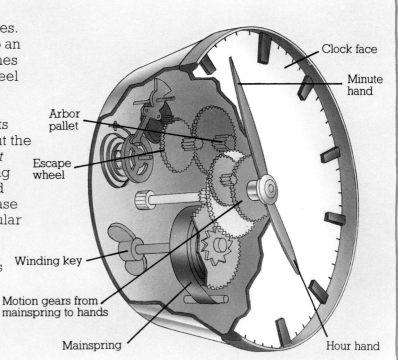

Clock face

Minute hand

Arbor pallet

Escape wheel

Winding key

Motion gears from mainspring to hands

Mainspring

Hour hand

## WARMTH AND WATER

The walls and ceilings of most modern houses conceal a maze of water pipes. There are two main systems: one for the water supply itself, from taps; and a separate circuit for the central-heating system. Water from the main flows under great pressure up into the roofspace, where it fills up the cold-water tank. Usually, one pipe runs from this incoming main to the kitchen cold tap, which is why this tap has such a powerful flow if you turn it on full! Water from the cold-water tank flows to the cold taps in the bath, shower and basin, and to the lavatory (page 16).

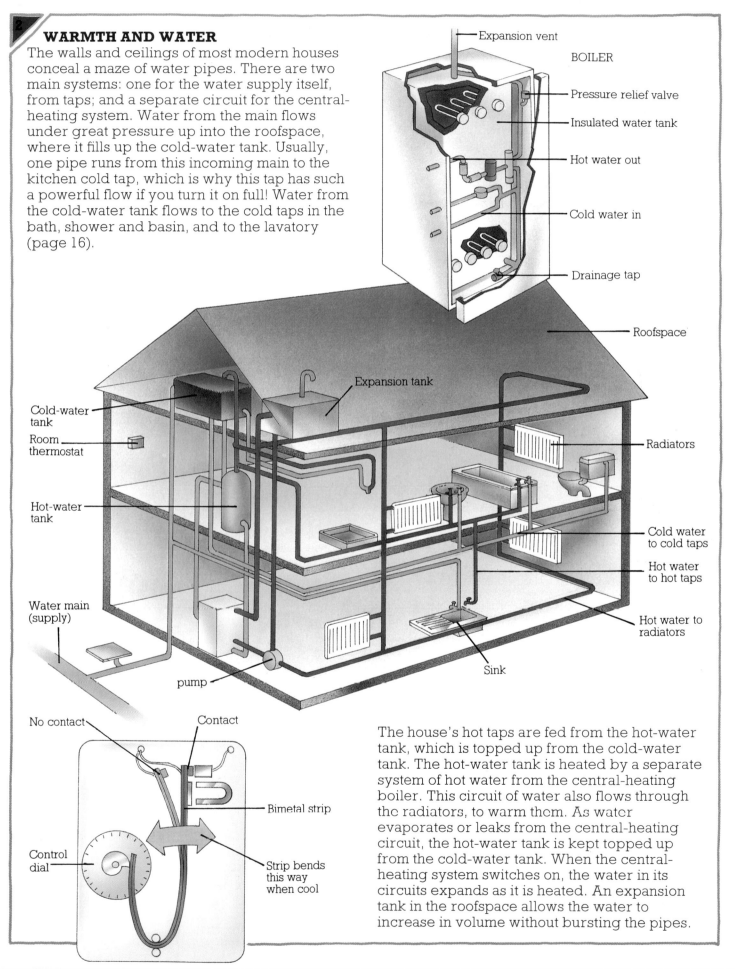

Expansion vent

BOILER

Pressure relief valve

Insulated water tank

Hot water out

Cold water in

Drainage tap

Roofspace

Expansion tank

Cold-water tank

Room thermostat

Hot-water tank

Water main (supply)

pump

Radiators

Cold water to cold taps

Hot water to hot taps

Hot water to radiators

Sink

No contact

Contact

Bimetal strip

Control dial

Strip bends this way when cool

The house's hot taps are fed from the hot-water tank, which is topped up from the cold-water tank. The hot-water tank is heated by a separate system of hot water from the central-heating boiler. This circuit of water also flows through the radiators, to warm them. As water evaporates or leaks from the central-heating circuit, the hot-water tank is kept topped up from the cold-water tank. When the central-heating system switches on, the water in its circuits expands as it is heated. An expansion tank in the roofspace allows the water to increase in volume without bursting the pipes.

## 3 TAP

We rarely think of what happens inside a tap, until it starts to drip. As you turn the handle, the screw mechanism inside, which presses a rubber washer onto the water pipe, lifts up. The pressure of the water trying to push through the pipe pushes the washer upwards, and so the water flows through. Water does not leak around the spindle because the spindle fits snugly inside the water-sealing nut.

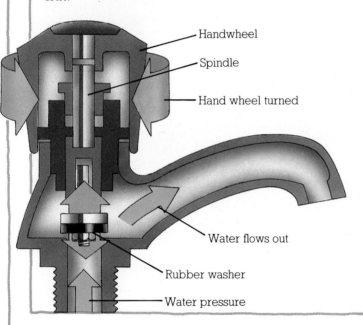

- Handwheel
- Spindle
- Hand wheel turned
- Water flows out
- Rubber washer
- Water pressure

## 4 HAIR DRIER

The drier contains a miniature electric heater to create your own warm wind. The heating element is made from special resistance wire. This partially resists the flow of electricity through it, and heat is produced as the electricity forces its way through. The fan blows moisture-laden air away from your hair, continuously replacing it with fresh, dry air.

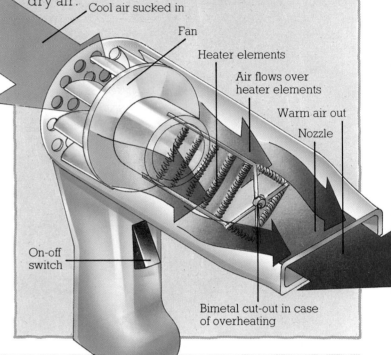

- Cool air sucked in
- Fan
- Heater elements
- Air flows over heater elements
- Warm air out
- Nozzle
- On-off switch
- Bimetal cut-out in case of overheating

## 5 LAVATORY

Most houses have several ballcocks, with one in each lavatory. As water fills the cistern, it lifts the large floating ball. Gradually the lever-arm attached to the ball closes a valve which stops the water. When you pull the handle, a large disc inside a bell lifts a quantity of water into the siphon tube. This water then falls down into the pan and 'pulls' with it the rest of the water in the cistern, by *siphonic action*. As the disc's edge wears, water leaks down past it when the handle is pulled. This is why a lavatory gradually becomes more awkward to flush.

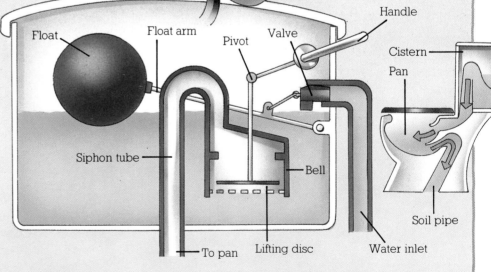

- Float
- Float arm
- Pivot
- Valve
- Handle
- Cistern
- Pan
- Siphon tube
- Bell
- Soil pipe
- To pan
- Lifting disc
- Water inlet

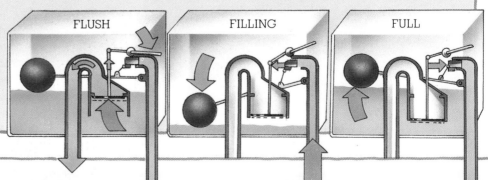

FLUSH    FILLING    FULL

## FLUORESCENT LIGHT

A fluorescent 'striplight' produces more light per amount of electricity than the light 'bulb' (page 140). The tube is filled with vapour of the silvery metal mercury (found in thermometers, page 115). The metal electrode at the end of the tube gives off a beam of invisible, electrically-charged particles, called electrons. When an electron hits a mercury atom, it momentarily knocks one of its own electrons out of position. This creates a burst of ultraviolet light, which is turned into visible light by the tube's internal coating (page 131).

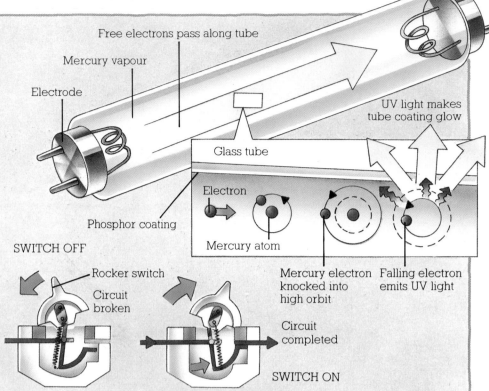

Free electrons pass along tube

Mercury vapour

Electrode

UV light makes tube coating glow

Glass tube

Phosphor coating

Electron

Mercury atom

Mercury electron knocked into high orbit

Falling electron emits UV light

SWITCH OFF

Rocker switch

Circuit broken

Circuit completed

SWITCH ON

## ZIP FASTENER

The zip is made of two rows of tiny teeth-and-sockets. These are opened and closed by wedges on the zip-pull. When you close the zip, the teeth come together at an angle as they slide past the upper wedge. They are then clipped together by the lower wedges, with each tooth fitting into the socket of the one in front. The first zip was invented by Whitcomb Judson in 1893.

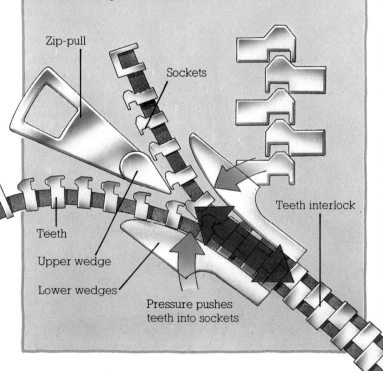

Zip-pull

Sockets

Teeth interlock

Teeth

Upper wedge

Lower wedges

Pressure pushes teeth into sockets

## AEROSOL SPRAY

The contents of an aerosol can include the product itself and the propellant that 'carries' it. They are under great pressure, and the outlet valve is kept closed both by this internal pressure and by a spring. As you push the button, the valve opens and allows the contents to flow. The outflow channel is very narrow and causes the product to break up into a fine, mist-like spray.

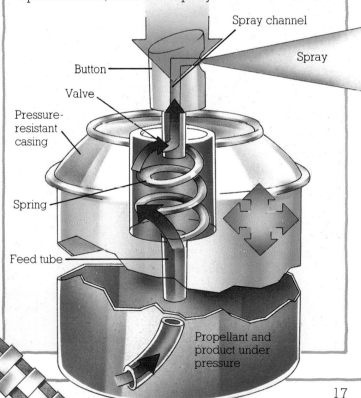

Spray channel

Spray

Button

Valve

Pressure-resistant casing

Spring

Feed tube

Propellant and product under pressure

# THE KITCHEN

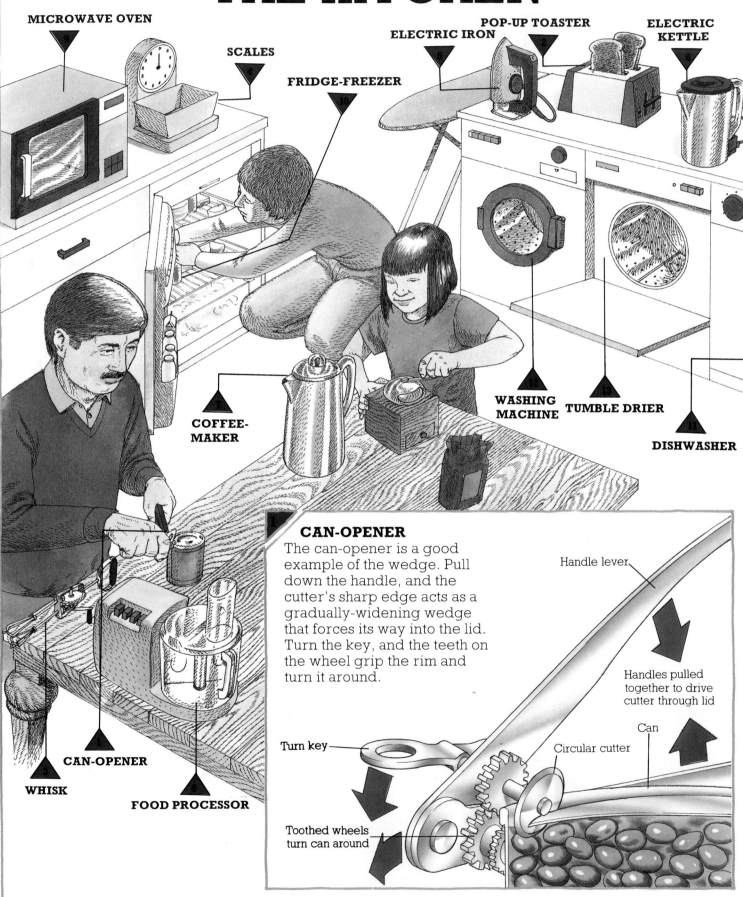

**MICROWAVE OVEN**

**SCALES**

**FRIDGE-FREEZER**

**ELECTRIC IRON**

**POP-UP TOASTER**

**ELECTRIC KETTLE**

**COFFEE-MAKER**

**WASHING MACHINE**

**TUMBLE DRIER**

**DISHWASHER**

**CAN-OPENER**

**WHISK**

**FOOD PROCESSOR**

## CAN-OPENER

The can-opener is a good example of the wedge. Pull down the handle, and the cutter's sharp edge acts as a gradually-widening wedge that forces its way into the lid. Turn the key, and the teeth on the wheel grip the rim and turn it around.

Handle lever

Handles pulled together to drive cutter through lid

Can

Turn key

Circular cutter

Toothed wheels turn can around

18

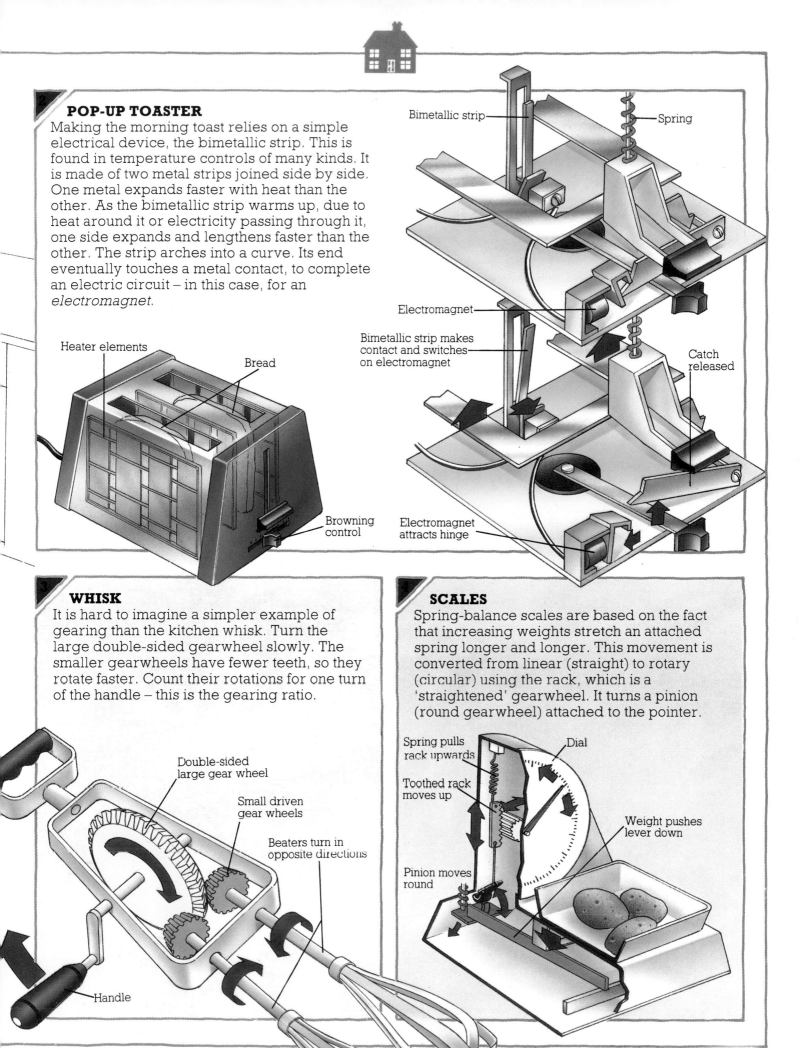

## POP-UP TOASTER

Making the morning toast relies on a simple electrical device, the bimetallic strip. This is found in temperature controls of many kinds. It is made of two metal strips joined side by side. One metal expands faster with heat than the other. As the bimetallic strip warms up, due to heat around it or electricity passing through it, one side expands and lengthens faster than the other. The strip arches into a curve. Its end eventually touches a metal contact, to complete an electric circuit – in this case, for an *electromagnet*.

Heater elements

Bread

Browning control

Bimetallic strip — Spring

Electromagnet

Bimetallic strip makes contact and switches on electromagnet

Catch released

Electromagnet attracts hinge

## WHISK

It is hard to imagine a simpler example of gearing than the kitchen whisk. Turn the large double-sided gearwheel slowly. The smaller gearwheels have fewer teeth, so they rotate faster. Count their rotations for one turn of the handle – this is the gearing ratio.

Double-sided large gear wheel

Small driven gear wheels

Beaters turn in opposite directions

Handle

## SCALES

Spring-balance scales are based on the fact that increasing weights stretch an attached spring longer and longer. This movement is converted from linear (straight) to rotary (circular) using the rack, which is a 'straightened' gearwheel. It turns a pinion (round gearwheel) attached to the pointer.

Spring pulls rack upwards

Dial

Toothed rack moves up

Weight pushes lever down

Pinion moves round

## ELECTRIC IRON

Old-fashioned 'smoothing irons' were warmed on a stand near the fire or hotplate. Today's electric version has its own heater element that warms the sole-plate. Most materials press more smoothly if they are damp, since moisture softens the tiny fibres in the material and makes them flexible. So the 'steam iron' sprays steam or a fine mist of hot water onto the material.

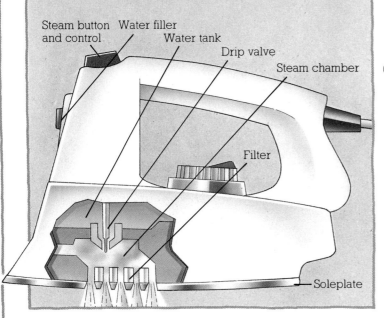

Steam button and control
Water filler
Water tank
Drip valve
Steam chamber
Filter
Soleplate

## ELECTRIC KETTLE

Like the iron, the modern kettle has its own electrical heater element. It also contains two failsafe circuit-breakers, or cut-outs. One stops the electric current to the heater when the water reaches boiling point. The other does the same if the kettle boils dry. The mains plug and socket must be designed so that water cannot drip into them and cause a short-circuit.

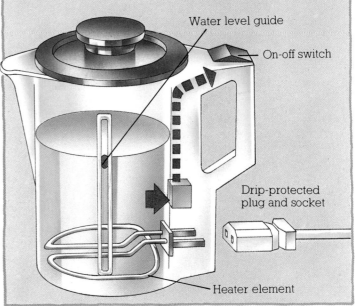

Water level guide
On-off switch
Drip-protected plug and socket
Heater element

## COFFEE-MAKER

In a coffee-grinder, beans slide down between two ridged metal surfaces that fit closely together. The turning motion crushes the beans into a fine powder, until the pieces are small enough to fall into the tray below. The percolator uses the principle that hot water gives off air bubbles and rises. The bubbles and hot water stream up the central spout, to create a fountain at the top. The hot water percolates, or oozes, back down through the ground coffee, dissolving the coffee-flavoured substances as it goes.

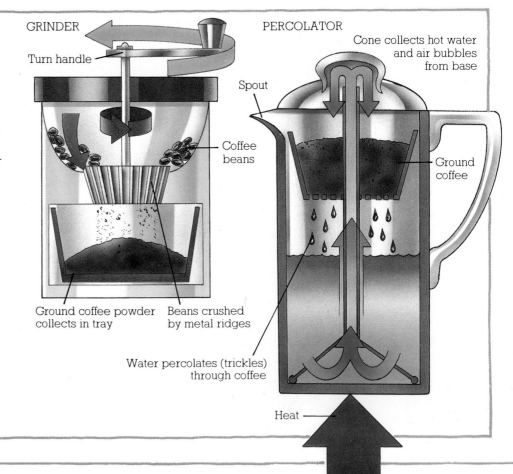

GRINDER
Turn handle
Coffee beans
Ground coffee powder collects in tray
Beans crushed by metal ridges

PERCOLATOR
Cone collects hot water and air bubbles from base
Spout
Ground coffee
Water percolates (trickles) through coffee
Heat

## FOOD PROCESSOR

The food processor is another kitchen device that uses electrical power instead of muscle power. Inside, the typical processor is relatively simple. An electric motor turns the spindle via a flexible toothed belt. Each differently-shaped attachment does a specific job, from slicing to shredding to beating to liquidizing. Ingredients are dropped into the feed tube, or pushed in using a plunger. This keeps fingers away from the whirling blades; safe design is a vital feature of many machines.

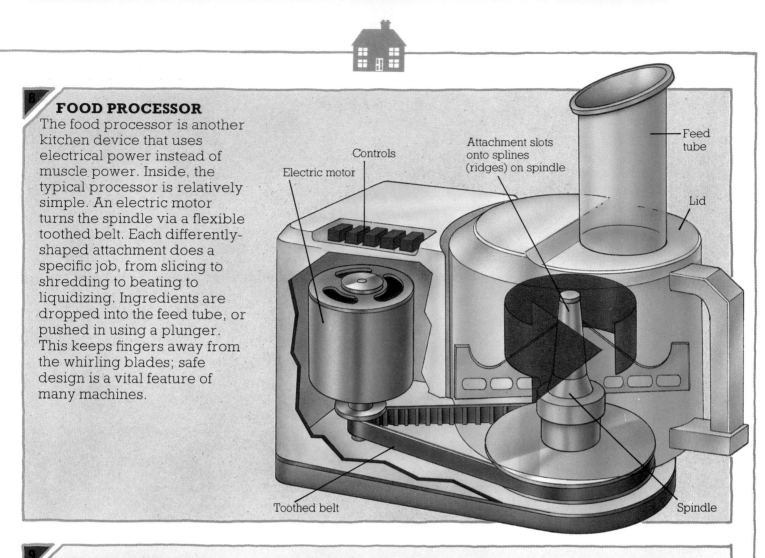

Controls
Electric motor
Attachment slots onto splines (ridges) on spindle
Feed tube
Lid
Toothed belt
Spindle

## MICROWAVE OVEN

Microwaves are part of the spectrum of *electromagnetic waves*, which includes light waves and X-rays. They have wavelengths from about 30 centimetres to one millimetre, which places them between the shortest radio waves and infra-red (heat) waves. One of their properties is to 'excite' molecules, especially in liquids, and make them vibrate and heat up. So foods with a large proportion of water, such as soups, cook quickest.

The waves are produced by a *magnetron*, a type of electron tube. They are scattered around the oven by a metal fan, for more even cooking. They pass through most types of china and glass, but not metals.

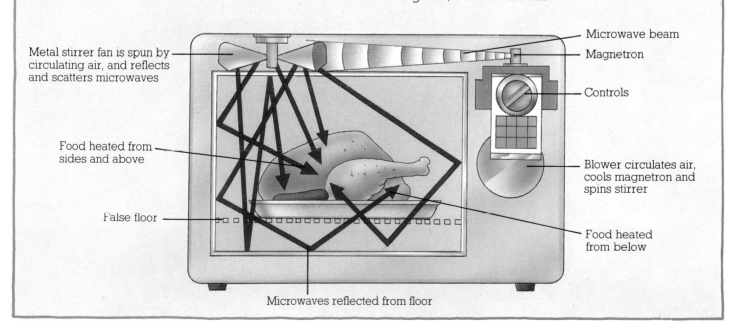

Metal stirrer fan is spun by circulating air, and reflects and scatters microwaves
Microwave beam
Magnetron
Controls
Food heated from sides and above
False floor
Blower circulates air, cools magnetron and spins stirrer
Food heated from below
Microwaves reflected from floor

## FRIDGE-FREEZER

The fridge-freezer does not make 'coldness' out of nothing. It works as a heat-exchanger, extracting warmth from the air inside the unit, and passing it into the air outside. The coolant is a special pressurized fluid that flows around a circuit, from evaporator to condenser. In the evaporator, inside the unit, the coolant boils under relatively high pressure. Being a boiling liquid, it draws heat from its surroundings. (In fact the coolant's boiling point is lower than water's freezing point.) It then flows under even higher pressure to the condenser. Here it turns from a gas back into a liquid, and gives out heat to the air as it does so.

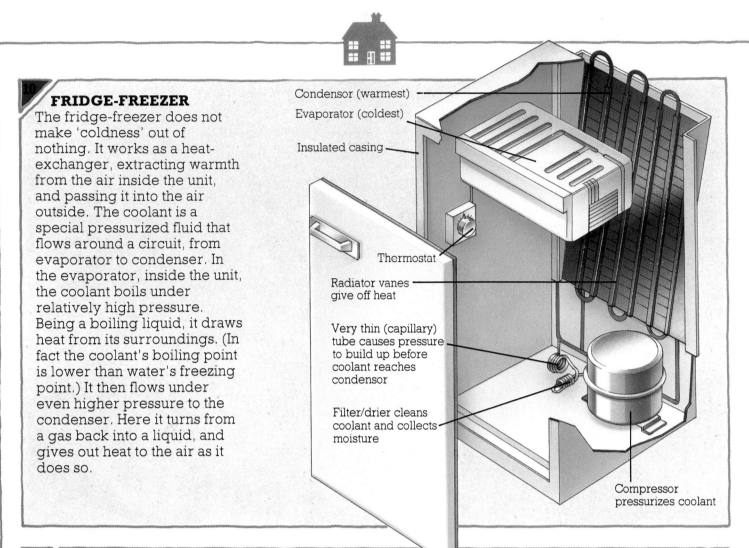

Condensor (warmest)
Evaporator (coldest)
Insulated casing
Thermostat
Radiator vanes give off heat
Very thin (capillary) tube causes pressure to build up before coolant reaches condensor
Filter/drier cleans coolant and collects moisture
Compressor pressurizes coolant

## DISHWASHER

Dirty crockery and cutlery are loaded into specially designed carriers, so that the water spray can reach all parts and the water can drain away freely afterwards. The pressure of the water itself makes the jets spin around. The first part of the cycle uses water containing detergent, to dissolve grease and grime. The detergent is loaded into a compartment in the lid. In the second part of the cycle, clean water rinses away the soapy water. Then a heating element warms and dries the load.

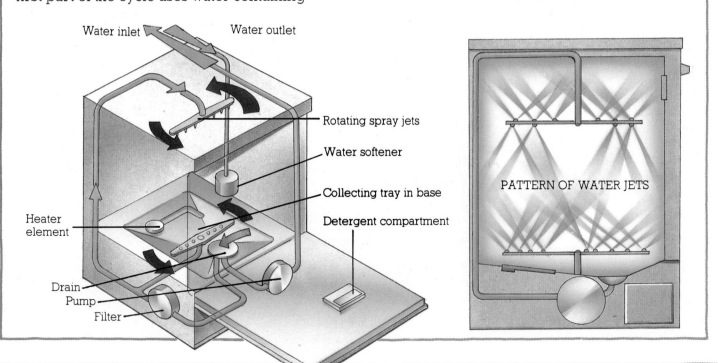

Water inlet
Water outlet
Rotating spray jets
Water softener
Collecting tray in base
Detergent compartment
Heater element
Drain
Pump
Filter

PATTERN OF WATER JETS

## WASHING MACHINE

A modern washing machine relies on several regulatory mechanisms in its operation. At the start of the cycle, water pours in through an electrically-controlled inlet valve. Once the water reaches a certain level in the drum, this is detected by a sensor that turns off the inlet valve. The pressure of the water in the inlet pipe helps to shut the valve firmly. The water is then heated by the machine's heater element. Once the pre-set temperature is reached, a *thermostat* switches off the electricity supply to the heater. A load of washing and water is very heavy, so the drum is stabilized by weights and suspended by heavy-duty springs.

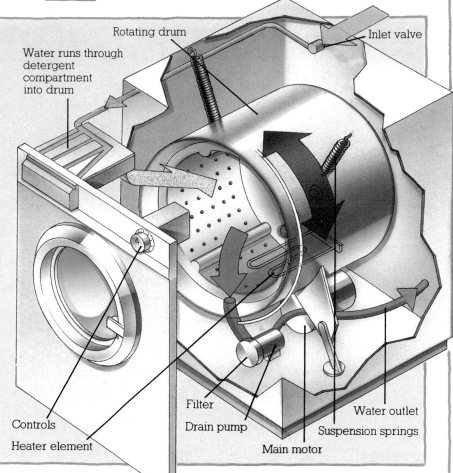

Rotating drum

Inlet valve

Water runs through detergent compartment into drum

Controls

Heater element

Filter

Drain pump

Main motor

Water outlet

Suspension springs

## TUMBLE DRIER

In most tumble driers, the electric motor is programmed to turn the drum one way, and then go into reverse and spin it the other way. This helps to shake and separate the contents. It prevents them from clumping together and leaving a still-damp patch in the middle, which the drying air cannot reach. Hot air is drawn through the unit by a blower fan. As it passes through the load, the air picks up dust and fibres; these are trapped by the filter screen. In order to heat such great volumes of air, tumble driers use lots of electricity. They have one of the highest running costs of all household machines.

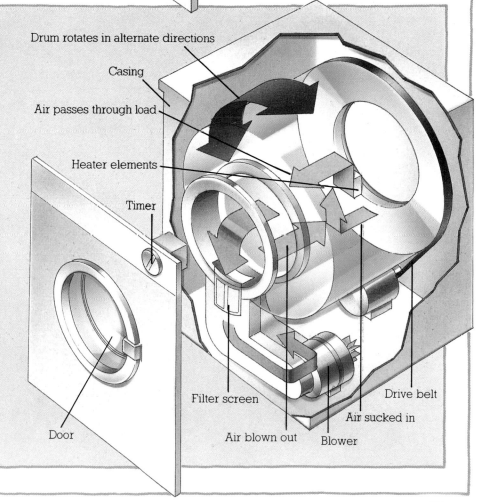

Drum rotates in alternate directions

Casing

Air passes through load

Heater elements

Timer

Door

Filter screen

Air blown out

Blower

Air sucked in

Drive belt

# THE GARDEN

**ELECTRIC DRILL** 6

**CHAINSAW** 5

**SCREWDRIVER** 2

**WHEELBARROW** 7

**GARDEN SHEARS** 8

**GREENHOUSE** 1

**LAWNMOWER** 3

**LAWN-SPRINKLER** 4

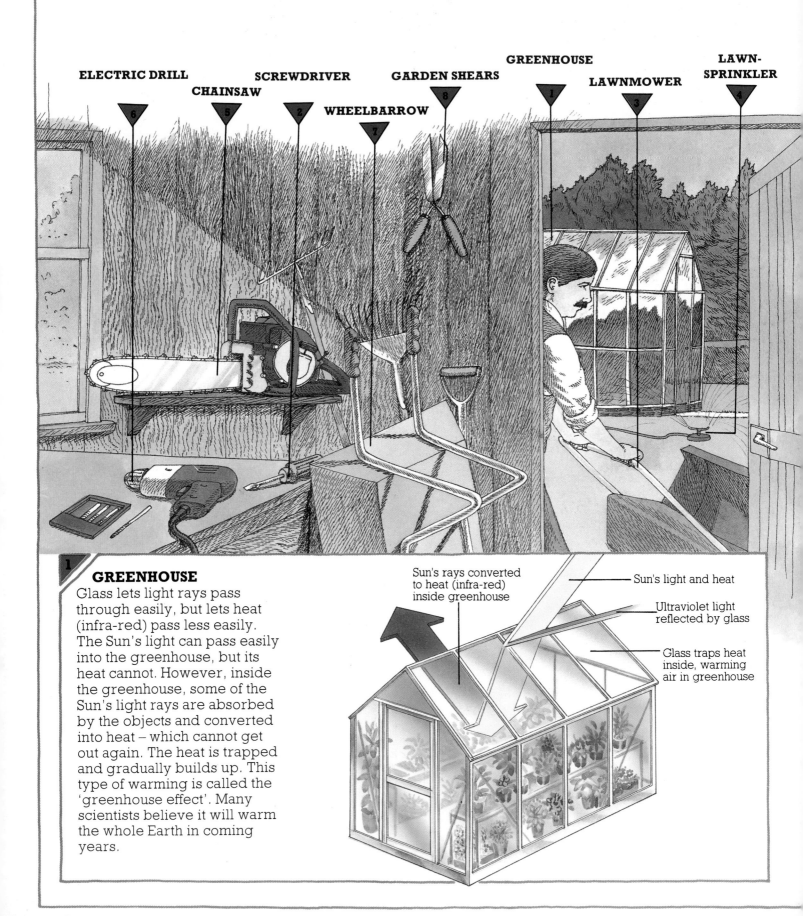

**1**

### GREENHOUSE

Glass lets light rays pass through easily, but lets heat (infra-red) pass less easily. The Sun's light can pass easily into the greenhouse, but its heat cannot. However, inside the greenhouse, some of the Sun's light rays are absorbed by the objects and converted into heat – which cannot get out again. The heat is trapped and gradually builds up. This type of warming is called the 'greenhouse effect'. Many scientists believe it will warm the whole Earth in coming years.

Sun's rays converted to heat (infra-red) inside greenhouse

Sun's light and heat

Ultraviolet light reflected by glass

Glass traps heat inside, warming air in greenhouse

## SCREWDRIVER

This acts like a kind of lever. Your hand moves in a large circle as you turn the handle. The turning force, or torque, is transmitted down the shaft and blade, into the screw head's slot. The screw turns in a smaller circle, but with greater turning power. Slot-headed screws are for general work. Cross-headed screws are less likely to let the blade slip out and damage the nearby surface.

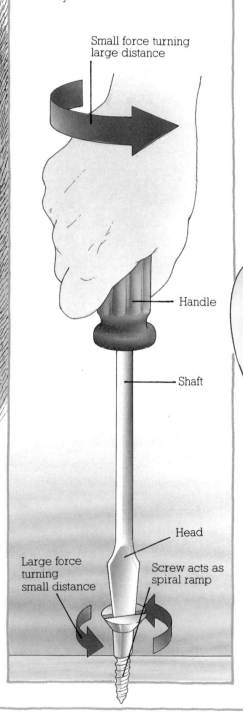

Small force turning large distance

Handle

Shaft

Head

Large force turning small distance

Screw acts as spiral ramp

## LAWNMOWER

Like the screwdriver, the lawnmower is a rotary machine. In the hand-pushed type, the heavy back roller is linked to the rotating blades by a chain. The rotating blades are angled in the form of a shallow helix, so that each one approaches the base blade with a scissor-like action. Grass is trapped between the two, snipped off, and thrown into the grass box.

The height of the cut is adjusted by lowering or raising the small front roller. In a motor mower, a small petrol engine drives the back roller and blades.

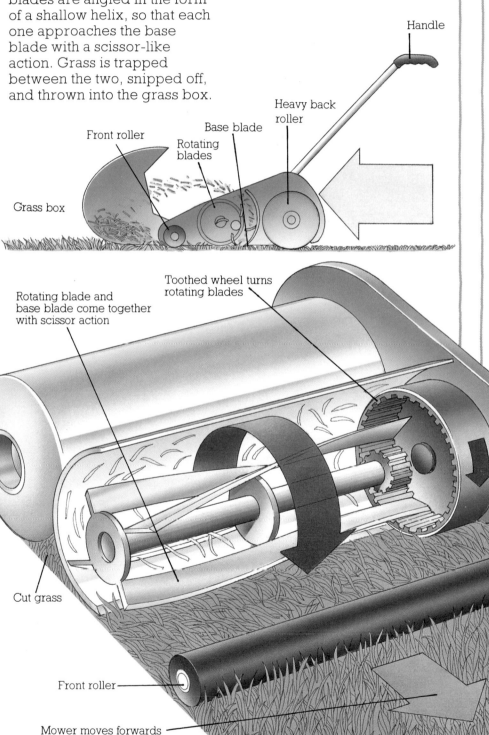

Handle

Heavy back roller

Front roller

Rotating blades

Base blade

Grass box

Toothed wheel turns rotating blades

Rotating blade and base blade come together with scissor action

Cut grass

Front roller

Mower moves forwards

Uncut grass

## LAWN-SPRINKLER

The oscillating sprinkler is based on the principle of the water wheel. The pressure of the water coming through the hosepipe turns a small fan-shaped water wheel, just as running water turns turbines in a giant hydroelectric power station (page 72). A series of gears slows down the spinning speed, and a crank fixed to a rotating wheel changes the circular motion to an oscillating one (swinging to and fro like a pendulum). By changing the length of the crank, the sprayer can be made to cover a wide or narrow area on either side.

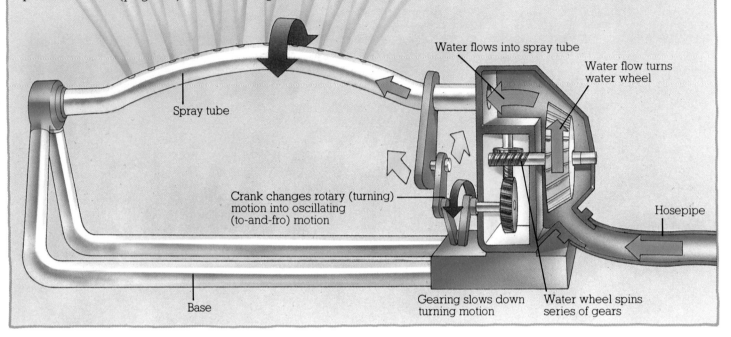

Water flows into spray tube

Water flow turns water wheel

Spray tube

Hosepipe

Crank changes rotary (turning) motion into oscillating (to-and-fro) motion

Base

Gearing slows down turning motion

Water wheel spins series of gears

## CHAINSAW

In a hand saw, the teeth oscillate (move to and fro). The chainsaw has a 'never-ending' blade, in the shape of a chain loop bearing teeth. A small engine, usually petrol-driven, turns the drive cog and makes the chain move around its loop. The chain soon becomes hot and tends to stick in its guides, so oil is regularly dripped onto it from a small tank, for cooling and lubrication. Safety is vital. Users wear strong gloves, protective goggles, shin-guards and thick boots, in case the cutting chain slips and falls.

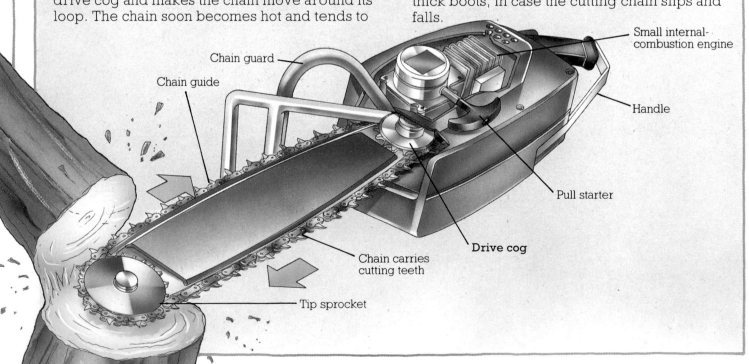

Chain guard

Chain guide

Small internal-combustion engine

Handle

Pull starter

**Drive cog**

Chain carries cutting teeth

Tip sprocket

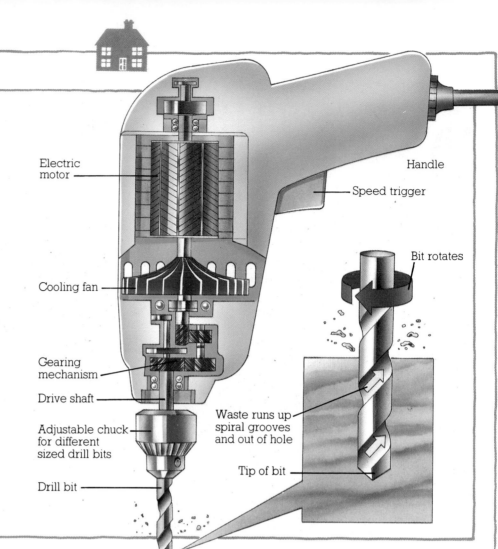

## 6 ELECTRIC DRILL

The small electric motor in a drill is extremely powerful, and its turning force is increased as it is slowed down by the gearing mechanism. Many drills have adjustable speeds, either by varying the electrical voltage fed to the motor, or by changing the gears in the gear train (page 90). Speeds of only a few hundred rpm (revolutions per minute) are suitable for tough materials such as concrete and hard metal. Several thousand rpm can be used in softer materials such as softwoods and plastics.

Electric motor

Handle

Speed trigger

Cooling fan

Bit rotates

Gearing mechanism

Drive shaft

Adjustable chuck for different sized drill bits

Waste runs up spiral grooves and out of hole

Tip of bit

Drill bit

## 7 WHEELBARROW

The wheelbarrow is one of the simplest examples of a lever. The pivot point, or fulcrum, is at one end. Using a wheelbarrow, you can lift a large weight over a small distance, by applying your small lifting effort over a large distance.

Effort moves greater distance

Fulcrum at wheel

Load moves small distance

## 8 GARDEN SHEARS

Two levers connected together give the shears plenty of cutting power. Shearing pressure is greatest near the fulcrum. The blades should be sharp and come together without gaps or twisting.

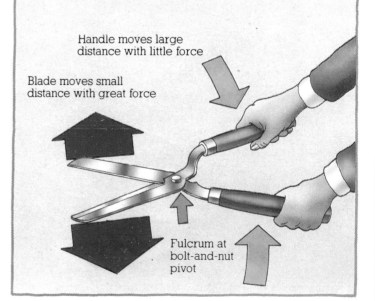

Handle moves large distance with little force

Blade moves small distance with great force

Fulcrum at bolt-and-nut pivot

# THE STREET

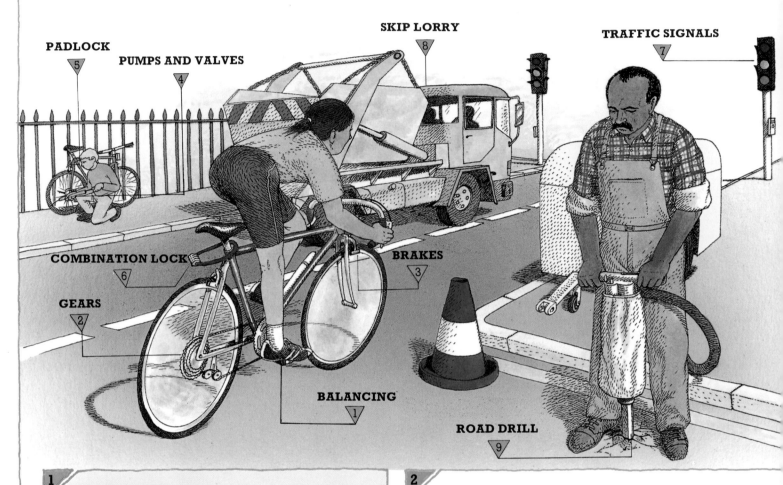

PADLOCK
5

PUMPS AND VALVES
4

SKIP LORRY
8

TRAFFIC SIGNALS
7

COMBINATION LOCK
6

GEARS
2

BRAKES
3

BALANCING
1

ROAD DRILL
9

---

**1**

## BALANCING

A spinning wheel acts as a simple gyroscope (page 45). It resists attempts to change position. Hold a rotating wheel as shown, and feel the resistance as you try to tip it. This *gyroscopic inertia* helps you to balance on a bicycle.

---

**2**

## GEARS

Pedalling downhill, the chain runs from the large front sprocket to the small rear one. For every turn of the pedals, the road wheel turns many times, but with limited turning force. Uphill, the chain runs from the small front

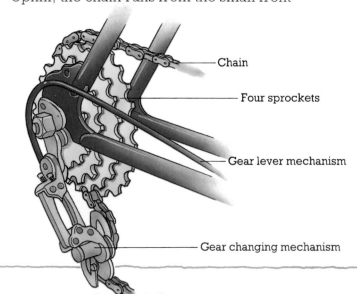

Chain

Four sprockets

Gear lever mechanism

Gear changing mechanism

## BRAKES

Brakes do not press on the bicycle tyre – they would soon wear a hole in it! They press on the wheel rim. The two metal arms, or yokes, work as levers. They close the blocks onto the rim with a scissor action, for even pressure on each side. Use the rear brake for routine braking, and both brakes in an emergency. Do not pull hard on the front brake alone. You could fly over the handlebars.

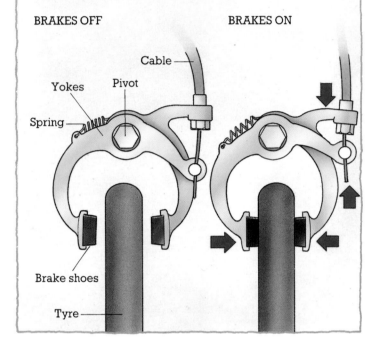

BRAKES OFF        BRAKES ON

Cable
Yokes
Pivot
Spring
Brake shoes
Tyre

sprocket to the large rear one. The road wheel turns more slowly but with greater force. Racing cyclists use gears to keep up their natural rate of pedalling whether going uphill or down.

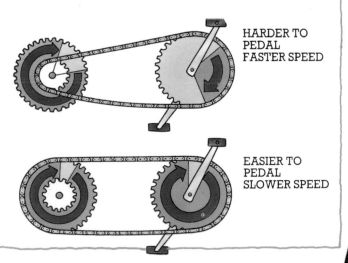

HARDER TO PEDAL FASTER SPEED

EASIER TO PEDAL SLOWER SPEED

## PUMPS AND VALVES

These are components of many machines, from taps to jet planes. The pump applies pressure to a fluid (gas or liquid), for example, by a piston (page 91). This makes the fluid flow to a region of lower pressure. Non-return valve designs are many and varied, but their main job is to allow fluid to flow one way but not the other. Some valves use hinged 'doors', others have flexible diaphragms or lever-operated closures.

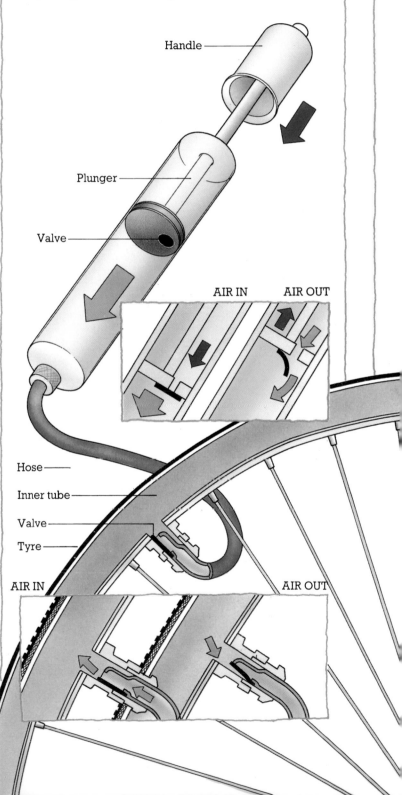

Handle

Plunger

Valve

AIR IN    AIR OUT

Hose
Inner tube
Valve
Tyre

AIR IN        AIR OUT

## 5 PADLOCK

This small security device has the same basic mechanism as a door lock or a car ignition. Grooves and ridges run lengthwise along the key, and the keyhole is shaped to accept only keys of a certain shape. When inserted, the key's V-cuts push small locking pins into exact alignment (a straight line), which permits the locking cylinder (barrel) to turn. A lever at its end drags back the locking bolt, thereby freeing the lock.

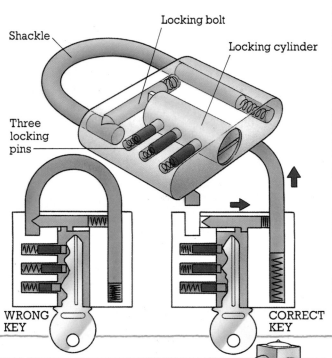

Shackle

Locking bolt

Locking cylinder

Three locking pins

WRONG KEY

CORRECT KEY

## 6 COMBINATION LOCK

Like the padlock, the combination lock relies on alignment. In this case, only when the tumblers are turned to the correct number combination, do the slots inside them line up. This lets you withdraw the key. With four number tumblers, and the numbers 0–9 on each one, how many possible number combinations are there?

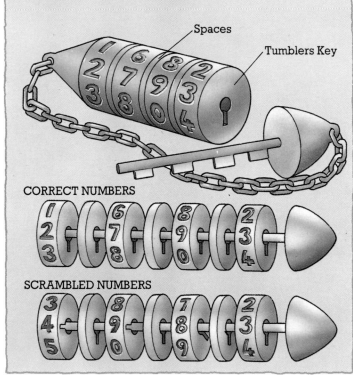

Spaces

Tumblers Key

CORRECT NUMBERS

SCRAMBLED NUMBERS

## 7 TRAFFIC SIGNALS

Older-type signals run to a pre-set timed cycle. If a car pulls up just as they change from green to red, it has to wait for the cycle to be completed before the lights will change to green again. Newer-style signals respond to a car's presence. The car's metal parts interfere with a weak magnetic field set up by the electrical wire buried in the road. The control box senses this and, if there are no cars waiting to move in the other directions, it switches the signals to green.

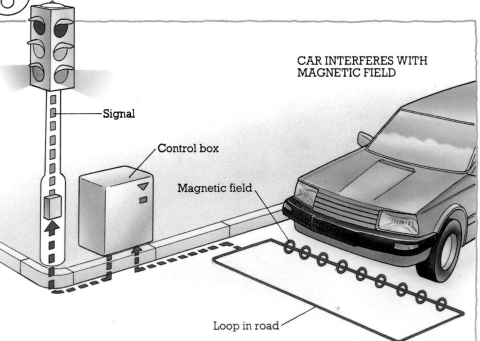

Signal

Control box

Magnetic field

CAR INTERFERES WITH MAGNETIC FIELD

Loop in road

## 8  SKIP LORRY

A skip lorry has a powerful hydraulic system enabling it to lift heavy loads. The power for the system is taken from the lorry's diesel engine via gearing and a control box. A hydraulic arm pushes the lifting arm; this is the effort moving the lever. The load is the skip, which moves in an arc as it is unloaded or loaded. If the tipping hooks are raised, they snag, or catch the base of the skip – and the skip truck becomes a tip-truck.

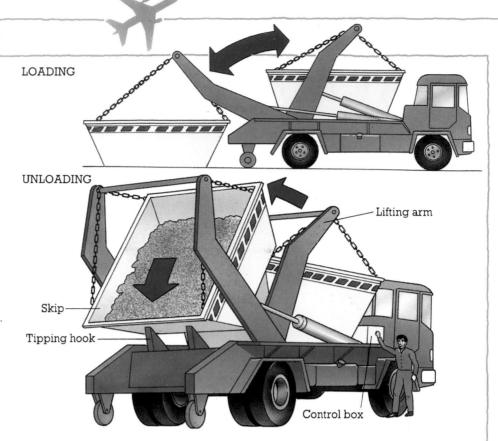

LOADING

UNLOADING

Lifting arm

Skip

Tipping hook

Control box

## 9  ROAD DRILL

Unlike the rotary electric drill (page 27), the road drill is pneumatic and percussive. 'Pneumatic' means that it is driven by compressed air (page 36). This is important for safety, since it means there are no trailing electrical wires. 'Percussive' refers to hitting. The drill breaks into the road surface using a fast series of hammer-blows. These are produced by a flip-flop diaphragm valve which re-routes the air many times each second, alternately raising and lowering the piston.

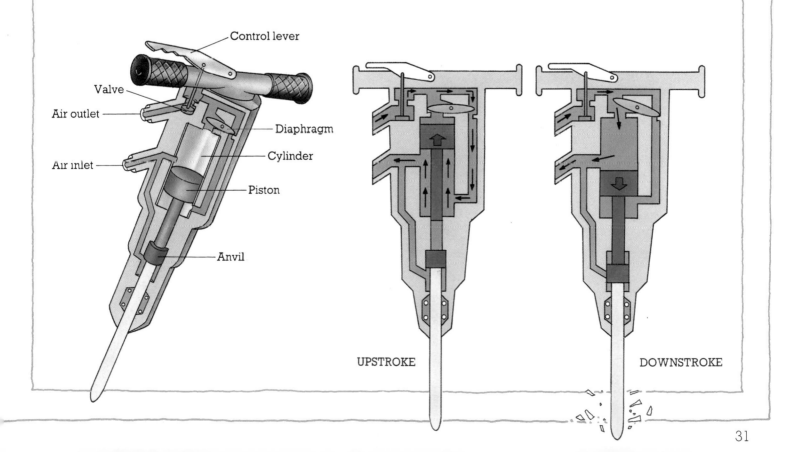

Control lever

Valve

Air outlet

Air inlet

Diaphragm

Cylinder

Piston

Anvil

UPSTROKE

DOWNSTROKE

# TAKING TO THE TRACKS

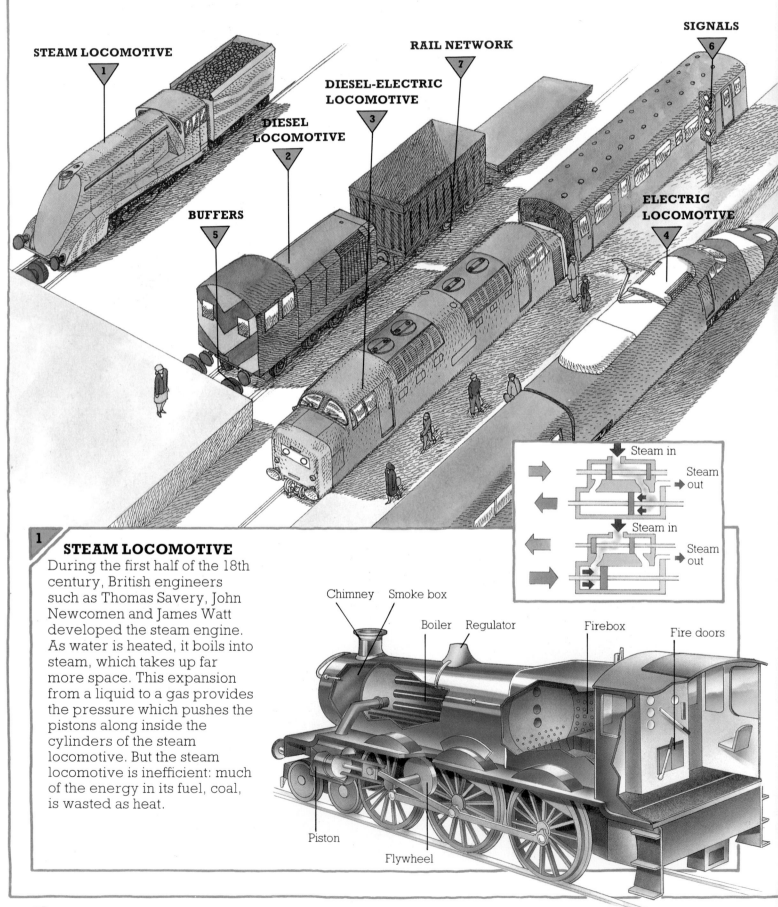

**STEAM LOCOMOTIVE** 1

**DIESEL LOCOMOTIVE** 2

**DIESEL-ELECTRIC LOCOMOTIVE** 3

**RAIL NETWORK** 7

**SIGNALS** 6

**ELECTRIC LOCOMOTIVE** 4

**BUFFERS** 5

Steam in
Steam out
Steam in
Steam out

1

### STEAM LOCOMOTIVE
During the first half of the 18th century, British engineers such as Thomas Savery, John Newcomen and James Watt developed the steam engine. As water is heated, it boils into steam, which takes up far more space. This expansion from a liquid to a gas provides the pressure which pushes the pistons along inside the cylinders of the steam locomotive. But the steam locomotive is inefficient: much of the energy in its fuel, coal, is wasted as heat.

Chimney  Smoke box

Boiler  Regulator

Firebox

Fire doors

Piston

Flywheel

## 2 DIESEL LOCOMOTIVE

The sources of power for this locomotive are diesel engines (page 89). The diesel engine was invented in the 1890s by the French-born German engineer Rudolf Diesel. Diesel engines are more efficient than steam ones: their fuel contains more energy per weight than coal, and their maintenance time and running costs are lower. Immense force is transmitted to the driving wheel through a hydraulic gearing system. The most powerful steam locomotives, American 'Big Boys', produced 7000 horsepower (about 5.25 million watts). Diesel locomotives are capable of similar feats.

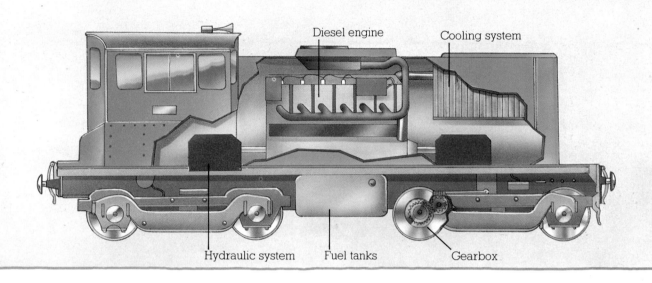

Diesel engine

Cooling system

Hydraulic system    Fuel tanks    Gearbox

## 3 DIESEL-ELECTRIC LOCOMOTIVE

This traction (pulling) unit is in effect an electric locomotive with its own source of electricity. The diesel engine turns a large generator, which produces electricity to drive electric motors. There is usually one electric motor on each axle. The motors are efficient and flexible, since they produce high turning force even at low speeds. This means that there is no need for an expensive and energy-wasting gear system. Union Pacific Railroad's turbo-charged diesel-electric locomotives are the most powerful, producing 6600 horsepower (about 4.95 million watts).

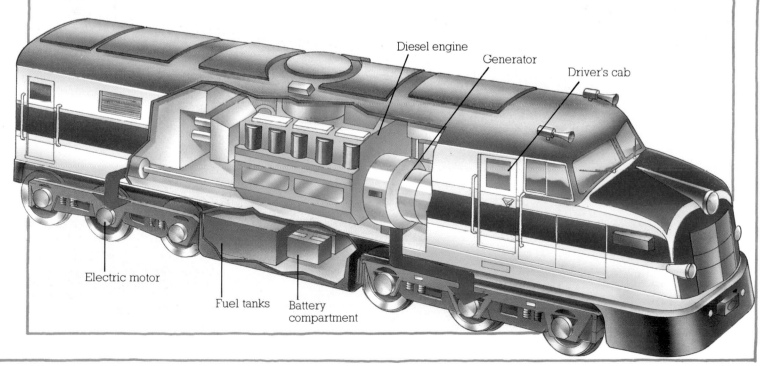

Diesel engine

Generator

Driver's cab

Electric motor

Fuel tanks    Battery compartment

## 4 ELECTRIC LOCOMOTIVE

The electric locomotive picks up electricity at 25,000 volts AC (alternating current) from overhead, or trackside, power lines. This is converted into DC (direct current) by *rectifiers* and *transformers*, and fed via motor control circuits to the drive motors. These are mounted in the locomotive, or 'power car', and they drive the wheels through a series of gears. The main disadvantage of this system is the high cost of building and maintaining the overhead power lines, and the fact that the train cannot go where there are no power lines.

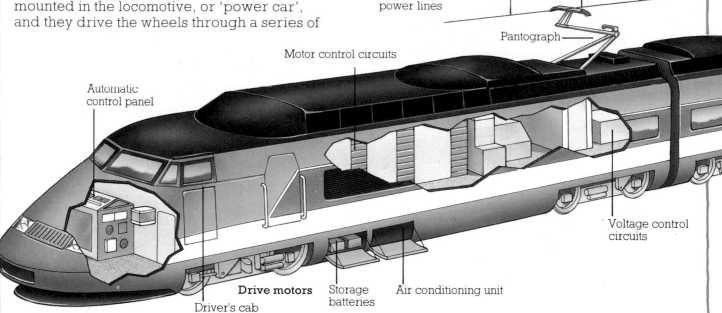

High voltage overhead power lines

Pantograph

Motor control circuits

Automatic control panel

Voltage control circuits

Drive motors

Driver's cab

Storage batteries

Air conditioning unit

## 5 BUFFERS

Stationary buffers are mounted at the end of a railway line. Buffers are also fitted to locomotives, passenger carriages and freight wagons. The metal spring and hydraulic damping fluid absorb the energy of the moving vehicle, causing it to slow down gradually without shocks or jarring.

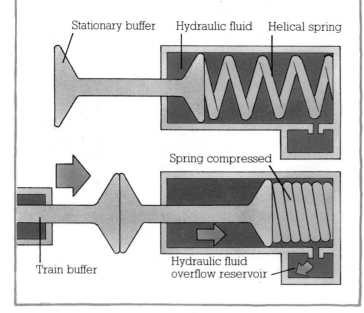

Stationary buffer    Hydraulic fluid    Helical spring

Spring compressed

Train buffer

Hydraulic fluid overflow reservoir

## 6 SIGNALS

Each rail network has its own signal design. The basic function of the signals is to inform the train driver that the line is clear, or to warn that it is not. The four-aspect system gives plenty of time for the driver to slow the train, so that passengers are not jerked by a sudden halt.

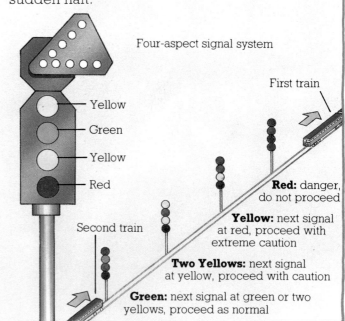

Four-aspect signal system

First train

Yellow

Green

Yellow

Red

Second train

**Red:** danger, do not proceed

**Yellow:** next signal at red, proceed with extreme caution

**Two Yellows:** next signal at yellow, proceed with caution

**Green:** next signal at green or two yellows, proceed as normal

# RAIL NETWORK

Today's railway system is a complicated maze of tracks, points, signals, crossings, passenger stations and freight yards. Most trains cannot climb steep gradients, so the tracks have to be made relatively level, by building cuttings through hills and embankments in valleys. The main signal boxes are the 'nerve centres' of the network, controlling the signals and the points. They can divert a slower goods train to allow through a passenger express, or switch a commuter train onto a local line for suburban stations.

There are approximately 440,000 kilometres of track in North America, 98,000 in South America, 420,000 in Europe, 145,000 in Asia, and 75,000 in Africa. The world's longest railway line runs across the USSR from Moscow to the Soviet east coast, a distance of almost 9500 kilometres with a journey time of more than eight days.

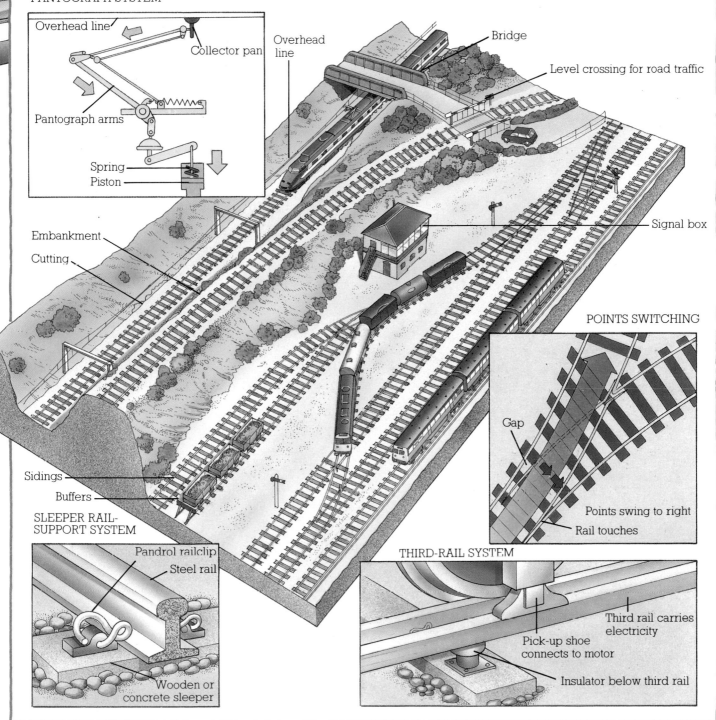

PANTOGRAPH SYSTEM

Overhead line

Collector pan

Pantograph arms

Spring

Piston

Overhead line

Bridge

Level crossing for road traffic

Signal box

Embankment

Cutting

POINTS SWITCHING

Gap

Points swing to right

Rail touches

Sidings

Buffers

SLEEPER RAIL-SUPPORT SYSTEM

Pandrol railclip

Steel rail

Wooden or concrete sleeper

THIRD-RAIL SYSTEM

Third rail carries electricity

Pick-up shoe connects to motor

Insulator below third rail

# THE MOTORWAY

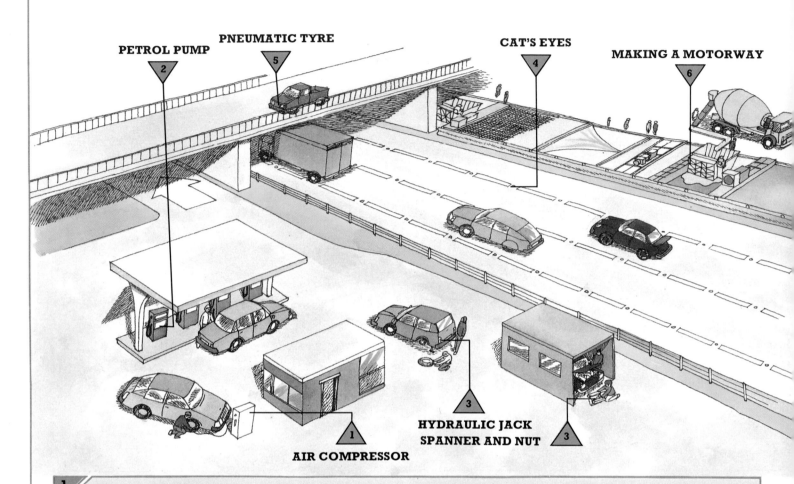

PETROL PUMP

2

PNEUMATIC TYRE

5

CAT'S EYES

4

MAKING A MOTORWAY

6

3

HYDRAULIC JACK
SPANNER AND NUT

3

1

AIR COMPRESSOR

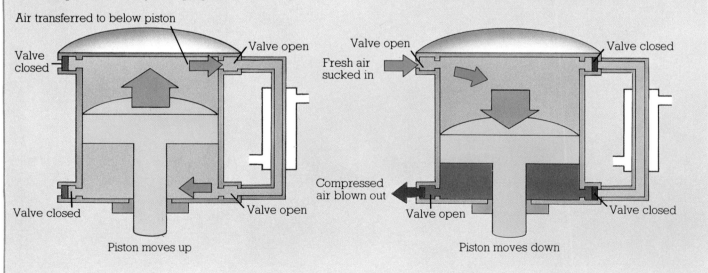

**1**

### AIR COMPRESSOR

The piston-based air compressor produces air at high pressure. This is used to operate machines such as the road drill (page 31) or the compressed-air nut-remover. It is also used to inflate pneumatic tyres (page 39). Air is pulled in above the piston, pushed around the bypass to below the piston, and then compressed and forced out as more air is pulled in above the piston. The piston is driven by an electric motor or internal combustion engine.

Air transferred to below piston

Valve closed

Valve open

Valve closed

Valve open

Piston moves up

Valve open

Fresh air sucked in

Valve closed

Compressed air blown out

Valve open

Valve closed

Piston moves down

## 2 PETROL PUMP

There are several main mechanisms within a petrol pump. One is the motor-driven pump itself, which draws up fuel from the large underground storage tank. Next is the filter to remove dirt and impurities, and the air separator which draws off bubbles of air and other gases. Then comes the meter that measures the volume, or quantity, of fuel passing through, and shows the amount on the dial or display. Finally, there is the hose and nozzle. There is often a detector in the hose, warning that the fuel tank of the vehicle is becoming full.

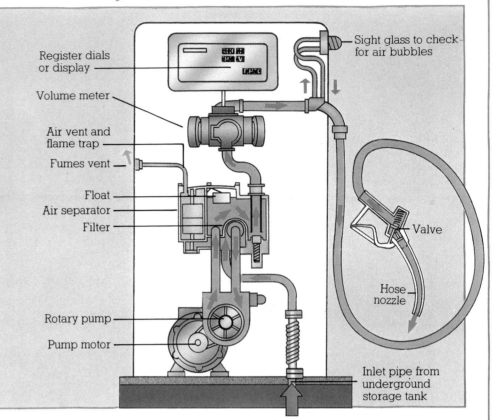

Register dials or display
Volume meter
Air vent and flame trap
Fumes vent
Float
Air separator
Filter
Rotary pump
Pump motor

Sight glass to check for air bubbles
Valve
Hose nozzle
Inlet pipe from underground storage tank

## 3 HYDRAULIC JACK

The vehicle jack converts a small force pushing a long way, into a large force pushing a short way. The jack's handle pushes a small piston a long way. This creates pressure in the hydraulic fluid, which presses on a secondary, or slave, piston. The slave piston has a much larger area, so it moves a short way but with greater total force. When the handle is pumped repeatedly, the jack gradually rises.

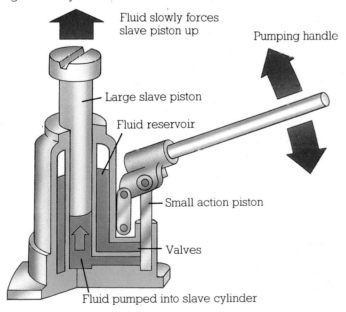

Fluid slowly forces slave piston up
Pumping handle
Large slave piston
Fluid reservoir
Small action piston
Valves
Fluid pumped into slave cylinder

## SPANNER AND NUT

The spanner's action is based on the lever principle: a small force moving a greater distance is converted into a greater force moving a small distance. The flat sides on the nut should fit snugly inside the corresponding slots in a spanner.

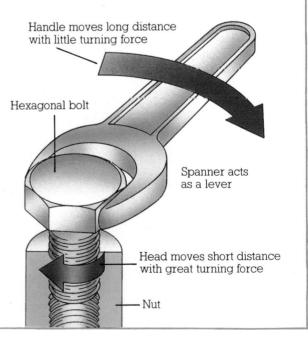

Handle moves long distance with little turning force
Hexagonal bolt
Spanner acts as a lever
Head moves short distance with great turning force
Nut

### 4 CAT'S EYES

Driving in the dark would be much more difficult without road reflectors to define the lane markings. The reflector contains a curved mirror and a half-spherical lens (page 77). When a light is shone on the reflector, the mirror and lens combine to focus and reflect the light rays back out, in the opposite direction to the way they came in. The device is called a 'cat's eye' because the eyes of a cat contain a special reflecting layer, the tapetum, so that they too 'glow' in the dark when a light is shone onto them.

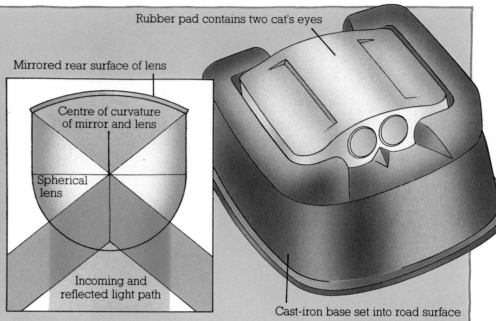

Rubber pad contains two cat's eyes

Mirrored rear surface of lens

Centre of curvature of mirror and lens

Spherical lens

Incoming and reflected light path

Cast-iron base set into road surface

### 6 MAKING A MOTORWAY

The roadway may not look very interesting as you speed along in a car, a metre or so above it. But road surfaces are the subject of constant research and improvement. They must have a combination of good strength, resistance to wear and to extremes of temperature and frost, excellent grip for tyres in dry and wet conditions, and a certain amount of flexibility so that they do not crack and flake. The main types of road surface today are based on asphaltic concrete, which is a mix of asphalt, gravel, sand and concrete. The surface has a 'camber', that is, a slight arched or domed shape in the centre, so that water drains off the sides.

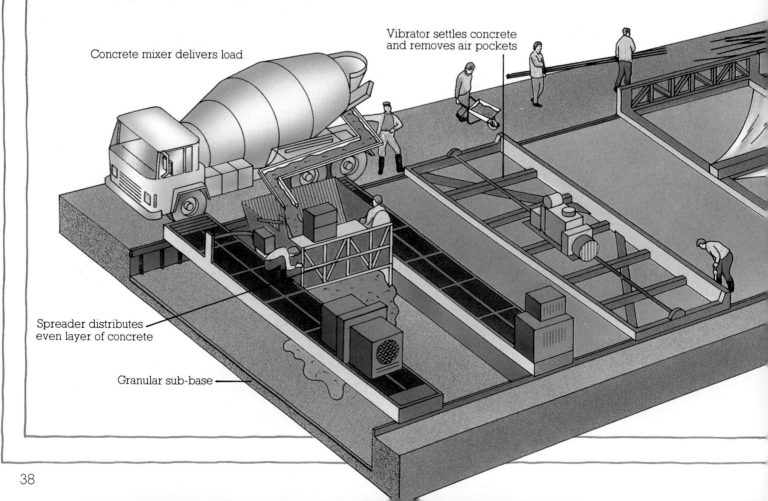

Concrete mixer delivers load

Vibrator settles concrete and removes air pockets

Spreader distributes even layer of concrete

Granular sub-base

## 5 PNEUMATIC TYRE

Unlike a liquid, a gas can be compressed. It stores the energy used to compress it, and releases this energy as a 'rebound' when the pressure eases. The air-filled pneumatic tyre works on this basis. The pressurized air inside the tyre carries nine-tenths of the load, and the flexible walls of the tyre carry the rest. The pressure of the air inside the tyre presses the bead, or inner edge, onto the wheel rim for an airtight fit. The first practical pneumatic tyres were invented by John Dunlop in 1888.

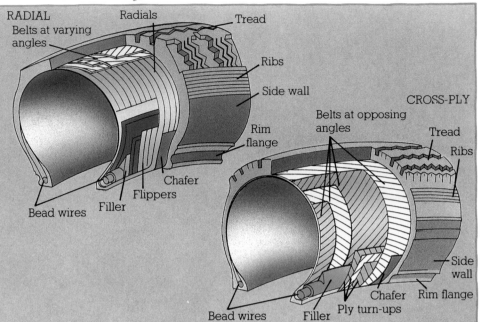

RADIAL

Belts at varying angles — Radials — Tread — Ribs — Side wall — Rim flange — Chafer — Flippers — Filler — Bead wires

CROSS-PLY

Belts at opposing angles — Tread — Ribs — Side wall — Rim flange — Chafer — Ply turn-ups — Filler — Bead wires

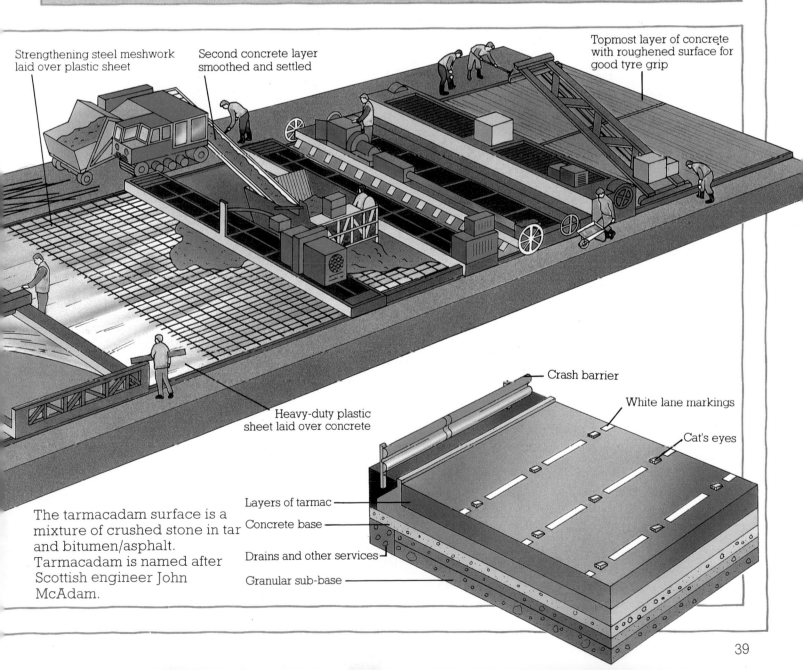

Strengthening steel meshwork laid over plastic sheet

Second concrete layer smoothed and settled

Topmost layer of concrete with roughened surface for good tyre grip

Heavy-duty plastic sheet laid over concrete

The tarmacadam surface is a mixture of crushed stone in tar and bitumen/asphalt. Tarmacadam is named after Scottish engineer John McAdam.

Crash barrier

White lane markings

Cat's eyes

Layers of tarmac

Concrete base

Drains and other services

Granular sub-base

# THE DOCKS

**SUBMARINE** 6

**MANOEUVRIN**

**PROPELLER** 1 2

**MAGNETIC COMPASS** 3

**ANEMOMETER** 4

**RO-RO FERRY** 5

**HOVERCRAFT** 7

**HYDROFOIL** 8

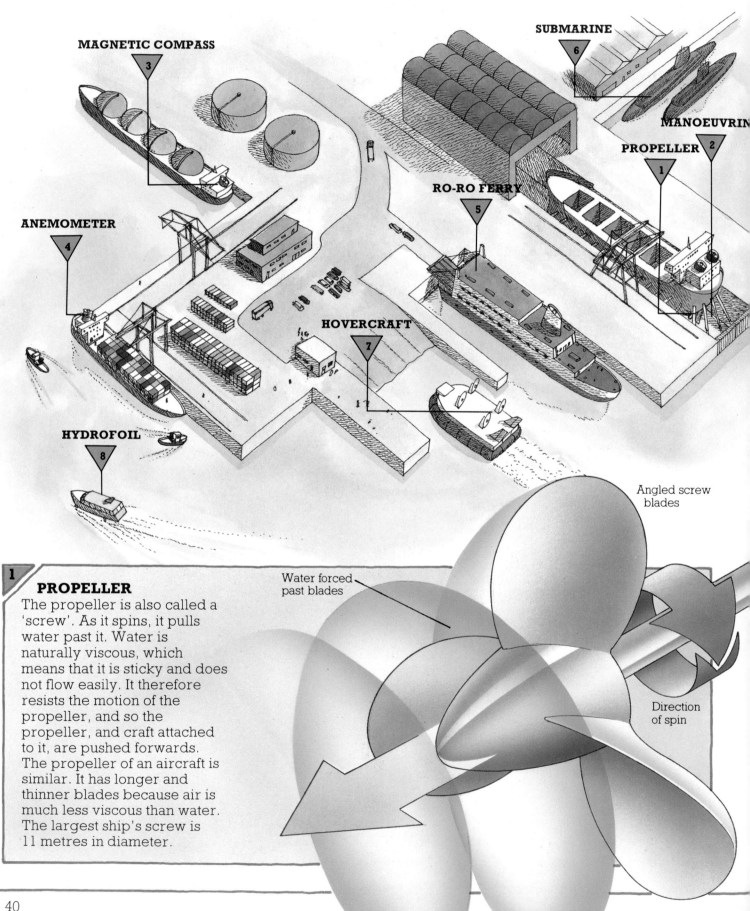

Angled screw blades

Water forced past blades

Direction of spin

### 1 PROPELLER

The propeller is also called a 'screw'. As it spins, it pulls water past it. Water is naturally viscous, which means that it is sticky and does not flow easily. It therefore resists the motion of the propeller, and so the propeller, and craft attached to it, are pushed forwards. The propeller of an aircraft is similar. It has longer and thinner blades because air is much less viscous than water. The largest ship's screw is 11 metres in diameter.

## 2 MANOEUVRING

Ships, planes and similar craft that move through fluids, change direction using control surfaces (page 47). The rudder is the control surface for steering to the left or right. If the rudder is angled into the flow of water (or air) past it, the moving water (or air) pushes against it (the action). To obey the first law of motion (page 94) there is a reaction, which pushes the control surface back and tries to make it parallel with the flow of the water or air. As the rudder swings round, so does the craft attached to it.

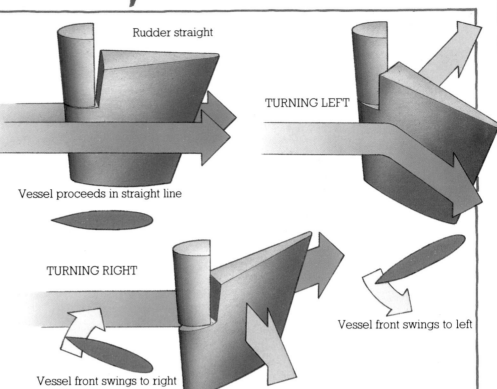

Rudder straight

Vessel proceeds in straight line

TURNING LEFT

Vessel front swings to left

TURNING RIGHT

Vessel front swings to right

## 3 MAGNETIC COMPASS

If a magnetized object is left to hang freely, the Earth's weak magnetic field acts on it, to make the object line up with the Earth's own lines of force. As only unlike poles of a magnet attract each other, it is the south pole of a magnetic compass that is pulled towards the Earth's own North Pole. A ship's compass floats on oil in order to remain steady in high seas.

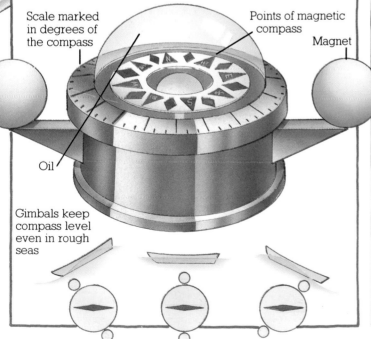

Scale marked in degrees of the compass

Points of magnetic compass

Magnet

Oil

Gimbals keep compass level even in rough seas

## 4 ANEMOMETER

Sailors need to know the wind speed, to calculate how far they are being blown off course, to warn of approaching storms, or to help them decide which sails to set. The anemometer's cups are spun by the wind. The faster they spin, the more electricity is produced in the small generator, and the higher is the dial or display reading.

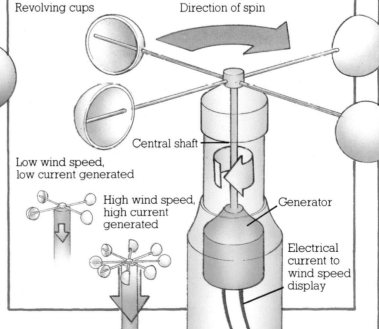

Revolving cups

Direction of spin

Central shaft

Low wind speed, low current generated

High wind speed, high current generated

Generator

Electrical current to wind speed display

## 5 RO-RO FERRY

The word ro-ro or 'Roll-On-Roll-Off' refers to the way that vehicles can drive in one end of the ferry along a ramp, and drive off a ramp at the other end, without being lifted by a crane or having to turn around inside. The ferry has propellers at both bow and stern (front and back), and often along the sides too, so that it can manoeuvre forwards, backwards and sideways. The heaviest vehicles are usually put on the ferry's lower decks. This gives the ferry a lower centre of gravity, which means that it has greater stability and is tossed around less in rough weather.

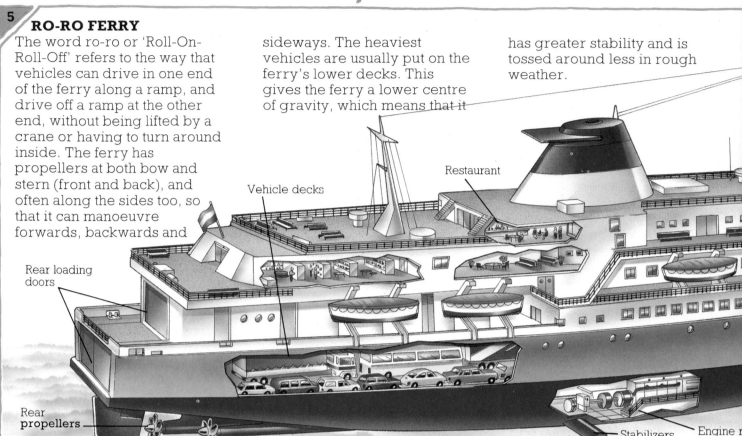

Vehicle decks

Restaurant

Rear loading doors

Rear propellers

Stabilizers

Engine r

## 6 SUBMARINE

Curved surfaces resist pressure better than flat ones (as in the aerosol can, page 17, and the bridge arch, page 56). The submarine can withstand great pressures as it dives beneath the waves. SONAR (SOund NAvigation and Ranging) enables the submarine to navigate and detect objects under water. High-pitched 'pings' of sound are given off by the transmitter, and a series of hydrophones (underwater microphones) listens for the returning echoes. From the direction of the echoes, and the time they take to return, computers on-board the submarine can calculate an object's direction, its distance or ranging, its size and shape. In passive sonar, the submarine simply listens for noises produced by other craft.

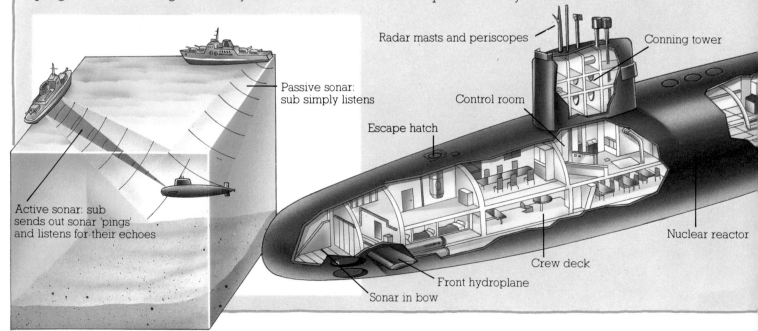

Passive sonar: sub simply listens

Active sonar: sub sends out sonar 'pings' and listens for their echoes

Radar masts and periscopes

Conning tower

Control room

Escape hatch

Nuclear reactor

Crew deck

Front hydroplane

Sonar in bow

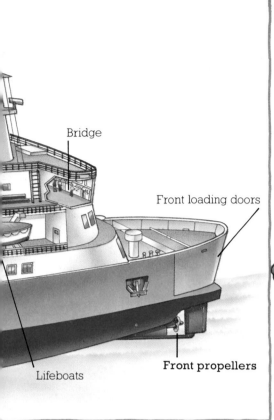

Bridge

Front loading doors

Front propellers

Lifeboats

## 7

## HOVERCRAFT

By skimming over waves, rather than through them, the hovercraft has several advantages over a normal ship. It can ride small waves more quickly and smoothly, and it can 'fly' straight up a ramp from water onto land.

The hovercraft is raised by downwards air currents blown from large lifting fans. The air currents are partly trapped within the flexible enclosing skirt. This produces the increased air pressure that forces the vehicle upwards.

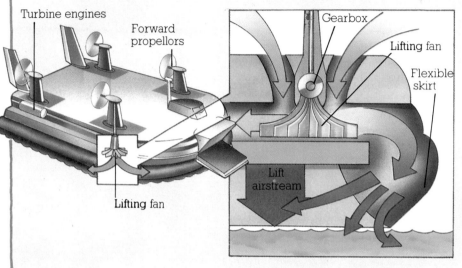

Turbine engines

Forward propellors

Gearbox

Lifting fan

Flexible skirt

Lift airstream

Lifting fan

## 8

## HYDROFOIL

The foil of the hydrofoil is shaped like an aircraft wing. As in a helicopter rotor blade (page 67), it converts forward motion into lift, and this raises the hull (the body of the vehicle) out of the water. Since the hull is clear of the water, the drag effect of the water (the force that slows things down) is removed. Hydrofoil ferries travel at up to 50 knots (90 km/h) and carry over 200 passengers.

Ultrasonic sensors detect the height and speed of the craft and the oncoming wave pattern, and tilt or adjust the foils as necessary to stay stable.

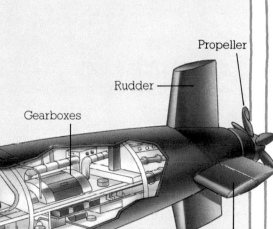

Propeller

Rudder

Gearboxes

Rear hydroplane

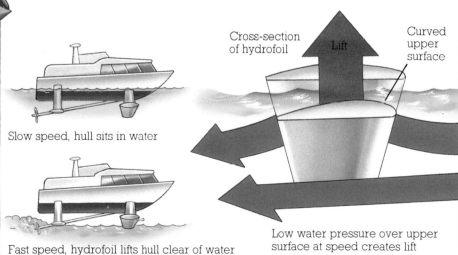

Slow speed, hull sits in water

Fast speed, hydrofoil lifts hull clear of water

Cross-section of hydrofoil

Lift

Curved upper surface

Low water pressure over upper surface at speed creates lift

# ON AN AIRLINER

**JUMBO JET** 4

**FLIGHT-DECK** 2

**RADIO AND RADAR** 1

**LIFEJACKET** 3

### RADIO AND RADAR

Aircraft navigate using radio in two ways. In RADAR (RAdio Detection And Ranging), the aircraft's transmitter sends out bursts of radio signals. These bounce off the ground and objects such as buildings and other aircraft. The aircraft detects the returning echoes with its receiver (the principle is the same as for SONAR, page 42). Radar equipment is usually hoisted in the radome, in the aircraft's nose (page 46). In addition ground stations send out radio signals. (Each station has a different code.) The receiver picks up these signals, and from their direction and strength, the flight-deck computers can pinpoint the plane's position.

RADAR — Transmitter/receiver — Reflective surface

Outward radio waves — Reflected radio waves

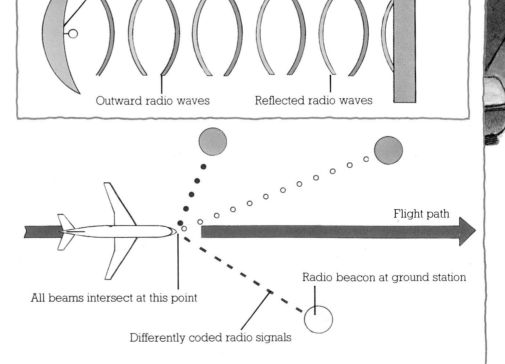

Flight path

All beams intersect at this point

Radio beacon at ground station

Differently coded radio signals

## 2 FLIGHT-DECK

The flight-deck of a modern jetliner has dozens of displays and controls. These are carefully designed and positioned so that the crew can concentrate on the most important ones; they notice the others only if a problem arises. The airspeed indicator shows the aircraft's speed through the air. The altimeter, which uses the same principle as a *barometer*, measures height above sea level. A *gyroscope* is linked to the 'attitude display' that shows whether the aircraft is flying level or tilted to one side.

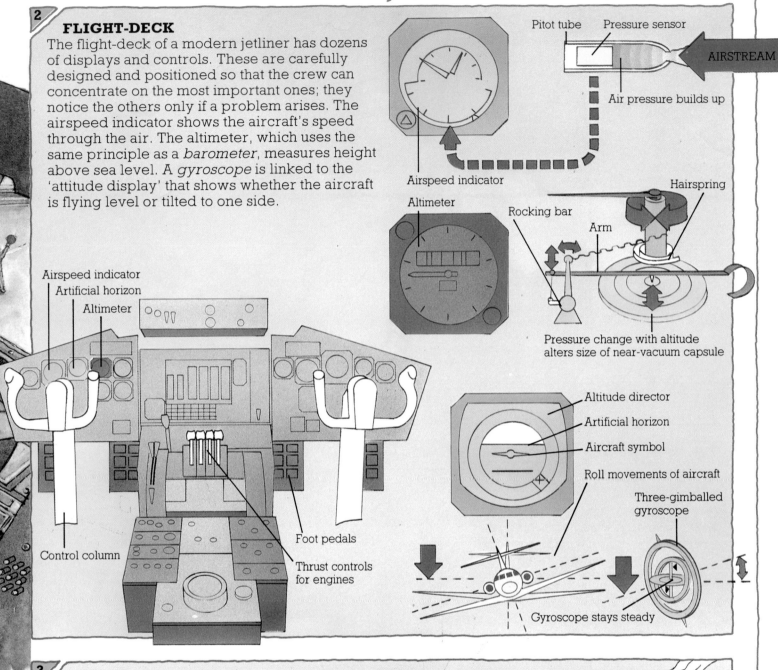

Pitot tube
Pressure sensor
AIRSTREAM
Air pressure builds up
Airspeed indicator
Altimeter
Rocking bar
Arm
Hairspring
Pressure change with altitude alters size of near-vacuum capsule

Airspeed indicator
Artificial horizon
Altimeter

Control column
Foot pedals
Thrust controls for engines

Altitude director
Artificial horizon
Aircraft symbol
Roll movements of aircraft
Three-gimballed gyroscope
Gyroscope stays steady

## 3 LIFEJACKET

Airliners carry lifejackets, and instructions to show passengers how to use them, for all journeys over water. Some jackets are blown up by the wearer, while others self-inflate when a cord is pulled. When the jacket enters sea water, a chemical reaction causes a light to flash. This signals to rescuers the position of the person needing help.

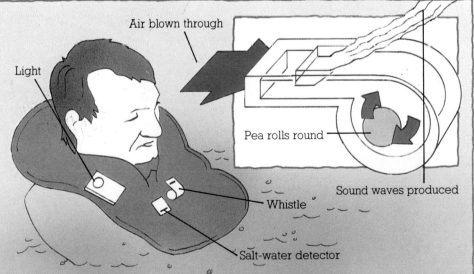

Air blown through
Light
Pea rolls round
Sound waves produced
Whistle
Salt-water detector

## 4 JUMBO JET

One of the most complex machines in the world, the airliner consists of several million separate parts – from turbine blades in the jet engines to passenger headphones for the movie soundtrack. The separate parts are grouped into a series of systems. The parts within each system work together to perform one overall function. The compressors, pistons and pressurized fluid in the hydraulic pipes, which work the various control surfaces and landing gear, make up the *hydraulic system*. The hundreds of kilometres of wiring that connect different parts all over the aircraft to the flight-deck controls and displays, make up the *electrical system*. The fuel tanks, pumps and pipes comprise the *fuel system*. The structural parts such as the fuselage, wings, tailplane and fin, make up the *airframe*.

Cruising at 1000 kilometres per hour, ten kilometres up, an airliner's wing provides lift, like a helicopter's rotor (page 67). When the plane takes off or comes in to land, various parts of its wing lift away. The shape of the wing as seen from the side – called the aerofoil section – changes, according to the speed of the aircraft. Spoilers at the front of the wing 'spoil', or interrupt the airflow over the front, or leading edge, while flaps at the back give extra lift at slower speeds.

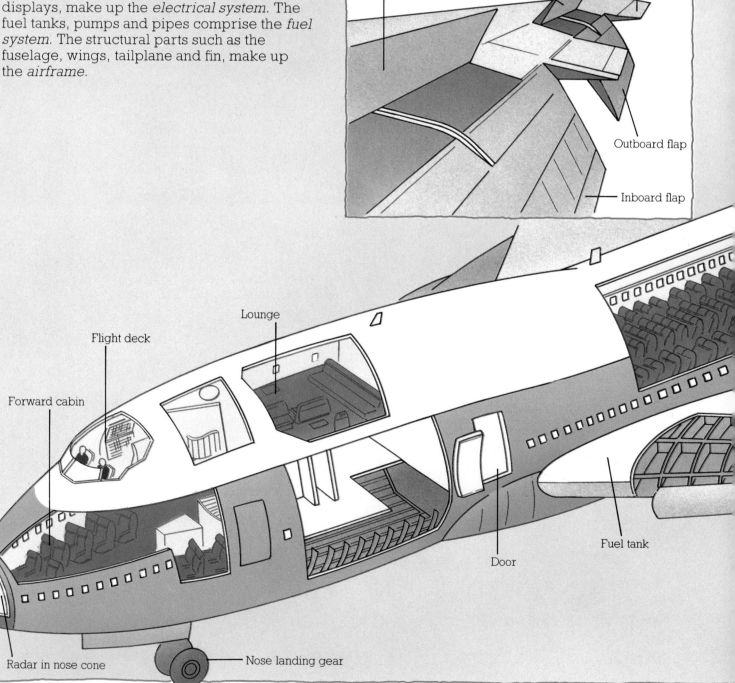

Inboard spoiler

Outboard spoiler

Outboard aileron

Outboard flap

Inboard flap

Lounge

Flight deck

Forward cabin

Door

Fuel tank

Radar in nose cone

Nose landing gear

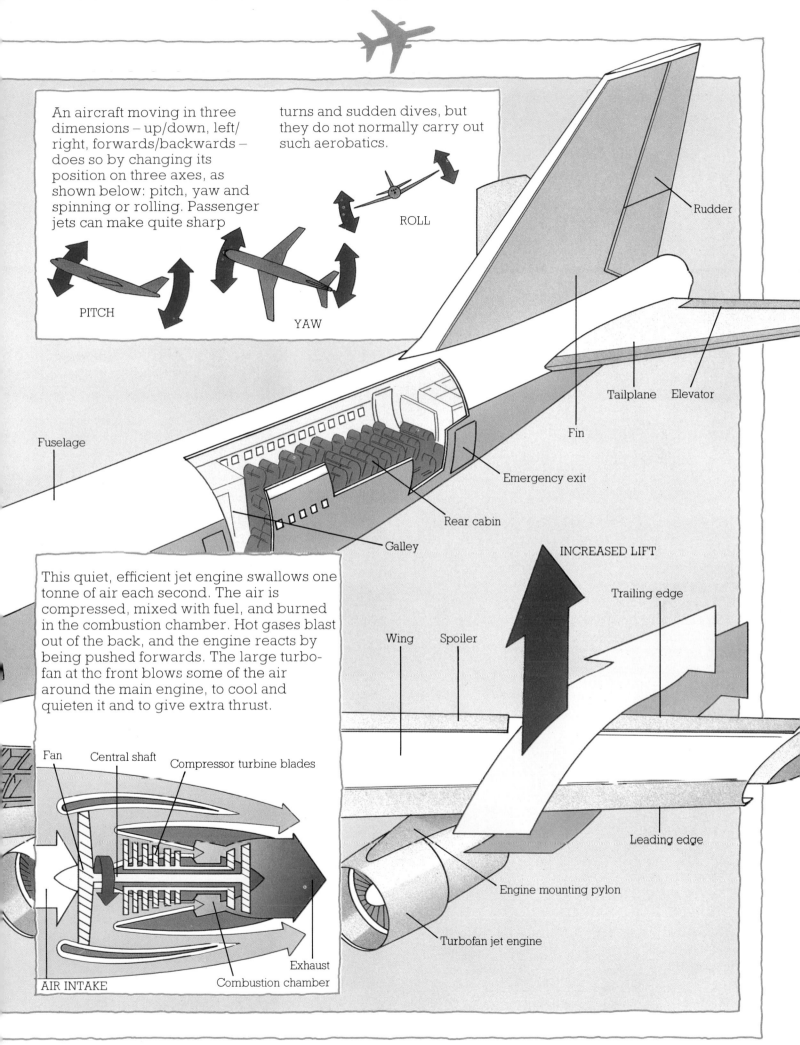

An aircraft moving in three dimensions – up/down, left/right, forwards/backwards – does so by changing its position on three axes, as shown below: pitch, yaw and spinning or rolling. Passenger jets can make quite sharp turns and sudden dives, but they do not normally carry out such aerobatics.

ROLL

PITCH

YAW

Rudder

Tailplane    Elevator

Fin

Emergency exit

Fuselage

Rear cabin

Galley

INCREASED LIFT

This quiet, efficient jet engine swallows one tonne of air each second. The air is compressed, mixed with fuel, and burned in the combustion chamber. Hot gases blast out of the back, and the engine reacts by being pushed forwards. The large turbo-fan at the front blows some of the air around the main engine, to cool and quieten it and to give extra thrust.

Trailing edge

Wing    Spoiler

Fan    Central shaft

Compressor turbine blades

Leading edge

Engine mounting pylon

Turbofan jet engine

Exhaust

AIR INTAKE    Combustion chamber

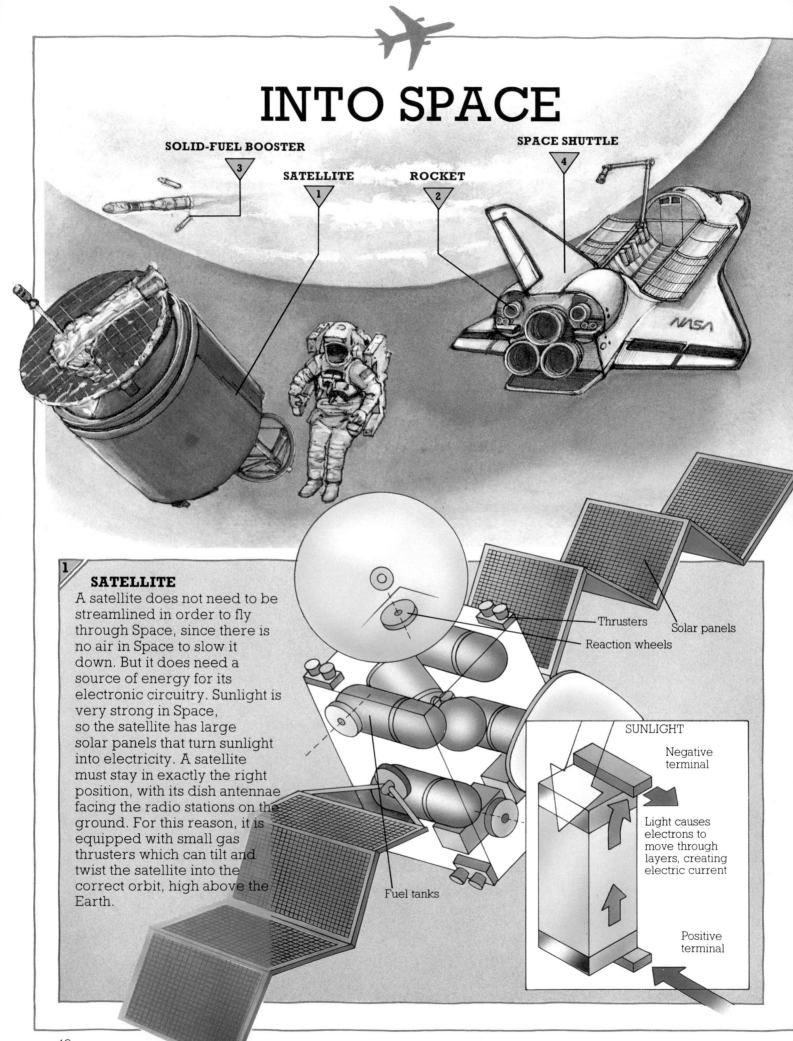

# INTO SPACE

**SOLID-FUEL BOOSTER** 3

**SATELLITE** 1

**ROCKET** 2

**SPACE SHUTTLE** 4

NASA

1

### SATELLITE

A satellite does not need to be streamlined in order to fly through Space, since there is no air in Space to slow it down. But it does need a source of energy for its electronic circuitry. Sunlight is very strong in Space, so the satellite has large solar panels that turn sunlight into electricity. A satellite must stay in exactly the right position, with its dish antennae facing the radio stations on the ground. For this reason, it is equipped with small gas thrusters which can tilt and twist the satellite into the correct orbit, high above the Earth.

Thrusters

Solar panels

Reaction wheels

Fuel tanks

SUNLIGHT

Negative terminal

Light causes electrons to move through layers, creating electric current

Positive terminal

## 2 ROCKET

A spacecraft must reach a speed of 40,000 kilometres per hour, before it can break free of Earth's gravity and head into Space. This is called the escape velocity. One huge rocket engine would make the spacecraft too heavy. The multi-stage launcher is designed to leave its engines and empty fuel tanks behind, stage by stage. As it climbs, smaller engines are sufficient to overcome the weakening pull of Earth's gravity. Nothing can burn without oxygen. Rocket fuel cannot therefore burn on its own in Space, since there is no oxygen (or any other gas). So the rocket takes its own supply, as oxidizer in super-cooled liquid form. The fuel and the oxidizer react in the combustion chamber (*see below*), in a kind of slow, controlled explosion.

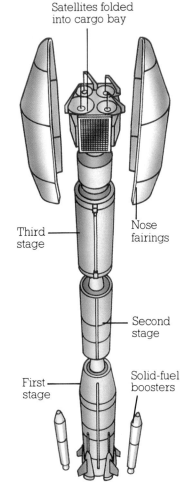

Satellites folded into cargo bay

Nose fairings

Third stage

Second stage

First stage

Solid-fuel boosters

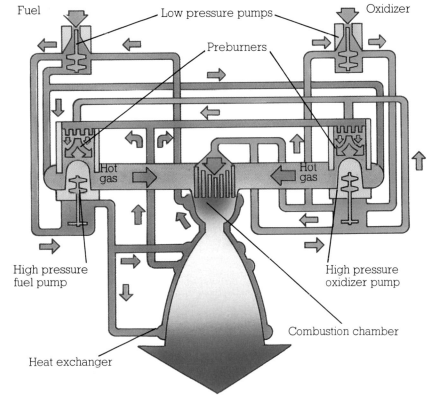

Fuel

Low pressure pumps

Oxidizer

Preburners

Hot gas

Hot gas

High pressure fuel pump

High pressure oxidizer pump

Combustion chamber

Heat exchanger

## 3 SOLID-FUEL BOOSTER

Instead of super-cooled fuel in liquid form, the solid-fuel booster has fuel 'cake' made of aluminium perchlorate, iron oxide, binders and curing chemicals. Once ignited, the booster fires steadily, but its burn cannot be altered or switched off. It 'boosts' acceleration at the start of the launch. The launcher *Ariane*'s boosters burn out and fall away 42 seconds after lift-off.

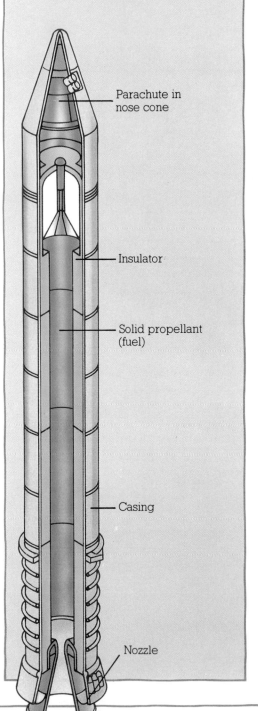

Parachute in nose cone

Insulator

Solid propellant (fuel)

Casing

Nozzle

Astronauts outside the spacecraft may wear a 'jet-pack' called a **manoeuvring unit**. Jets of nitrogen from a compressed-nitrogen tank are 'squirted' from sets of nozzles, using hand controls. In this way the astronaut can move in all three dimensions: up/down, left/right, and forwards/backwards. But there is no air to slow the astronaut, so he or she must squirt a jet of nitrogen in the opposite direction in order to stop moving.

Satellites can be launched from the spacecraft's cargo bay using a remote-controlled **robot arm** to position them precisely in orbit. Satellites which are broken or out of position can be 'captured' by the arm.

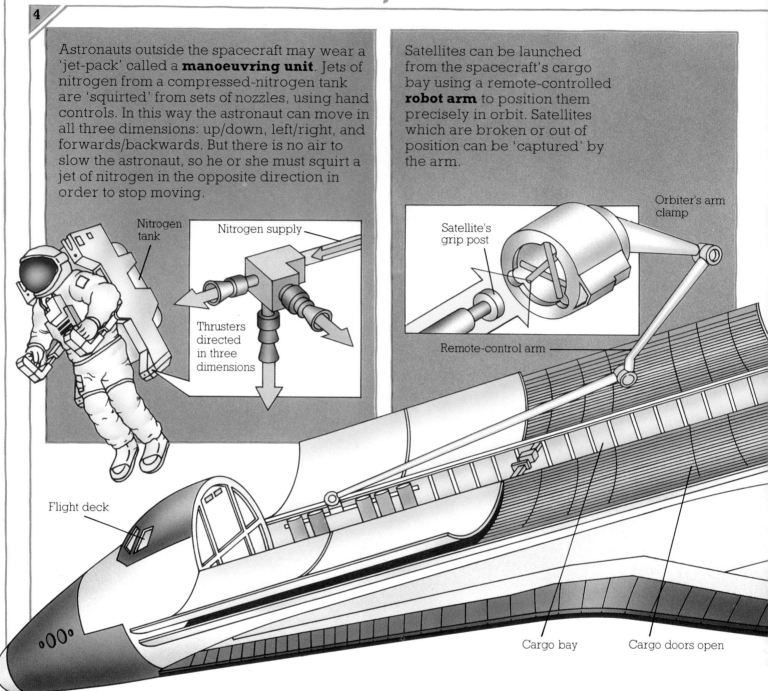

Nitrogen tank

Nitrogen supply

Thrusters directed in three dimensions

Orbiter's arm clamp

Satellite's grip post

Remote-control arm

Flight deck

Cargo bay

Cargo doors open

### SPACE SHUTTLE

Rockets such as *Ariane* and *Apollo V*, which launched the manned mooncrafts in the 1960s and 70s, are ELV's or Expendable Launch Vehicles. They are designed for use only once, and their parts fall to Earth or burn up in the atmosphere. The Space Shuttle is an RLV – a re-usable launch vehicle. The part that goes into space, the 'spaceplane' itself, is known as the orbiter. At lift-off, it is helped by two solid-fuel boosters, each 45.5 metres long and producing 1200 tonnes of thrust. These fall away after 2 minutes and 12 seconds. Fuel for the orbiter's three main engines is contained in a gigantic

fuel tank 47 metres long, which is emptied and falls away 8 minutes and 50 seconds after lift-off. At launch, the weight of the orbiter, boosters and fuel tank is 2000 tonnes! The orbiter has a wingspan of 23.8 metres and a length of 37.2 metres, and it travels around the Earth at heights of between 100 and 300 kilometres. Two pilots fly the orbiter from the flight-deck. Other crew members are the mission specialists, who carry out experiments in Space or help to launch and capture satellites.

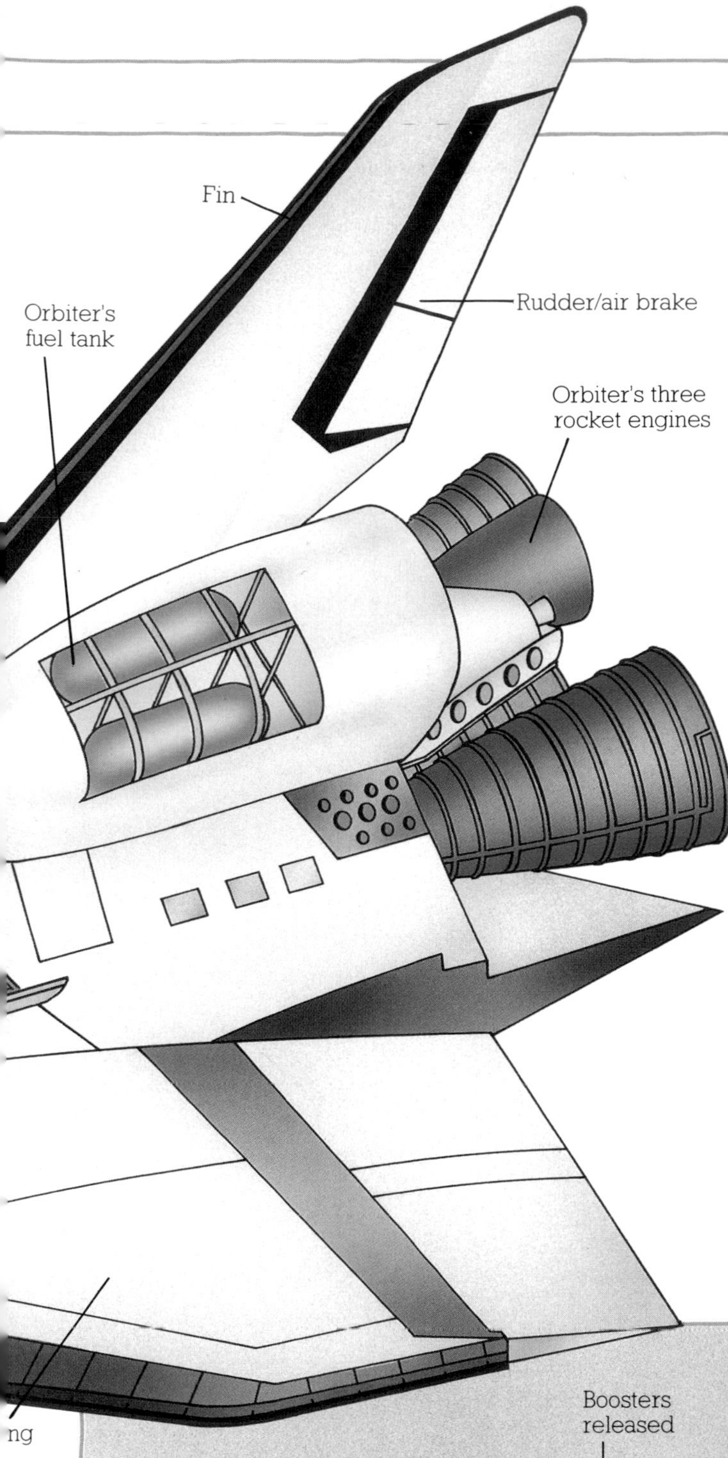

Fin

Rudder/air brake

Orbiter's fuel tank

Orbiter's three rocket engines

In order to move about in Space, the astronaut wears a 'personal spacecraft' – the **spacesuit**. This has an inner water-cooled suit, and an outer pressure-suit that protects against the Sun's glare and radiation and also the tiny meteorites (fragments of rock or metal) that speed through Space. The backpack provides oxygen to breathe and circulates cooling water around the inner suit.

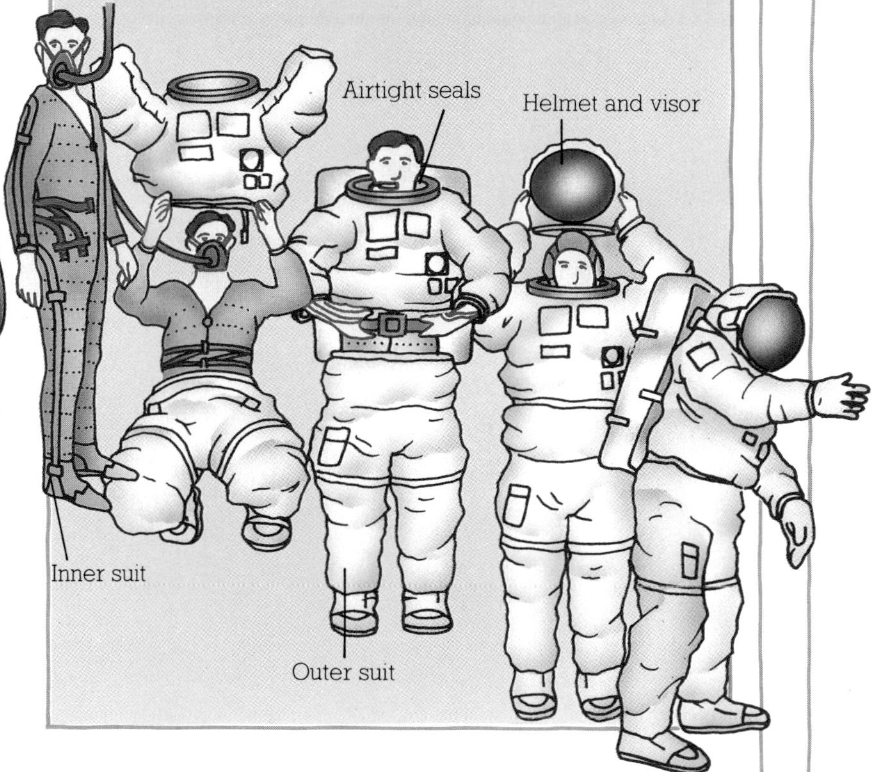

Airtight seals

Helmet and visor

Inner suit

Outer suit

ng

After launch, the orbiter usually stays in space for several days. At the end of the mission, it comes back down into the Earth's atmosphere at tremendous speed, and friction with the ever-thickening air, creates enormous heat. The orbiter is protected from burning up by special ceramic tiles fixed to the lower fuselage. As it comes in to land on the runway, the Shuttle is the world's biggest glider.

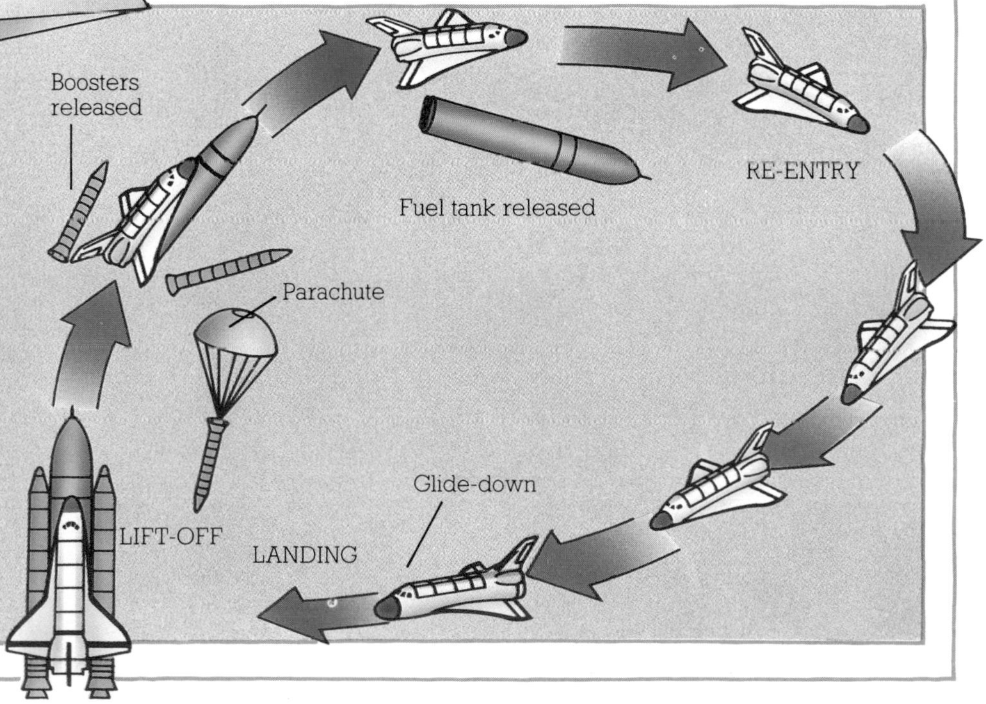

Boosters released

Fuel tank released

RE-ENTRY

Parachute

LIFT-OFF

LANDING

Glide-down

# THE BUILDING SITE

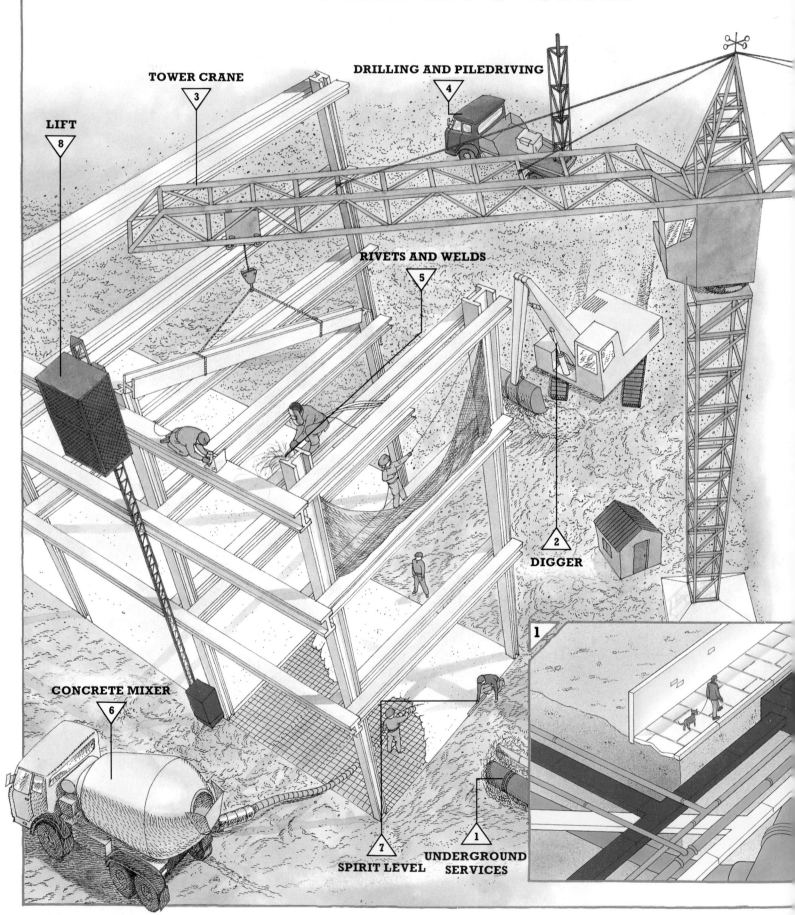

**LIFT**
8

**TOWER CRANE**
3

**DRILLING AND PILEDRIVING**
4

**RIVETS AND WELDS**
5

**DIGGER**
2

**CONCRETE MIXER**
6

**SPIRIT LEVEL**
7

**UNDERGROUND SERVICES**
1

## 2 DIGGER

The multipurpose digger makes trenches and holes, loads materials into trucks, and can bulldoze areas level. The arms, and their buckets, are operated by hydraulic pistons. As hydraulic fluid is pumped under great pressure into the cylinder, it pushes the piston along. The piston is connected to a lever that moves the arm or bucket. These hydraulic pistons can only push. Like the muscles in the human body they are arranged in opposing pairs.

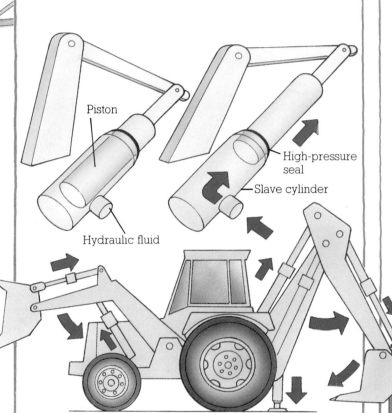

Piston

High-pressure seal

Slave cylinder

Hydraulic fluid

Stabilizing stands

## 3 TOWER CRANE

Towering over the building site, this crane can lift objects over a large area. Its main jib swivels round, and the hook-carrying trolley is winched along the jib by cables and a motor. The crane is 'self-erecting'. After its base is installed, it uses a special extending section, into which it fits a new section of tower. The extending section then 'crawls' up the tower section, fits another tower section into itself and so on, until it is the correct height.

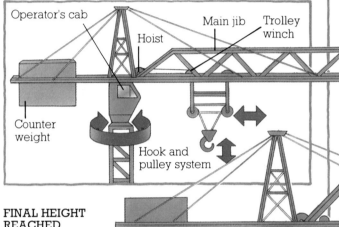

Operator's cab

Hoist

Main jib

Trolley winch

Counter weight

Hook and pulley system

FINAL HEIGHT REACHED

TOWER SECTION FITTED

EXTENDING SECTION FITTED

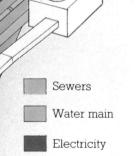

Under the city streets is a maze of tunnels, pipes, wires and cables, known collectively as 'services'. They include underground gas pipes, telephone lines and water mains. Before any new building is erected, planners must check with the city records office to see where they can and cannot dig. They must also look for places where they can 'tap in' to services for the new building.

Sewers

Water main

Electricity

Telecommunications

Gas

## 4 DRILLING AND PILEDRIVING

To stop a building toppling, cracking or sinking, it must be built on firm foundations. The taller the building, the deeper the foundations. Columns or piles can be sunk deep into the ground by drilling or driving. The piledriver is a large weight that is repeatedly raised and dropped onto a driving wedge or pile, hammering it deep into the earth. The earthdrill, a rotary device in a derrick tower, works like an oil rig drill (page 63). London's tallest building, the NatWest Tower, has main foundations 18 metres deep, and 375 piles a further 24 metres deep.

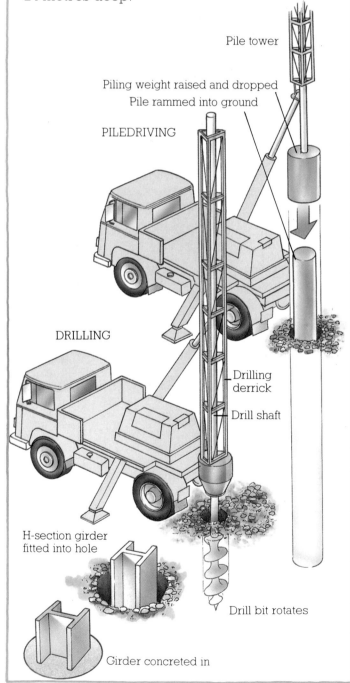

Pile tower

Piling weight raised and dropped
Pile rammed into ground

PILEDRIVING

DRILLING

Drilling derrick

Drill shaft

H-section girder fitted into hole

Drill bit rotates

Girder concreted in

## 5 RIVETS AND WELDS

There are numerous ways of joining girders, plates and other pieces of buildings and machinery. These include screws, nuts and bolts, adhesives, rivets and welds. A rivet is a metal pin with a flattened head at one end. It is pushed by its flat head into holes in the parts to be fastened. A rivet gun then hammers the other

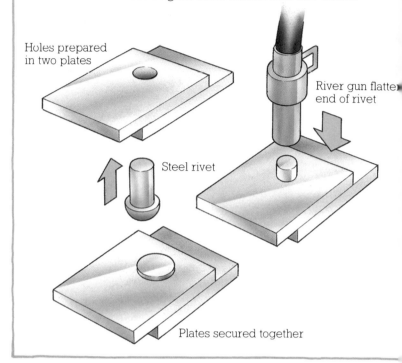

Holes prepared in two plates

River gun flatte end of rivet

Steel rivet

Plates secured together

## 6 CONCRETE MIXER

In a premixed concrete truck, the Archimedes screw keeps the concrete or mortar circulating as it is carried from the mixing depot to the building site. The screw is essentially a spiral or helical ramp (page 18) wound around inside a drum. The same device was used in Ancient Egypt, to lift water out of ditches for irrigating the fields beyond.

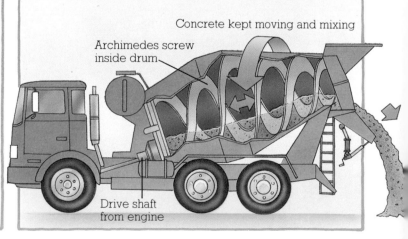

Concrete kept moving and mixing

Archimedes screw inside drum

Drive shaft from engine

end flat, squeezing and securing the parts together.

In a weld, the very high temperature created by an electric arc or flame melts the two metal parts at the join. The liquefied metals run together, and after the heat is removed they solidfy and fuse together.

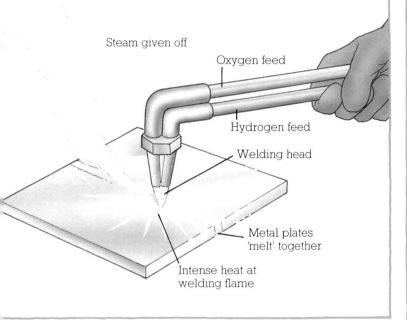

Steam given off
Oxygen feed
Hydrogen feed
Welding head
Metal plates 'melt' together
Intense heat at welding flame

## 7 SPIRIT LEVEL

In the spirit level, a bubble of air floats in oil or a spirit-based fluid, inside a transparent container. The air, being much less dense than the fluid, always finds the highest part of the container and floats on top of the fluid. When the device is level, the bubble rests in the middle of the container, midway between the two marks.

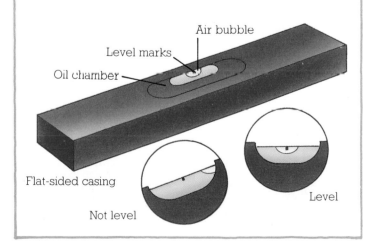

Air bubble
Level marks
Oil chamber
Flat-sided casing
Not level
Level

## 8 LIFT

The goods and materials lift on a building site works in the same way as the passenger lift inside a tall building. The lift car runs up and down a guide tower, or between the guide rails of a lift shaft. It is winched up by the lifting motor, which does not have to lift the whole weight of the car since this is balanced by a counterweight. A safety brake locks the car to the rails or tower if the cable snaps.

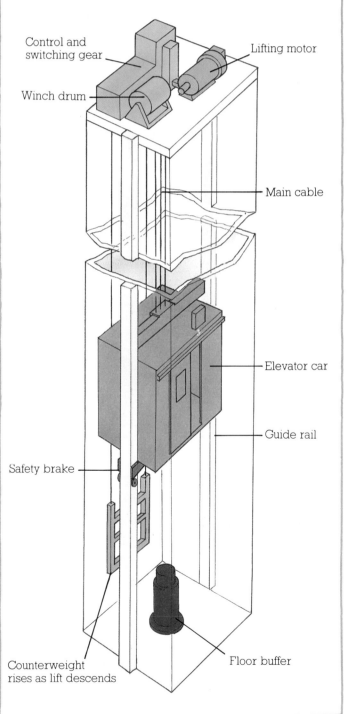

Control and switching gear
Lifting motor
Winch drum
Main cable
Elevator car
Guide rail
Safety brake
Counterweight rises as lift descends
Floor buffer

# BRIDGES

**SPANNING THE RIVER**
2

**TYPES OF BRIDGE**
1

**NUTS AND BOLTS**
3

1 ◁ **TYPES OF BRIDGE**
Four main types of bridge design are shown on the right. Each has advantages. The beam design can be simple and inexpensive, but it needs regular supports along its length. It is not suitable for a wide, deep river. In the cantilever design, each pair of side spans projects beyond their supporting tower, balancing each other for better stability.

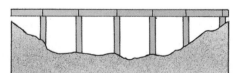
Beam

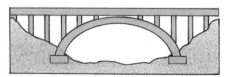
Single-span arch

Suspension

Cantilever

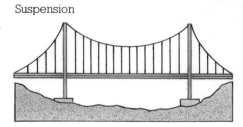

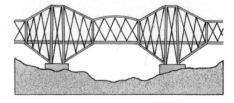

## 2 SPANNING THE RIVER

In a suspension bridge, the deck hangs by suspending cables from the enormously thick main cables. New York's Verrazano-Narrows Bridge has four main cables, each 0.9 of a metre thick, spun from hundreds of thinner steel wires. The main cables transmit the pull of the roadway, over the towers, to the cable anchorages in the ground at either end.

The world's longest single-span suspension bridge is 1410 metres long, over the Humber Estuary in north-east England.

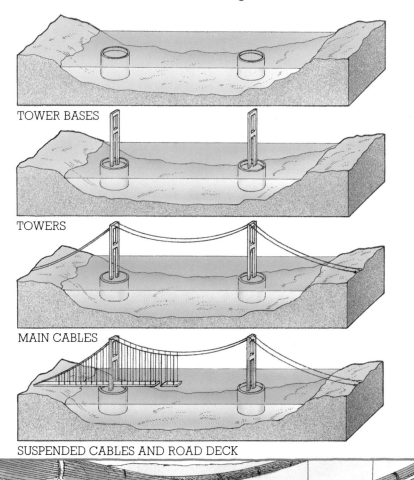

TOWER BASES

TOWERS

MAIN CABLES

SUSPENDED CABLES AND ROAD DECK

## 3 NUTS AND BOLTS

The thread of a bolt winds around the shaft in a helical pattern. (A screw thread has a spiral pattern, page 25.) As it turns, it works like a ramp to force the nut along its length. This changes a rotary force into a longitudinal (lengthwise) force.

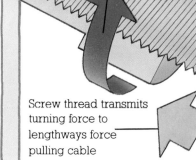

Force turning nut

Nut attached to bridge

Screw thread transmits turning force to lengthways force pulling cable

## 4 THEODOLITE

Marker rule

Angle measured between marks on rule

Theodolite

This surveying instrument measure angles. It is mounted on an adjustable tripod, and has spirit levels (page 55) to show when it is horizontal. The main target is sighted through the eyepiece of the main telescope. A second eyepiece is aimed at the second target, and the angle between these two lines of sight is read off. The surveyor then uses the geometry of triangles to calculate distances and other measurements.

# TUNNELS

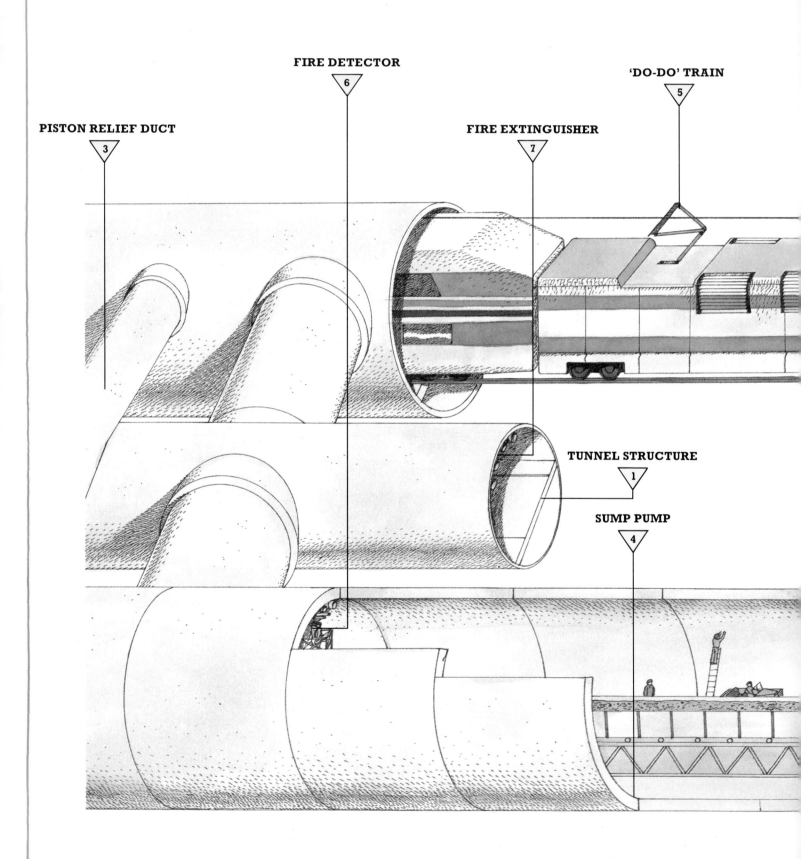

PISTON RELIEF DUCT
3

FIRE DETECTOR
6

FIRE EXTINGUISHER
7

'DO-DO' TRAIN
5

TUNNEL STRUCTURE
1

SUMP PUMP
4

## 1 TUNNEL STRUCTURE

The Eurotunnel between Britain and France is, in fact, three tunnels. The two main shafts, each 7.6 metres across, will convey locomotives pulling wagons of vehicles, freight and passengers. Between them is the smaller service tunnel, 4.8 metres in diameter. This will carry services such as electrical cables and water pipes. It will also be used for access and maintenance, and escape in emergencies.

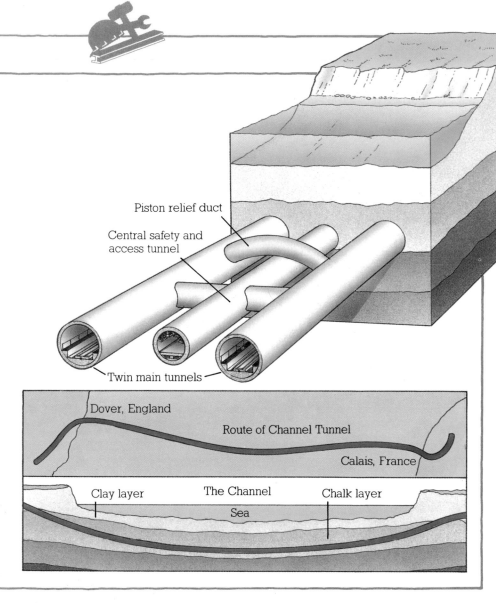

Piston relief duct

Central safety and access tunnel

Twin main tunnels

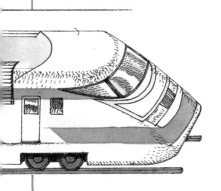

Dover, England

Route of Channel Tunnel

Calais, France

Clay layer

The Channel

Chalk layer

Sea

## 2 TUNNEL-BORING MACHINE

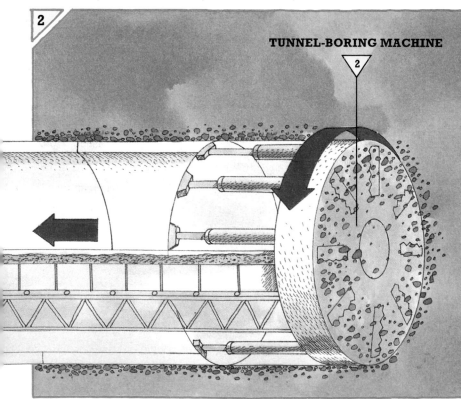

TUNNEL-BORING MACHINE

2

Eurotunnel's rotating cutter head is like a giant drill (page 27). It bears over 100 cutting rollers to chew up the rock, and 200 teeth, made of the very hard metal tungsten. The head goes round about twice each minute, depending on the material being drilled. Hydraulic rams guide the cutting head, steered by laser beams. The gripper ring pushes against the tunnel wall as rams force the machine forwards. A system of conveyors takes away the spoil at a rate of 70 cubic metres (almost two large dumper trucks) for every one metre of tunnel drilled.

### 3 PISTON RELIEF DUCT

As a train travels through the Eurotunnel at 160 kilometres per hour, it will push air in front of it. This will gradually increase the air pressure, like air being forced along a cylinder by a piston (page 89). It could even damage passengers' ears. So there are regular smaller cross-shafts, known as *piston relief ducts*, between the two main tunnels. Air pushed by the speeding locomotive will circulate through these, back along the other tunnel, and then into the main tunnel behind the locomotive. In this way the pressure build-up is avoided.

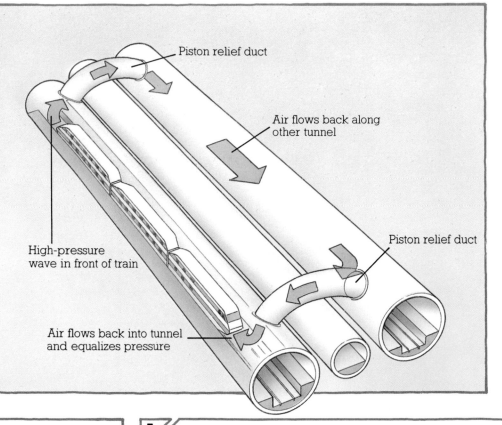

Piston relief duct

Air flows back along other tunnel

Piston relief duct

High-pressure wave in front of train

Air flows back into tunnel and equalizes pressure

### 4 SUMP PUMP

It is impossible to prevent rainwater, drips of oil and fuel, and various other fluids from collecting along the tunnel bottoms. Among other problems, this could create a fire hazard. The sump pump is specially designed to collect these various wastes. It is worked by high-pressure water that rotates the vanes and draws up the wastes, to be pumped away along the outlet pipe.

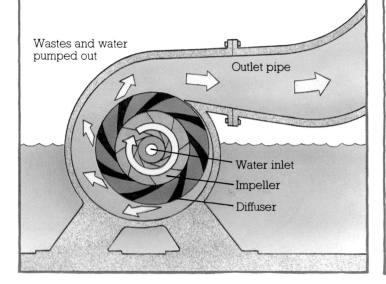

Wastes and water pumped out

Outlet pipe

Water inlet

Impeller

Diffuser

### 5 'DO-DO' TRAIN

With the fastest trip under the Channel taking only 35 minutes, loading and unloading could take up a large proportion of the total journey time. So, like the Ro-Ro ferry (page 42), the Do-Do train is designed for a speedy and convenient turnaround of vehicles and freight. Cars can 'Drive On and Drive Off' without having to be loaded by cranes or turn around in

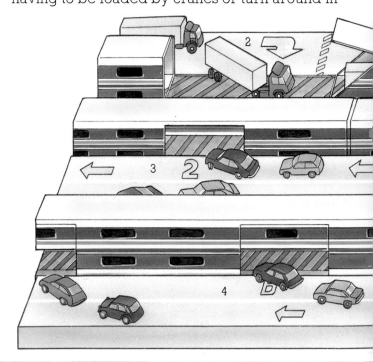

## 6 FIRE DETECTOR

The fire detectors are fitted at regular intervals along the tunnel. They contain a specially-developed *alloy* (mixture of metals) that melts at temperatures only a little above normal. The melted blob completes an electric circuit and sets off the alarm.

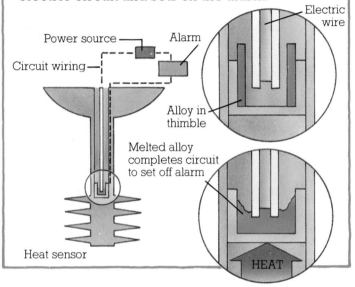

Power source

Alarm

Circuit wiring

Electric wire

Alloy in thimble

Melted alloy completes circuit to set off alarm

Heat sensor

HEAT

## 7 FIRE EXTINGUISHER

This is a carbon dioxide ($CO_2$)-type extinguisher. When the strike knob is hit, the piercer punctures the pressure-release disc and allows the pressurized carbon dioxide to escape. This gas is heavier than air and it settles over the fire, smothering it like a blanket, and keeping away the oxygen that flames need to burn. Deprived of oxygen, the fire gradually goes out.

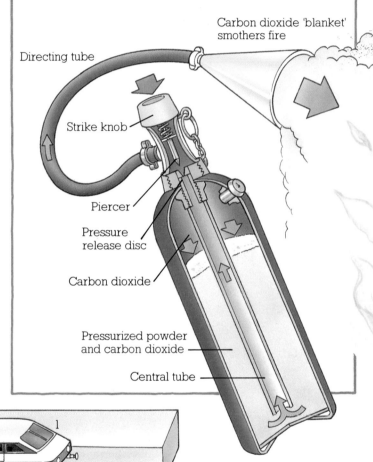

Carbon dioxide 'blanket' smothers fire

Directing tube

Strike knob

Piercer

Pressure release disc

Carbon dioxide

Pressurized powder and carbon dioxide

Central tube

wagons. Eurotunnel's car wagons are 25 metres long. There are about 30 in the standard tourist 'shuttle train', which travels back and forth between the two terminals.

The freight wagons are 18 metres in length and each train consists of about 25 of these. There will also be bulk-freight wagons to carry loads such as grain.

1. High-speed electric locomotive

2. Trucks and container-freight loading bay

3. Upper car deck loading ramp

4. Lower car deck loading ramp

5. High and special loads

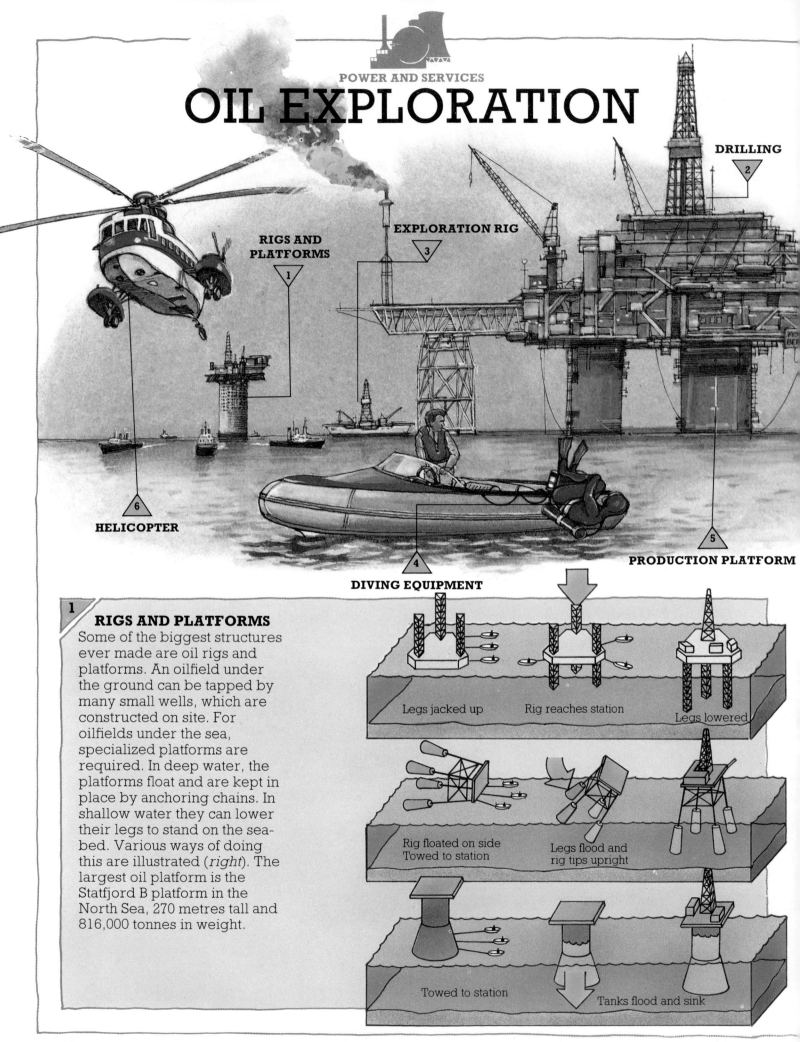

# OIL EXPLORATION

**DRILLING** ▽ 2

**RIGS AND
PLATFORMS** ▽ 1

**EXPLORATION RIG** ▽ 3

6

**HELICOPTER**

5

**PRODUCTION PLATFORM**

4

**DIVING EQUIPMENT**

## 1   RIGS AND PLATFORMS

Some of the biggest structures ever made are oil rigs and platforms. An oilfield under the ground can be tapped by many small wells, which are constructed on site. For oilfields under the sea, specialized platforms are required. In deep water, the platforms float and are kept in place by anchoring chains. In shallow water they can lower their legs to stand on the sea-bed. Various ways of doing this are illustrated (*right*). The largest oil platform is the Statfjord B platform in the North Sea, 270 metres tall and 816,000 tonnes in weight.

Legs jacked up    Rig reaches station    Legs lowered

Rig floated on side
Towed to station    Legs flood and
rig tips upright

Towed to station    Tanks flood and sink

## 2 DRILLING

The drilling derrick is a tower that supports the drill pipes. It lowers them as the drill is gradually lengthened, by adding extra sections of pipe (*below right*). It also raises them section by section when the drill bit needs to be changed. The drill pipes contain several channels (*right*). A special mixture of mud is pumped at high pressure down one channel. It cools and lubricates the rotary drill bit (*far right*) and carries pieces of drilled rock back up to the surface, through the outer pipe channel. The high-pressure mud also prevents underground water from leaking into the borehole. Once the oil-bearing rocks are reached (*below*), the drilling pipes are withdrawn and casing pipes are inserted into the bore. These form the tube up which the oil flows to the surface. Sometimes powerful acids or explosives are used to start the oil flowing.

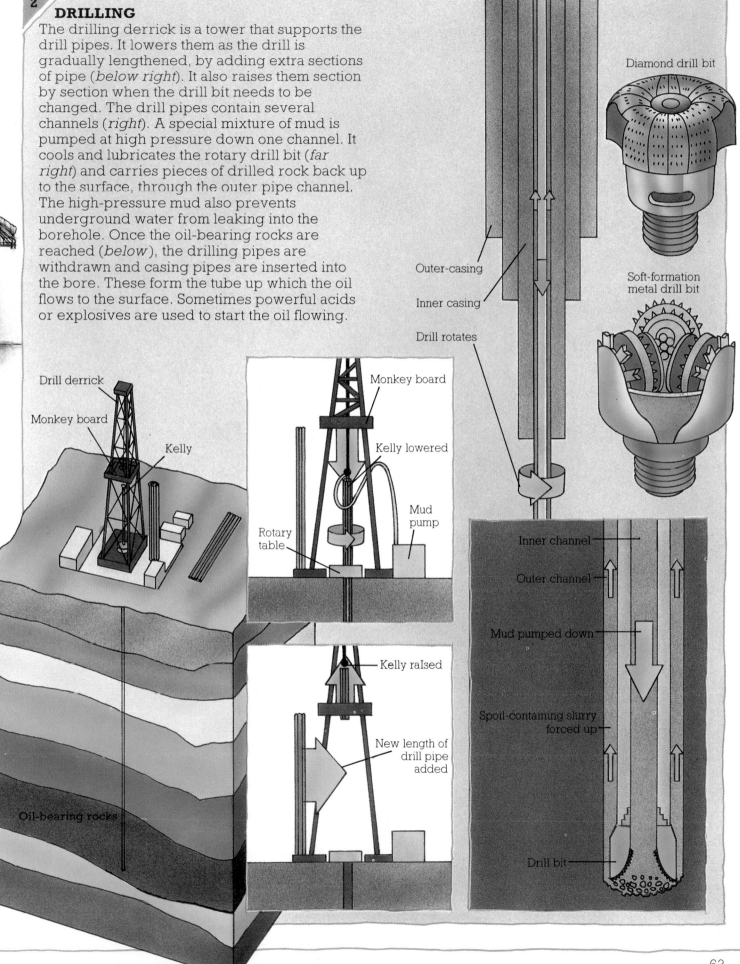

Diamond drill bit

Soft-formation metal drill bit

Outer-casing

Inner casing

Drill rotates

Inner channel

Outer channel

Mud pumped down

Spoil-containing slurry forced up

Drill bit

Drill derrick

Monkey board

Kelly

Monkey board

Kelly lowered

Rotary table

Mud pump

Kelly raised

New length of drill pipe added

Oil-bearing rocks

## 3 EXPLORATION RIG

Searching for oil (petroleum) is immensely costly. Before drilling starts, scientists study the sea-bed and the underground rocks using techniques such as *seismology*, to see if they are likely to contain oil. Then the smaller, mobile exploration rig drills a series of test bores, to mark out the extent and depth of the oilfield. If there is enough oil to make extraction worthwhile, a production platform is installed (*opposite*).

Present drill site

Exploratory rig

Past drill sites

Extent of oil field

Rock strata

## 4 DIVING EQUIPMENT

The underwater parts of oil rigs, drills and pipelines must be checked for corrosion, and maintained and serviced. Highly trained divers carry out this hazardous work. They can descend to depths of 100 metres using specialist scuba gear. (Scuba stands for Self-Contained Underwater Breathing Apparatus.) The scuba's breathing mechanism is shown on the right. As the diver breathes in, gas from the aqualung's pressure tank passes through valves and a diaphragm which form an 'airlock', to reduce its pressure. Breathed-out gases bubble into the water.

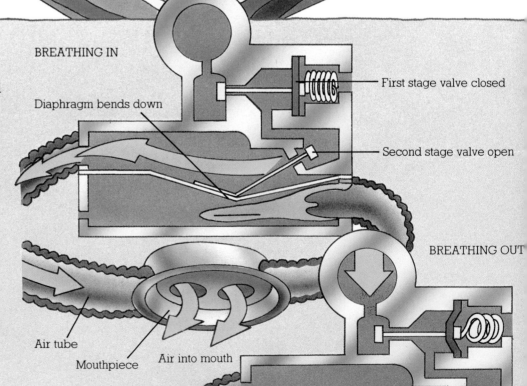

BREATHING IN

Diaphragm bends down

First stage valve closed

Second stage valve open

BREATHING OUT

Air tube

Mouthpiece

Air into mouth

Diaphragm bends up

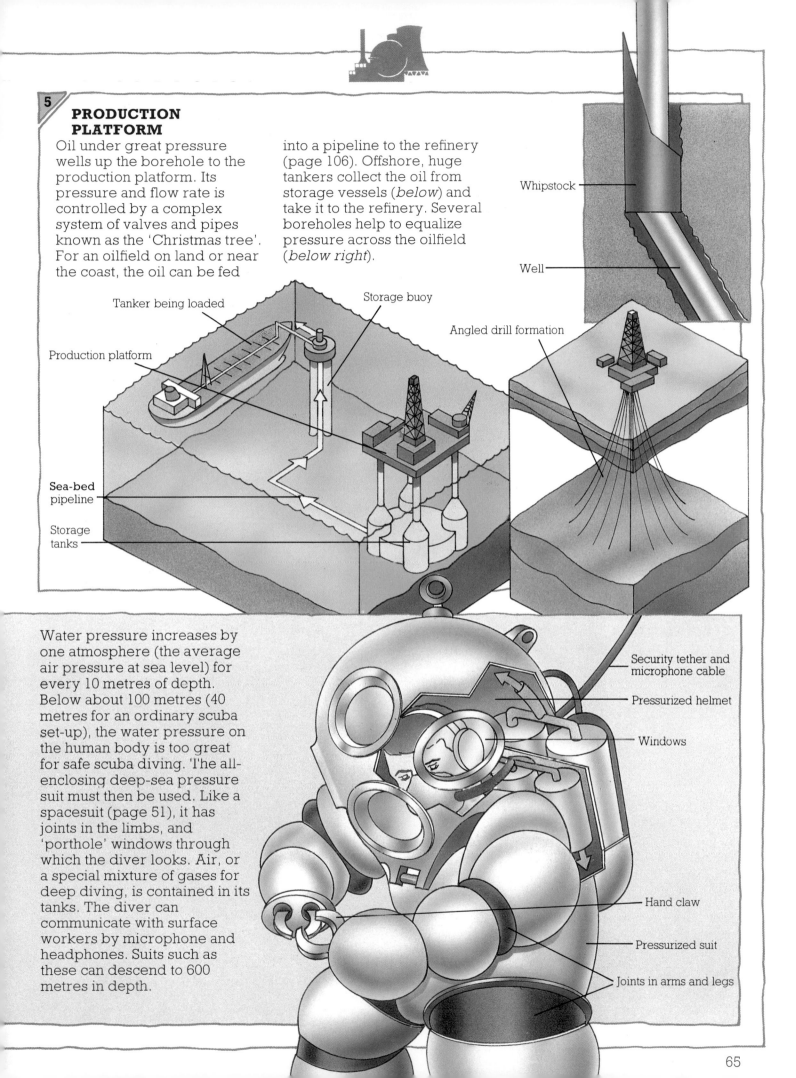

## PRODUCTION PLATFORM

Oil under great pressure wells up the borehole to the production platform. Its pressure and flow rate is controlled by a complex system of valves and pipes known as the 'Christmas tree'. For an oilfield on land or near the coast, the oil can be fed into a pipeline to the refinery (page 106). Offshore, huge tankers collect the oil from storage vessels (*below*) and take it to the refinery. Several boreholes help to equalize pressure across the oilfield (*below right*).

Whipstock

Well

Tanker being loaded

Storage buoy

Angled drill formation

Production platform

Sea-bed pipeline

Storage tanks

Water pressure increases by one atmosphere (the average air pressure at sea level) for every 10 metres of depth. Below about 100 metres (40 metres for an ordinary scuba set-up), the water pressure on the human body is too great for safe scuba diving. The all-enclosing deep-sea pressure suit must then be used. Like a spacesuit (page 51), it has joints in the limbs, and 'porthole' windows through which the diver looks. Air, or a special mixture of gases for deep diving, is contained in its tanks. The diver can communicate with surface workers by microphone and headphones. Suits such as these can descend to 600 metres in depth.

Security tether and microphone cable

Pressurized helmet

Windows

Hand claw

Pressurized suit

Joints in arms and legs

# HELICOPTER

Helicopters are used to ferry supplies and people to oil rigs, and also to rescue them in an emergency (as shown here). They can fly backwards, forwards, both up and down and also remain hovering stationary in the air. Instead of a fixed wing, helicopters have a set of rotating blades which act as long, thin wings. These can be tilted to control the direction the helicopter takes. The pilot's control stick alters the angle of the blades via a swash plate. The diagram below shows how the pilot's controls are connected to the swashplate and then to the rotor blades.

The rotors spin round very fast in one direction and the natural reaction is for the rest of the machine to spin round in the opposite direction. A small rotor mounted on the tail acts as a propeller whose thrust cancels out this tendency. Some helicopters have two sets of main rotors that spin in opposite directions, so each blade cancels the spinning force of the other.

Unlike aeroplanes, helicopters have no natural stability. They require constant adjustments to the controls to keep them in level flight.

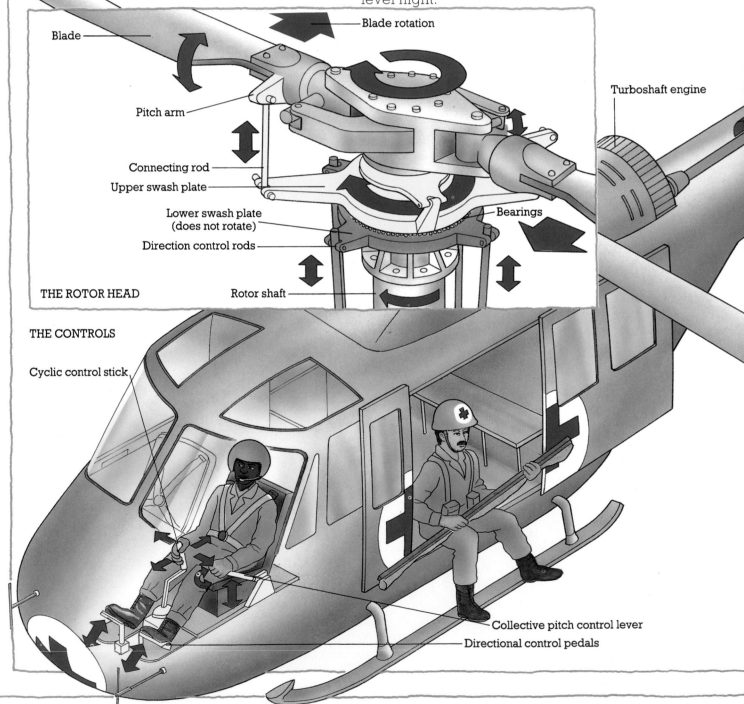

Blade

Blade rotation

Pitch arm

Connecting rod

Upper swash plate

Lower swash plate (does not rotate)

Direction control rods

Turboshaft engine

Bearings

Rotor shaft

THE ROTOR HEAD

THE CONTROLS

Cyclic control stick

Collective pitch control lever

Directional control pedals

## THE TAIL ROTOR

Tail rotor direction

Tail plane

Tail rotor transmission shaft

## CREATING LIFT

The shape of the helicopter's rotor forces air to pass over the top surface faster than it does below. The air pressure above the rotor falls and the helicopter is pushed upwards. Since the pressure rises equally below the blades, the helicopter can also be thought of as riding on a bed of compressed air. To fly higher the pilot tilts the rotor blades, making air flow even faster aross the top surface. This increases the lifting force and pushes the helicopter higher.

Lift

Rotor direction

Air flow faster

Air flow slower

Rotor blade

## MANOEUVRING

To take off and hover the helicopter pilot pulls the collective pitch lever, so increasing the lift of the main rotor blades. The lift is directed downwards and the helicopter rises straight up. To fly ahead the pilot pushes the cyclic control lever forwards. This increases the lift of the blades as they pass behind the pilot and decreases their lift when in front. The helicopter tilts its nose down and the rearward thrust pushes it along.

UP

FORWARD

RIGHT

Direction

Rotor force

Tail rotor force

Engine force

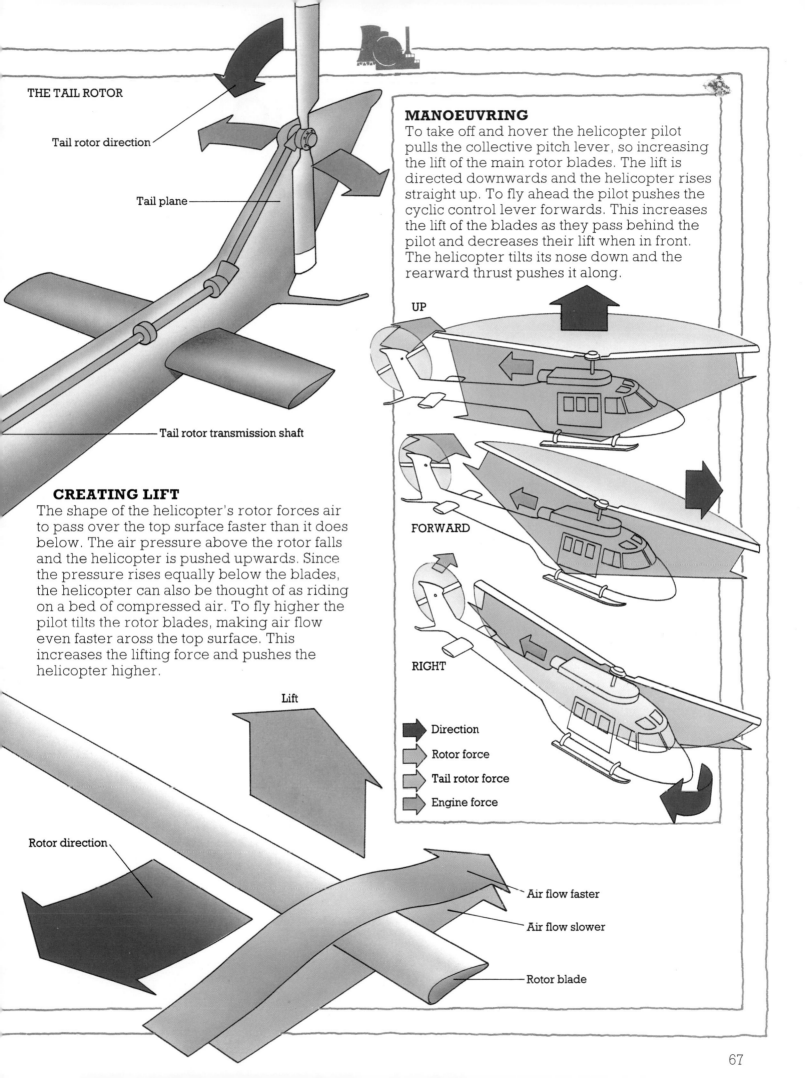

# POWER STATIONS

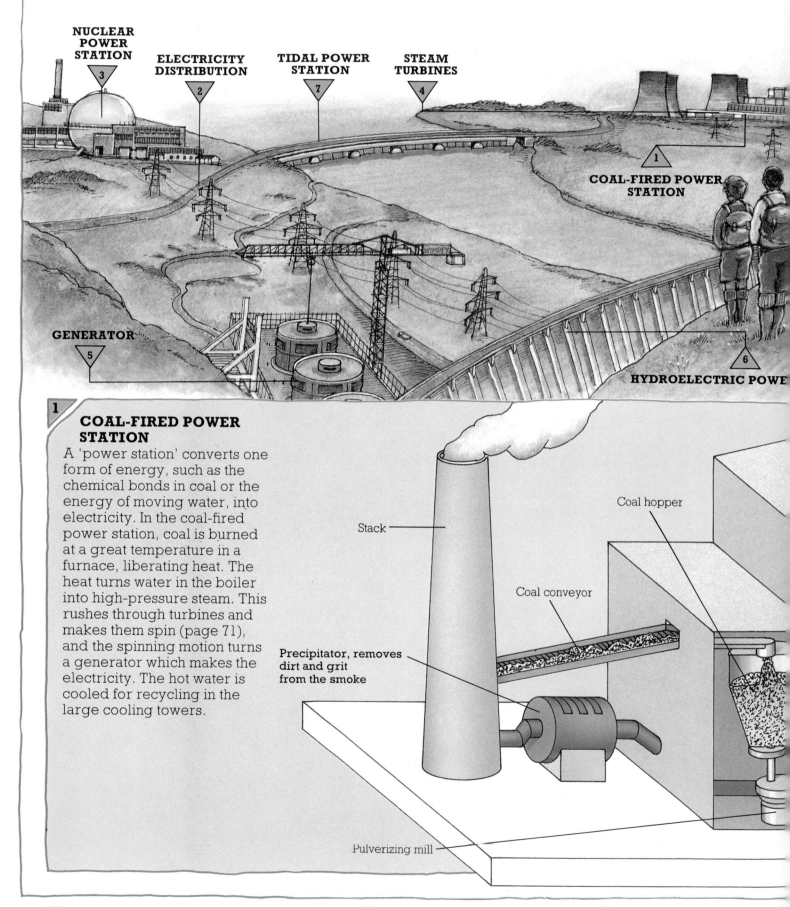

**NUCLEAR POWER STATION**
3

**ELECTRICITY DISTRIBUTION**
2

**TIDAL POWER STATION**
7

**STEAM TURBINES**
4

**COAL-FIRED POWER STATION**
1

**GENERATOR**
5

**HYDROELECTRIC POWE**
6

---

**1**

## COAL-FIRED POWER STATION

A 'power station' converts one form of energy, such as the chemical bonds in coal or the energy of moving water, into electricity. In the coal-fired power station, coal is burned at a great temperature in a furnace, liberating heat. The heat turns water in the boiler into high-pressure steam. This rushes through turbines and makes them spin (page 71), and the spinning motion turns a generator which makes the electricity. The hot water is cooled for recycling in the large cooling towers.

Stack

Coal hopper

Coal conveyor

Precipitator, removes dirt and grit from the smoke

Pulverizing mill

## ELECTRICITY DISTRIBUTION

Large amounts of electricity are carried by overhead lines at very high voltages – 500,000,000 volts or more. (High voltages lose less power when carried over long distances.) Substation transformers change the voltage to a few thousand volts, and then to about 110 or 220–240 volts for home use. The transformer works by *inductance*. If the output coil has twice as many windings as the input coil, it produces twice the voltage – but at only half the current. The total power, measured in *watts* (which equals volts multiplied by amps), stays the same.

Three windings    Metal core    Six windings

TRANSFORMER

100 volts at 10 amps

200 volts at 5 amps

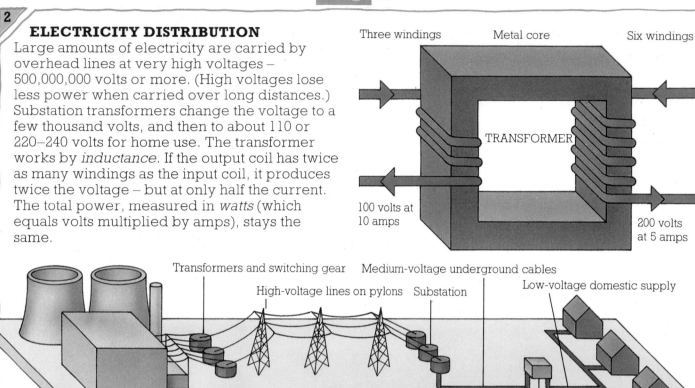

Transformers and switching gear    Medium-voltage underground cables

High-voltage lines on pylons    Substation    Low-voltage domestic supply

Power station    Transformer

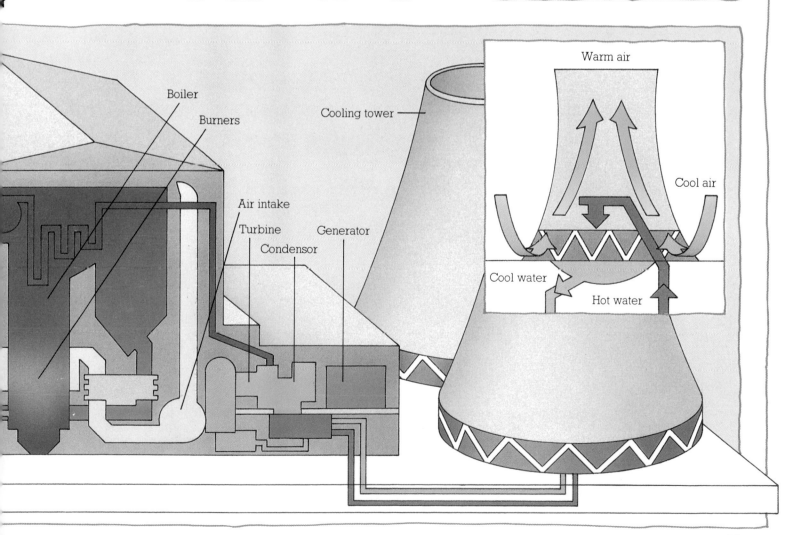

Boiler

Burners

Cooling tower

Air intake

Turbine    Generator

Condensor

Warm air

Cool air

Cool water    Hot water

## NUCLEAR POWER STATION

The various designs of nuclear power stations work on the principle that tiny amounts of matter can be changed into enormous quantities of energy. A nucleus is the small, dense, central part of each atom. The nuclei of certain substances are unstable and ready to split (called nuclear fission) if stimulated in some way. The stimulus can be bombardment by other atomic particles or rays. When this happens, the nucleus splits into two or more parts. The total mass, or weight, of these parts does not add up to the mass of the original intact nucleus. The difference in mass appears as heat energy. For example, if the nucleus of Uranium-235 is hit by one neutron particle, it splits into two other substances (krypton and barium), plus energy, plus about two more neutrons. These neutrons continue the reaction by splitting more Uranium-235 nuclei, and so on, in a chain reaction. The reaction is stopped from getting out of hand by control rods that absorb extra neutrons.

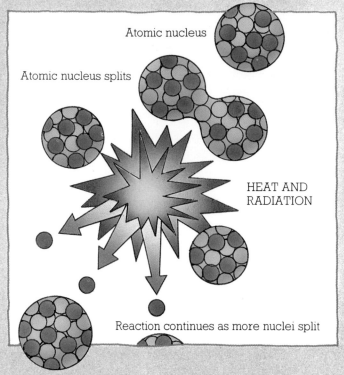

Atomic nucleus

Atomic nucleus splits

HEAT AND RADIATION

Reaction continues as more nuclei split

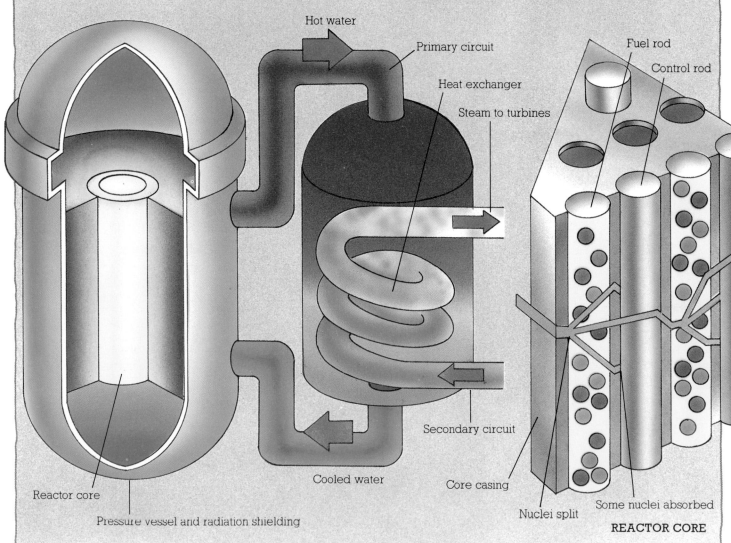

Hot water

Primary circuit

Heat exchanger

Steam to turbines

Fuel rod

Control rod

Secondary circuit

Cooled water

Core casing

Reactor core

Pressure vessel and radiation shielding

Nuclei split

Some nuclei absorbed

**REACTOR CORE**

## 4 STEAM TURBINES

Turbines are fan-like blades mounted on a central shaft. Because they are set at an angle, they turn when a fluid (liquid or gas) flows past them. The principle is the same as when you blow at a toy windmill. Your breath is like the steam, and the windmill sails act like turbine blades. Steam turbines are spun by high-pressure steam produced from boiling water, which has been heated in the boiler of a power station. As the steam loses pressure, it flows past different sizes and angles of blades, each designed to extract the maximum energy from the steam at that point. The central shaft of the turbines is connected to the generator (*below*).

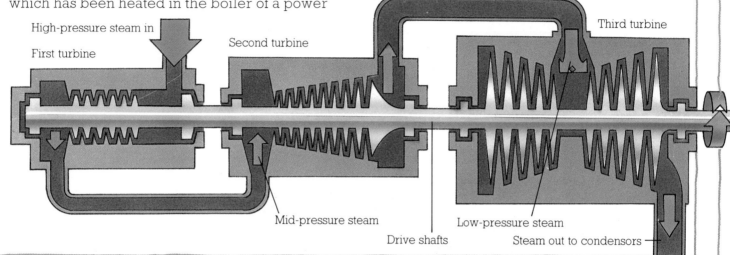

High-pressure steam in

First turbine

Second turbine

Third turbine

Mid-pressure steam

Low-pressure steam

Drive shafts

Steam out to condensors

## 5 GENERATOR

The mechanical energy of a spinning shaft is converted into electrical energy by this device. A central magnet, or rotor, turns around inside a series of electrical coils, called the *stator*. As the magnetic field of the rotor passes through the stator coils, it creates electricity in the windings, by inductance. The rotor is an electromagnet that itself needs electricity to make its magnetic field. This is conveyed to its own coils by brushes that press against slip-rings on the spinning shaft. But it is a small amount of electricity compared to the total quantity generated.

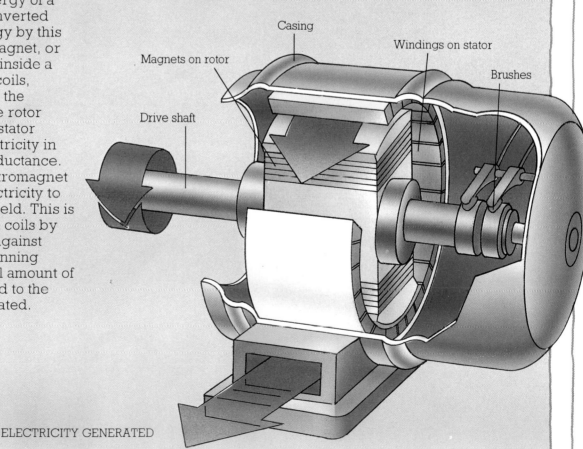

Casing

Windings on stator

Magnets on rotor

Brushes

Drive shaft

ELECTRICITY GENERATED

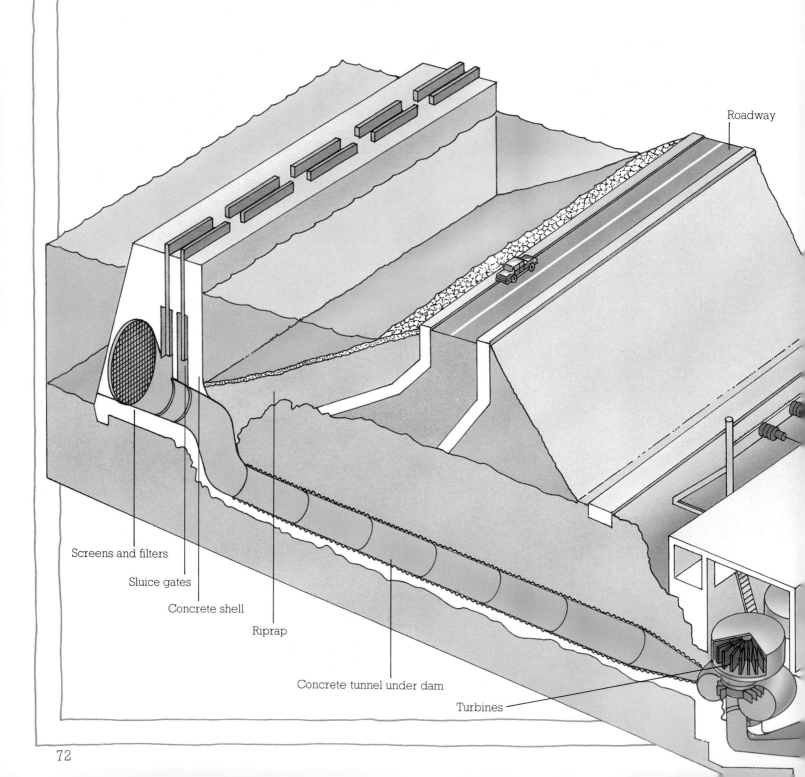

# HYDROELECTRIC POWER STATION

The force of gravity pulls water along a river to the sea. The hydroelectric power station 'taps into' this flow of falling water and uses it to turn turbine blades. Under the turbine is a *draft tube* that allows water to fall away from the blades quickly. This creates a vacuum effect that sucks more water in, thereby increasing the efficiency of the turbine. The turbine is connected to electricity generators. A river that is in full flood in the wet season, but then shrinks in the dry season, is too unreliable by itself for

hydroelectricity. Therefore a dam is usually built at the site. This holds back the water in times of plenty, and uses this stored water to drive the turbines during dry spells. The dam creates a lake behind it which makes water available for irrigation. Three-quarters of South America's electricity is hydroelectricity. This type of power generation does not pollute the atmosphere like a coal-fired station, and it does not create hazardous and long-lasting radioactive wastes as do nuclear power stations.

Roadway

Screens and filters

Sluice gates

Concrete shell

Riprap

Concrete tunnel under dam

Turbines

One design of hydroelectric turbine is the Francis reaction turbine (*below*). Water pushes the blades around as it streams through the adjustable vanes and then falls downwards. Another design, the Kaplan turbine, looks like a ship's propeller (page 40).

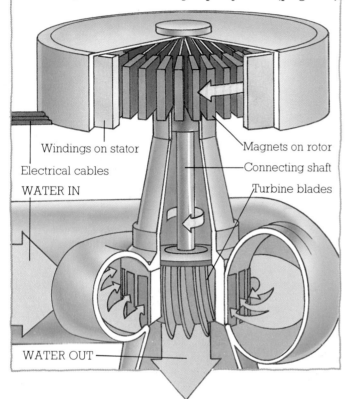

Windings on stator

Magnets on rotor

Electrical cables

Connecting shaft

WATER IN

Turbine blades

WATER OUT

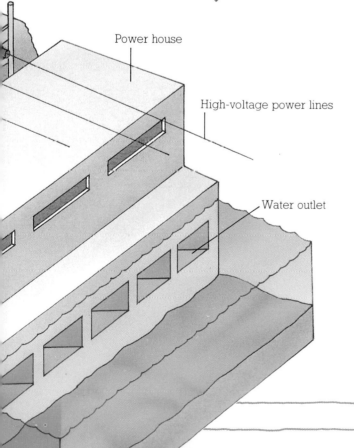

Power house

High-voltage power lines

Water outlet

## TIDAL POWER STATION

The Sun and the Moon both pull on the Earth due to their gravitational forces. The movements of the Earth around the Sun, and the Moon around the Earth, pull 'bulges' of sea water around our planet. As the bulge passes a certain place on the shore, we call it a high tide. The trough before the next bulge is the low tide. Tides can be turned into electricity by a tidal power station, that operates in a similar way to the hydroelectric power station (*opposite*). The dam for the turbines is built at the coast, across the mouth of a river. As the tide rises, sea water flows through the dam tunnels into the river, and spins the turbines. When the tide flows out the turbine blades spin in the other direction.

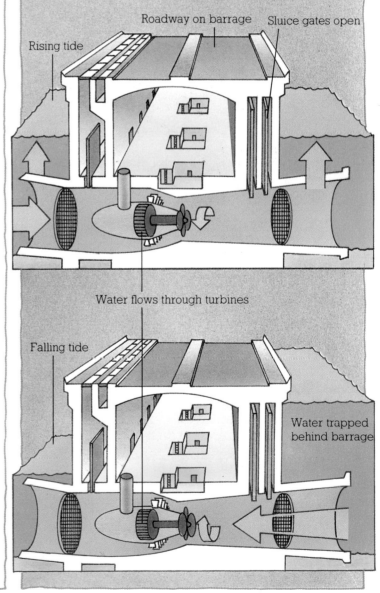

Roadway on barrage    Sluice gates open

Rising tide

Water flows through turbines

Falling tide

Water trapped behind barrage

# THE NEWSROOM

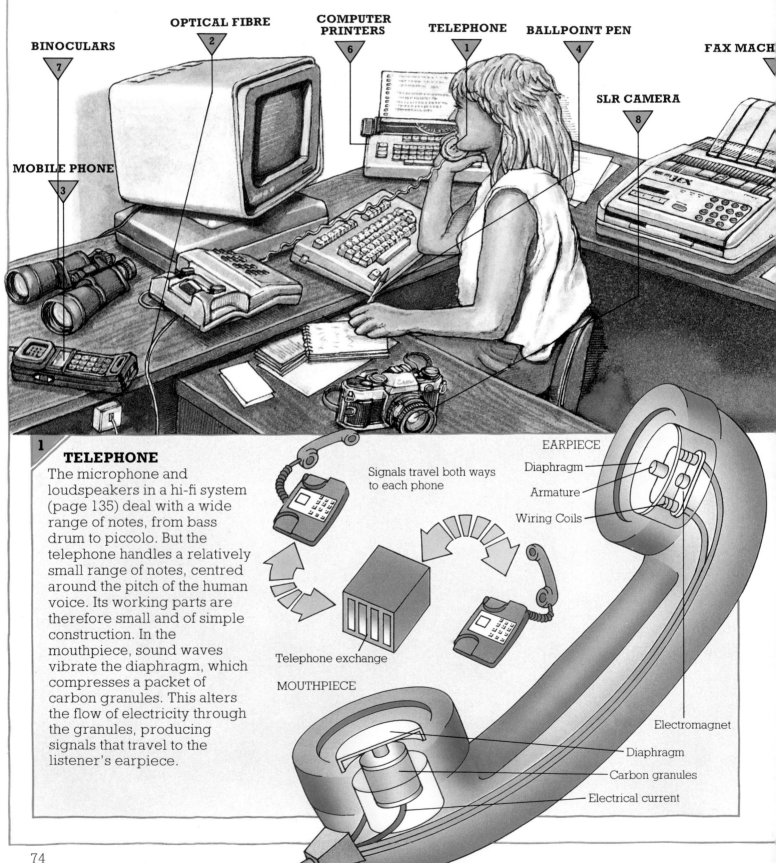

**OPTICAL FIBRE** 2

**BINOCULARS** 7

**COMPUTER PRINTERS** 6

**TELEPHONE** 1

**BALLPOINT PEN** 4

**FAX MACH**

**SLR CAMERA** 8

**MOBILE PHONE** 3

## 1 TELEPHONE

The microphone and loudspeakers in a hi-fi system (page 135) deal with a wide range of notes, from bass drum to piccolo. But the telephone handles a relatively small range of notes, centred around the pitch of the human voice. Its working parts are therefore small and of simple construction. In the mouthpiece, sound waves vibrate the diaphragm, which compresses a packet of carbon granules. This alters the flow of electricity through the granules, producing signals that travel to the listener's earpiece.

Signals travel both ways to each phone

Telephone exchange

MOUTHPIECE

EARPIECE

Diaphragm

Armature

Wiring Coils

Electromagnet

Diaphragm

Carbon granules

Electrical current

## 2 OPTICAL FIBRE

Inside an optical fibre, light rays reflect repeatedly off the inner surface. They can travel around bends as a series of short straight lines. Many telephone networks now use optical fibres. These hair-thin fibres can carry more light signals more efficiently than electrical signals in a wire.

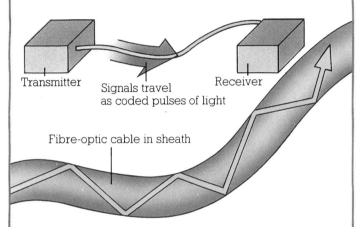

Transmitter

Signals travel as coded pulses of light

Receiver

Fibre-optic cable in sheath

## 3 MOBILE PHONE

An area covered by a cellphone network is divided into a number of smaller areas or 'cells'. Each cell has a transceiver (transmitter/receiver) station. The mobile phone sends and receives messages by radio waves. The signals travel between stations via the standard telephone network.

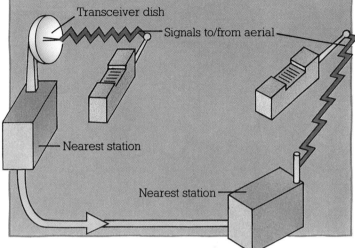

Transceiver dish

Signals to/from aerial

Nearest station

Nearest station

## 4 BALLPOINT PEN

Oil-based ink flows down the refill tube onto the ball as it rotates, and smears onto the paper beneath. The ball and its seating are made from very hard metals such as tungsten, to minimize wear.

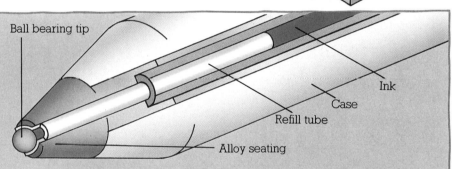

Ball bearing tip

Ink

Case

Refill tube

Alloy seating

## 5 FAX MACHINE

'Fax' is short for 'facsimile', which means a copy or reproduction. The fax machine both sends and receives. It can transmit any marks on paper, from a sketchy drawing to typeset words (page 78). The scanner 'reads' the paper line by line, detecting any dark patches and coding these as electrical signals. The signals travel via the telephone network to the receiving machine. There, a printer puts the same pattern of marks as tiny dots onto the paper – a fraction of a second later.

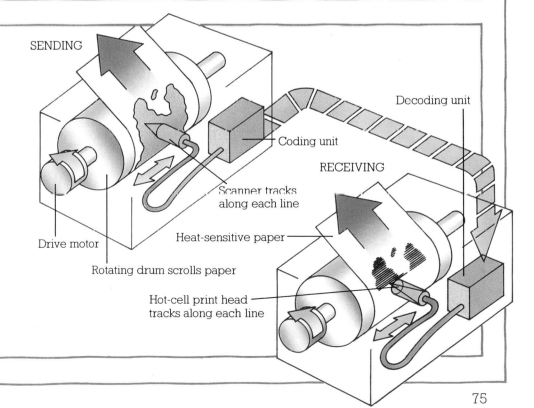

SENDING

Decoding unit

Coding unit

RECEIVING

Scanner tracks along each line

Heat-sensitive paper

Drive motor

Rotating drum scrolls paper

Hot-cell print head tracks along each line

## 6 COMPUTER PRINTERS

In the printout from a dot-matrix printer, the words or pictures are made up from patterns of tiny dots. These dots are made by little pins in the print head, which hammer against an inked ribbon as the head whizzes along, line by line, making ink spots on the paper. The pins are worked by miniature electromagnets. In a daisy-wheel printer, each letter or number is a raised ridge on the print head. The wheel twirls round until the correct letter is aligned with the hammer, which then punches it against an inked ribbon to mark the paper. The wheel spokes are supposed to resemble the petals of a daisy, hence the name.

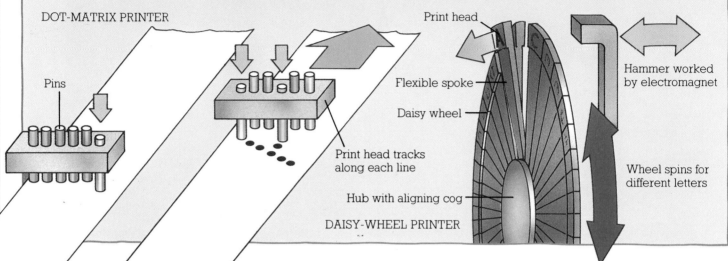

DOT-MATRIX PRINTER

Pins

Print head tracks along each line

Print head

Flexible spoke

Daisy wheel

Hammer worked by electromagnet

Wheel spins for different letters

Hub with aligning cog

DAISY-WHEEL PRINTER

## 7 BINOCULARS

A telescope gives a two-dimensional image with no 'depth', but a pair of binoculars lets you see in three dimensions. Each barrel contains a lens system that magnifies the view, and prisms which 'fold' the light rays, thereby allowing the barrel to be quite short. The prisms also turn the image the correct way up for the eye. Look through one eyepiece only, and you see a 'flat' scene, like through a telescope. When you look through both barrels, your brain combines the slightly different views from each eye into one three-dimensional scene, just as it does in normal sight.

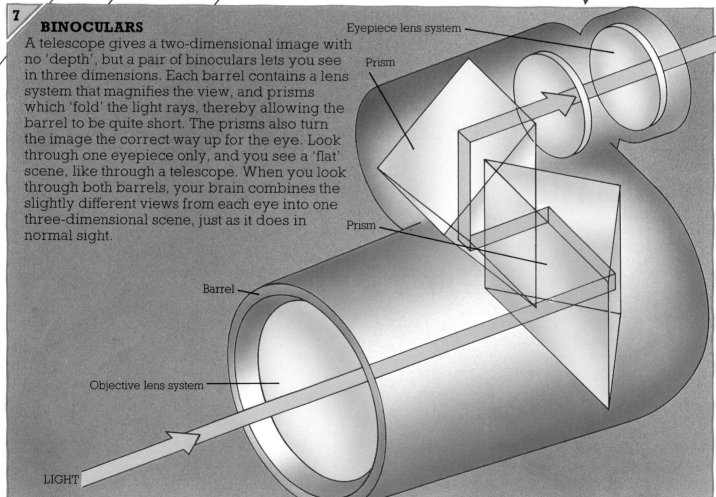

Eyepiece lens system

Prism

Prism

Barrel

Objective lens system

LIGHT

## SLR CAMERA

SLR means Single Lens Reflex. The 'single lens' refers to the fact that the scene through the viewfinder is exactly the same as the scene that appears on the film, because they are both seen through the same lens. (In some cameras, the viewfinder has a separate lens, to one side of the main lens.) This is achieved by a mirror in front of the film, that reflects light rays up to a five-sided pentaprism. The prism turns the image the correct way up by reflecting the light rays around a series of corners – this is the 'reflex' part. It then sends the rays on to the eye. When the shutter button is pressed, the mirror swings up out of the way, and the light rays momentarily fall onto the film before the mirror swings down again.

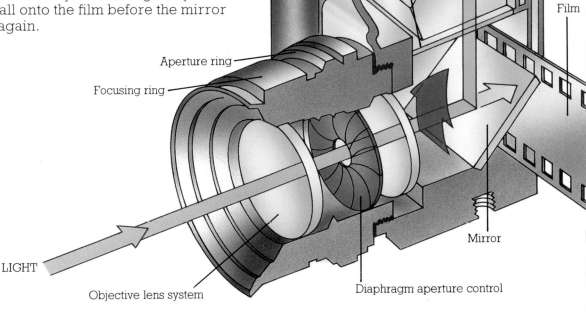

Shutter button

Focusing plate

Prism

Spool winder

Eyepiece

Film

Aperture ring

Focusing ring

LIGHT

Objective lens system

Diaphragm aperture control

Mirror

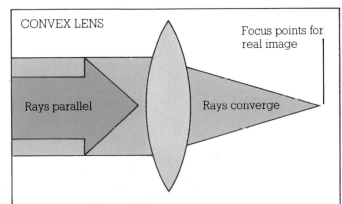

CONVEX LENS

Focus points for real image

Rays parallel

Rays converge

The two basic types of lens are concave and convex lenses. As light rays pass from air into the glass of the lens, they are bent slightly or *refracted*. They are refracted again as they leave the glass and enter the air on the other side of the lens. The curvature of a convex lens bends the rays inwards, making them converge.

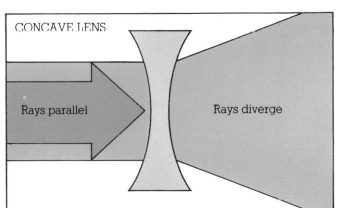

CONCAVE LENS

Rays parallel

Rays diverge

The curved surfaces of the concave lens diverges the light rays, bending them outwards. Lenses are vital to optical instruments such as cameras, binoculars, telescopes and microscopes. Such lenses are usually made from special optical glass. They are arranged in groups, called lens systems, to reduce image distortion.

# PRINTING A BOOK

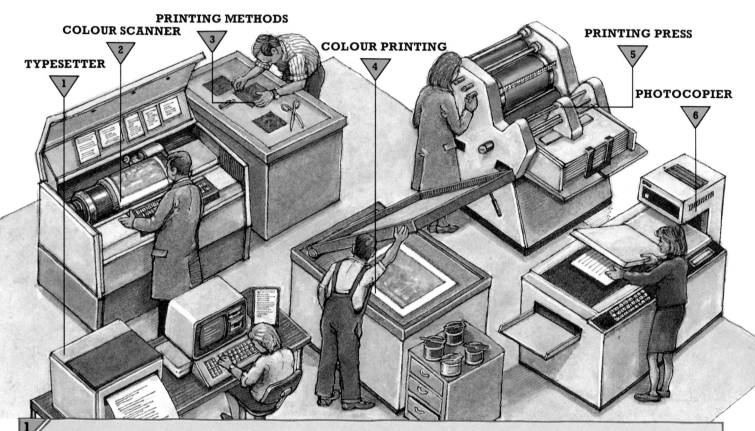

TYPESETTER
1

COLOUR SCANNER
2

PRINTING METHODS
3

COLOUR PRINTING
4

PRINTING PRESS
5

PHOTOCOPIER
6

---

**1** ### TYPESETTER

Printed words like the ones you are reading now are the result of a series of processes, starting with the typesetter. This machine stores in its computer memory the sizes and shapes of various typefaces – the different styles and 'designs' of letters and numbers. The words in this book are in the typeface called Rockwell.

To typeset the letters, the computer controls the movements of a laser beam that etches the shapes of the letters onto a rotating drum of special printing paper or printing film (page 80). Highly magnified, the letters are seen to be made up of numerous lines (*below*).

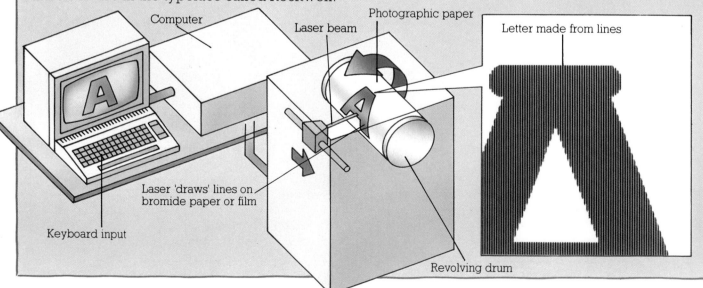

Computer

Laser beam

Photographic paper

Letter made from lines

Laser 'draws' lines on bromide paper or film

Keyboard input

Revolving drum

## 2 COLOUR SCANNER

To prepare a colour photograph or illustration for printing, it must first be 'separated' into its primary colours, so that each may be printed separately (page 80). This is a job for the colour scanner. The laser beam scans line by line as the photograph revolves on a drum. During each scan the frequency of the light in the laser is changed to correspond with each of the primary colours, so that it detects only the parts of the photograph which are of that particular colour. This is repeated four times: once for each of the three primary colours (cyan (blue), magenta (red), yellow), and once for black. The information about which colours are where on the photograph is coded as electrical signals. It can be converted into four separate printing films, or stored in a computer memory.

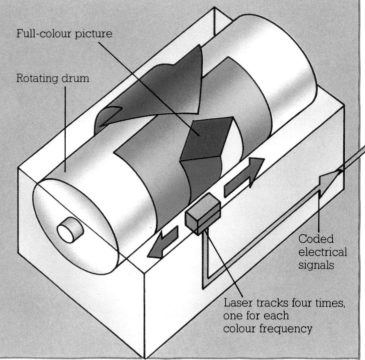

Full-colour picture

Rotating drum

Coded electrical signals

Laser tracks four times, one for each colour frequency

## 3 PRINTING METHODS

Since the German goldsmith Johann Gutenberg invented the first proper printing press, in about 1450, there have been various developments in printing techniques. Four methods of printing are shown here. Each depends on passing paper over an inked roller or plate, so that the ink comes off the roller or plate and sticks to the paper. Offset lithography is described on page 80. In letterpress, the image exists as a raised area on a lower base. Only the raised part receives the printing ink. In gravure, the image is a shallow 'hole' below the surface of the plate or roller, and ink is scraped from the raised, non-printing part by a doctor blade. Silk-screen printing involves forcing ink through a very fine net-like screen onto the paper; the shape of the stencil forms the image.

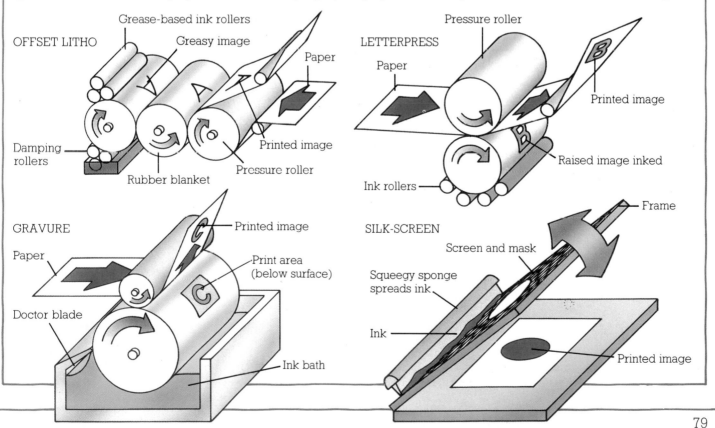

OFFSET LITHO
- Grease-based ink rollers
- Greasy image
- Paper
- Damping rollers
- Rubber blanket
- Printed image
- Pressure roller

LETTERPRESS
- Pressure roller
- Paper
- Printed image
- Raised image inked
- Ink rollers

GRAVURE
- Printed image
- Paper
- Print area (below surface)
- Doctor blade
- Ink bath

SILK-SCREEN
- Frame
- Screen and mask
- Squeegy sponge spreads ink
- Ink
- Printed image

## 4  COLOUR PRINTING

The colour pictures in this book are made from patterns of tiny ink dots. There are four colours of dots. These are the three primary printing colours of cyan, magenta and yellow, plus black. Each is printed from a separate piece of printing film on the press (*shown below*). From a distance, the eye sees the separate dots as areas of continuous ink. It also merges the different combinations of primary colours to see all the other colours of the spectrum.

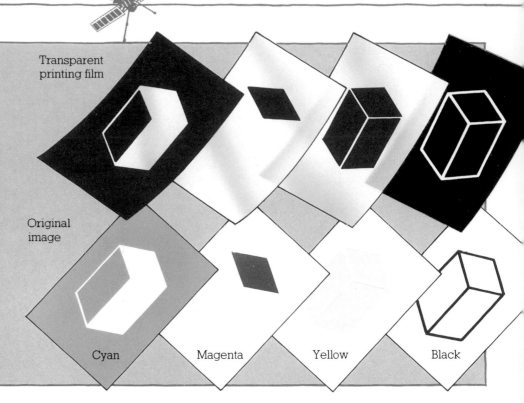

Transparent printing film

Original image

Cyan

Magenta

Yellow

Black

## 5  PRINTING PRESS

On the offset lithography press, each primary colour is printed separately. The image on the plate or roller exists as a part of its surface that has been treated, or 'etched', to attract grease-based printing ink – and to repel water. For areas that are not to be printed, the surface is treated to attract water but to repel the greasy ink. The ink roller puts ink onto the image parts of the surface, while the damping rollers put water onto the non-printing areas. The ink is then transferred to another, intermediate roller bearing a rubber blanket. This presses the ink onto the paper. 'Offset' refers to the transfer of the inked image to an intermediate roller.

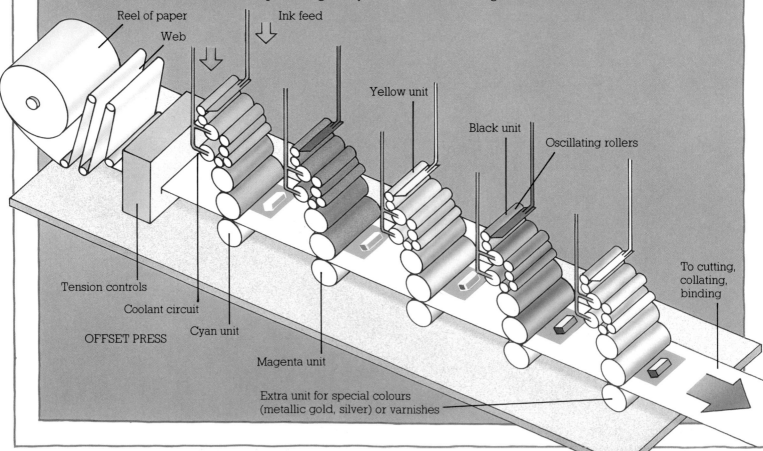

Reel of paper

Web

Ink feed

Yellow unit

Black unit

Oscillating rollers

Tension controls

Coolant circuit

Cyan unit

OFFSET PRESS

Magenta unit

To cutting, collating, binding

Extra unit for special colours (metallic gold, silver) or varnishes

## 6 PHOTOCOPIER

This fairly recent method of copy-printing is suitable for a few tens or perhaps hundreds of copies. But it becomes expensive for larger numbers, compared to other printing processes. Photocopying is based on the principle that static electricity attracts objects. This happens when you rub a balloon on a dry woollen jumper. The friction of rubbing generates static electricity that makes the balloon 'stick' to the jumper. The photocopier has a large electrostatic drum that is charged with static electricity in the same way. The image to be copied is beamed down from the platen onto the drum by a series of mirrors and lenses, and it alters the pattern of charges. The charged parts attract the toner, usually granules or ink. This is transferred to a sheet of paper and then fixed in place, usually by heat.

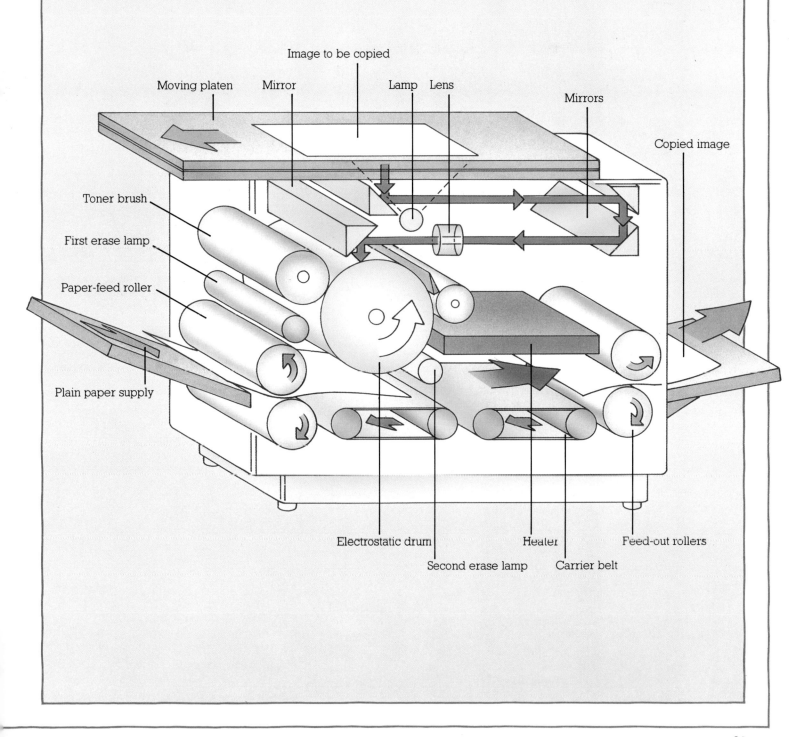

Image to be copied

Moving platen    Mirror    Lamp    Lens    Mirrors

Copied image

Toner brush

First erase lamp

Paper-feed roller

Plain paper supply

Electrostatic drum    Heater    Feed-out rollers

Second erase lamp    Carrier belt

# THE TELEVISION STUDIO

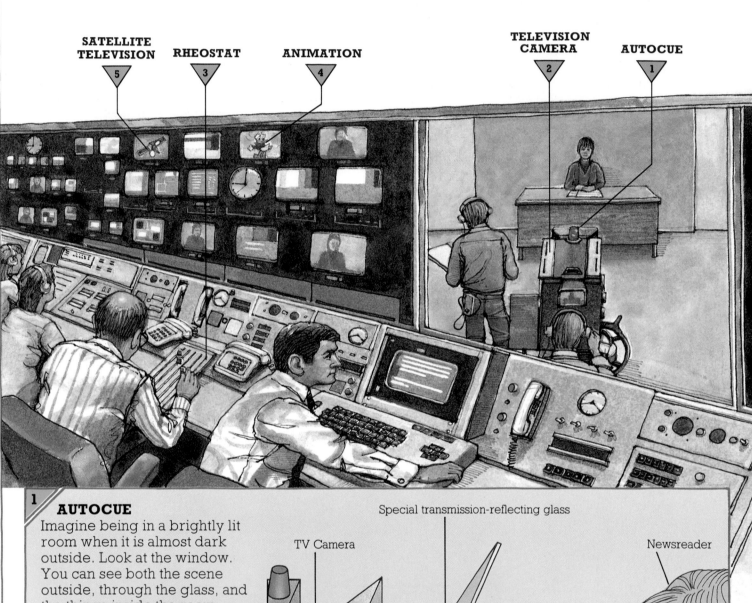

SATELLITE
TELEVISION
5

RHEOSTAT
3

ANIMATION
4

TELEVISION
CAMERA
2

AUTOCUE
1

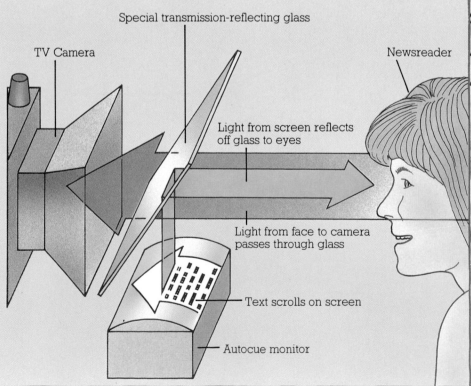

## 1 AUTOCUE

Imagine being in a brightly lit room when it is almost dark outside. Look at the window. You can see both the scene outside, through the glass, and the things inside the room, reflected in the glass. The autocue machine works along the same lines. There is a glass sheet between the newsreader and the screen. The camera 'sees' the newsreader through the glass. The newsreader sees the camera – and also the reflections of the words on the monitor screen. Are the words on the screen upside down, or in 'mirror writing'?

Special transmission-reflecting glass

TV Camera

Newsreader

Light from screen reflects off glass to eyes

Light from face to camera passes through glass

Text scrolls on screen

Autocue monitor

## TELEVISION CAMERA

White light is made up of a mixture of different colours, which can be separated by a prism to form the colours of the spectrum. The prism in one type of television camera is designed to split light from the scene into three colours: red, green and blue. It does this by *refraction*. Each colour of light consists of rays of a slightly different wavelength. The different wavelengths are refracted by slightly different amounts as they pass into and out of the glass of the prism.

The angles of the prism's faces are arranged so that the three main colours are separated from each other and shone out of the prism in different directions. Each colour is beamed into a detector that scans the image and converts the patterns of light rays into electrical signals. The camera operator watches the scene through the viewfinder, a small TV screen mounted on the camera. In the television set, the three colours are recombined on the screen (page 131).

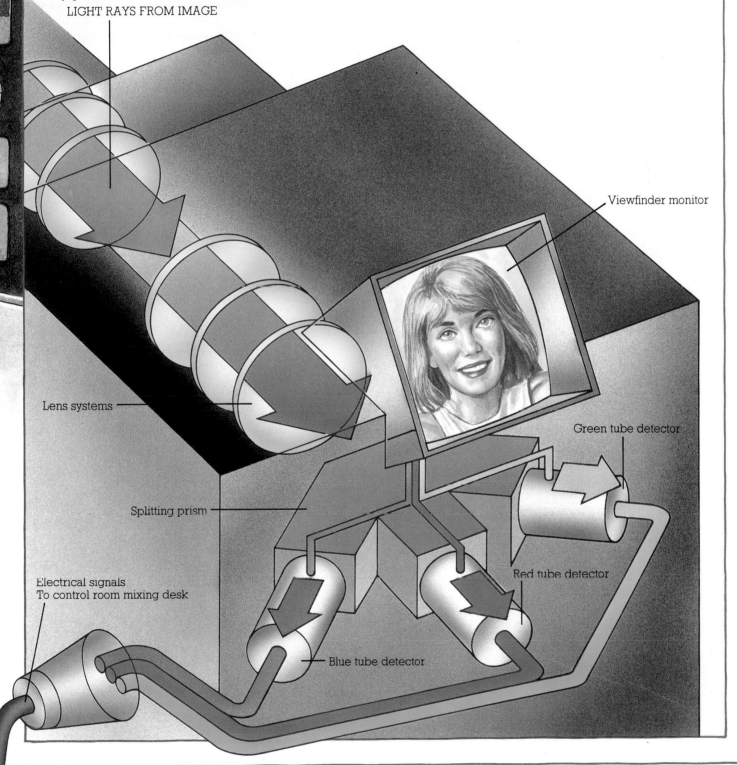

LIGHT RAYS FROM IMAGE

Viewfinder monitor

Lens systems

Green tube detector

Splitting prism

Red tube detector

Electrical signals
To control room mixing desk

Blue tube detector

## 3 RHEOSTAT

Many of the knobs and sliders on electrical equipment operate rheostats. The basic rheostat is a coil of resistance wire, touched by a sliding contact on one side, which forms part of an electrical circuit. When the electricity passes through only a few turns of the coil, it meets only a slight resistance. If the contact is slid to the other end, there is much more resistance wire included in the circuit, and the electricity is thereby reduced. A similar device works by turning a metal wiper around an arc-shaped resistance bar to 'tap off' varying amounts of electricity.

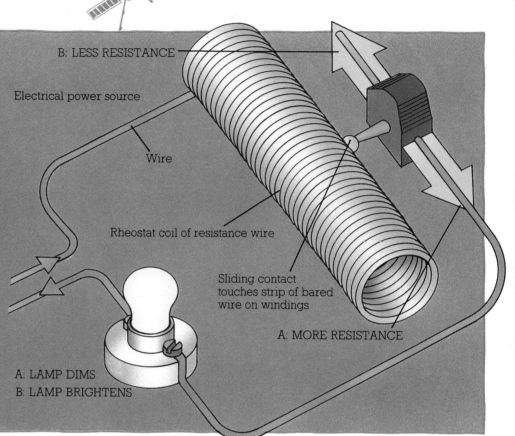

B: LESS RESISTANCE

Electrical power source

Wire

Rheostat coil of resistance wire

Sliding contact touches strip of bared wire on windings

A: MORE RESISTANCE

A: LAMP DIMS
B: LAMP BRIGHTENS

## 4 ANIMATION

A television or cinema screen does not show a continuously moving image. It shows a number of still images in rapid succession, many each second. The eye blurs together these quickly-changing still images and sees them as a 'moving picture'. Animation is the technique of making a 'moving picture' from a series of still images created by artists, or by models, or photographs, or computerized graphics. Cartoons are one familiar example. Each image, or frame, is drawn and coloured as a separate piece of artwork. These are recorded one by one, as individual frames on cine film or videotape (pages 132, 139). When played back at normal speed, the frames blur together and create the illusion of movement.

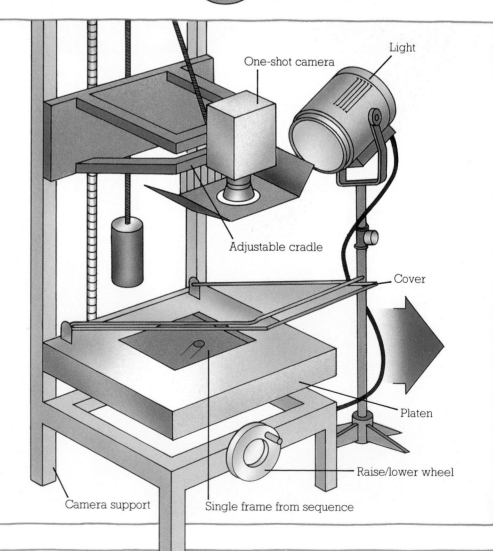

Light

One-shot camera

Adjustable cradle

Cover

Platen

Raise/lower wheel

Camera support

Single frame from sequence

## 5 | SATELLITE TELEVISION

A broadcasting aerial on the ground can beam signals only a limited distance. Even if the aerial is on a tall mast, hills and valleys in the landscape can soon block the signals. The TV satellite can be thought of as an aerial on an incredibly tall mast – so tall that it is in space! Its dish aerial broadcasts the signals over a very wide area. Receiving dishes on the ground collect and focus the signals and feed them to the television set. The satellite orbits at a speed which corresponds to the Earth's rotation, so that it 'hangs' in the same spot in the sky.

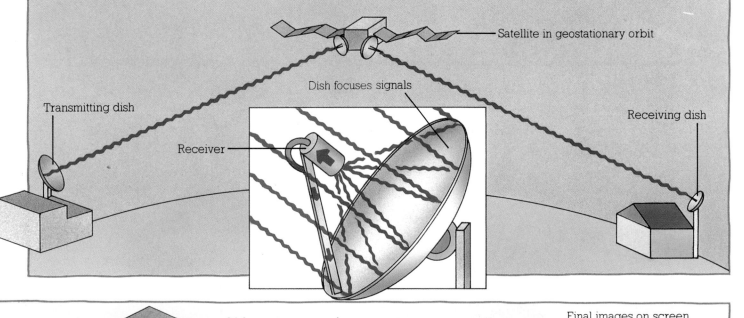

Satellite in geostationary orbit

Transmitting dish

Dish focuses signals

Receiver

Receiving dish

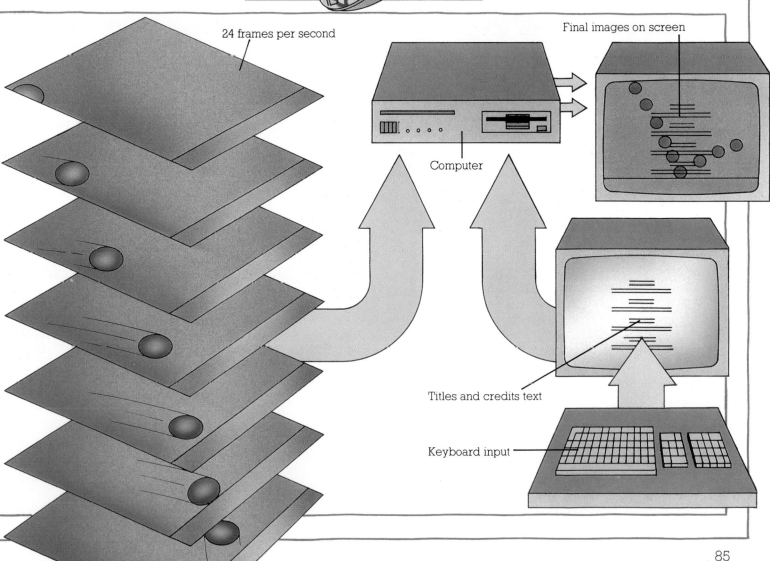

24 frames per second

Final images on screen

Computer

Titles and credits text

Keyboard input

# GRAND PRIX CIRCUIT

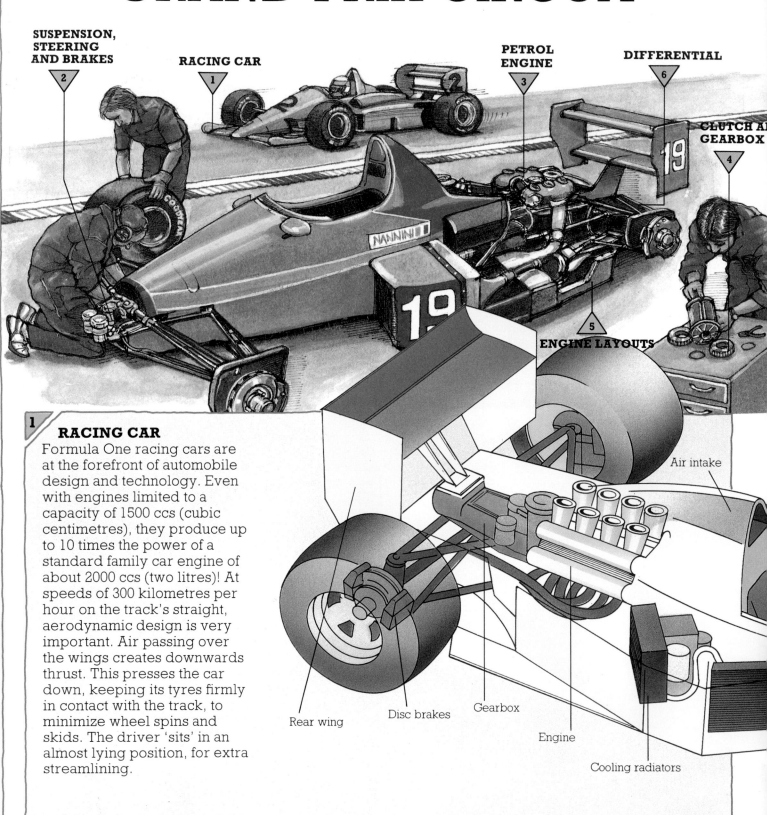

**SUSPENSION, STEERING AND BRAKES**

2

**RACING CAR**

1

**PETROL ENGINE**

3

**DIFFERENTIAL**

6

**CLUTCH A GEARBOX**

4

**ENGINE LAYOUTS**

5

NANNINI

## 1 RACING CAR

Formula One racing cars are at the forefront of automobile design and technology. Even with engines limited to a capacity of 1500 ccs (cubic centimetres), they produce up to 10 times the power of a standard family car engine of about 2000 ccs (two litres)! At speeds of 300 kilometres per hour on the track's straight, aerodynamic design is very important. Air passing over the wings creates downwards thrust. This presses the car down, keeping its tyres firmly in contact with the track, to minimize wheel spins and skids. The driver 'sits' in an almost lying position, for extra streamlining.

Air intake

Rear wing

Disc brakes

Gearbox

Engine

Cooling radiators

# SUSPENSION, BRAKES AND STEERING

The car's suspension system helps to absorb bumps and hollows in the road, giving a smoother ride. It also allows the car body to tilt slightly as it goes round a bend, for better cornering. A typical suspension unit has both a coil spring and a hydraulic damper unit, where fluid moves into and out of the cylinder and 'dampens' the vibrations. Formula One cars and other performance cars have disc brakes. Stationary brake pads attached to the chassis press on a disc that revolves with the roadwheel. The disc brake is more effective and stays cooler than the drum brake, in which curved brake shoes press outwards onto the inside of a revolving drum attached to the roadwheel. Both types work by hydraulic pressure (page 52). In rack-and-pinion steering, the steering wheel turns a shaft that ends in a small pinion gear. This meshes with the rack, which is a 'straightened' gear wheel. As the pinion rotates it makes the rack slide along, moving levers that turn the roadwheels.

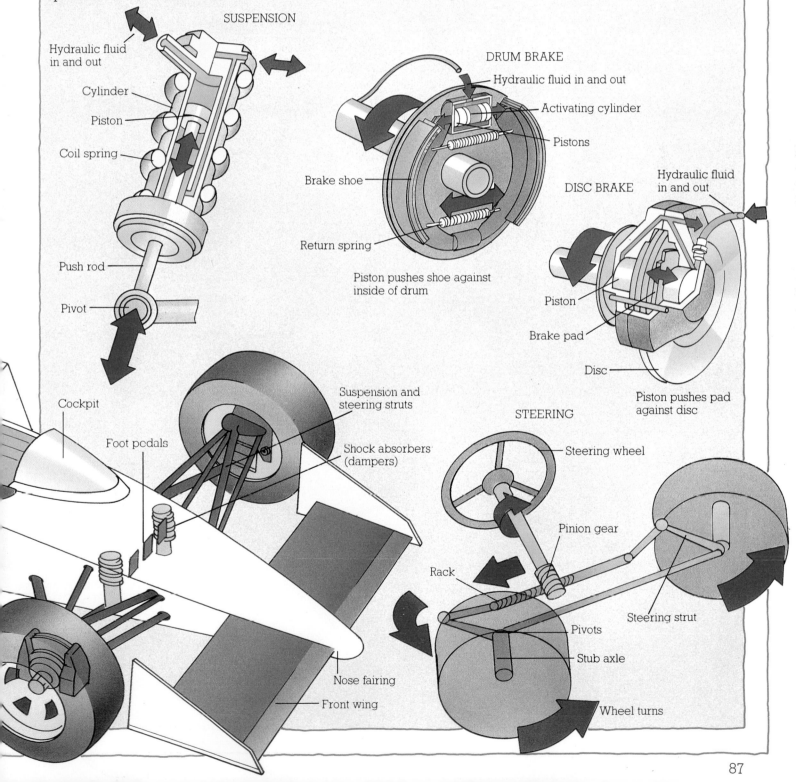

SUSPENSION

Hydraulic fluid in and out

Cylinder

Piston

Coil spring

Push rod

Pivot

DRUM BRAKE

Hydraulic fluid in and out

Activating cylinder

Pistons

Brake shoe

Return spring

Piston pushes shoe against inside of drum

DISC BRAKE

Hydraulic fluid in and out

Piston

Brake pad

Disc

Piston pushes pad against disc

Cockpit

Foot pedals

Suspension and steering struts

Shock absorbers (dampers)

STEERING

Steering wheel

Pinion gear

Rack

Steering strut

Pivots

Stub axle

Nose fairing

Front wing

Wheel turns

## PETROL ENGINE

In the type of internal combustion engine that runs on petrol the energy comes from chemical substances in the petrol, which has been purified from crude petroleum (page 101). Inside each cylinder of the engine, a mixture of petrol vapour and air is ignited by an electrically-produced spark (*opposite*). This produces a mini-explosion, or combustion, which forces the piston down inside the cylinder. The piston is linked to a crankshaft that transforms an oscillating (to-and-fro) movement into a rotary one. Most ordinary car engines have four or six cylinders. As each piston moves inside its cylinder, from its lowest to its highest position, it pushes or *displaces* a certain volume of air from the cylinder. Add together these displacement volumes for all the cylinders in the engine, and this gives the capacity for the engine, usually measured in cubic centimetres (ccs). If each piston in a four-cylinder engine displaces 500 ccs, then the capacity of the engine is $4 \times 500 = 2000$ ccs (two litres).

The carburettor mixes air with fuel to give the correct explosive mixture for the cylinder. Each piston on its *induction* stroke (*opposite*) sucks in air from the atmosphere. The air flows through a narrowed part of the carburettor, the *venturi*, where it speeds up and sucks in fuel from the fuel pipe. A tapered needle moves up or down inside a tube to control the amount of fuel entering the carburettor.

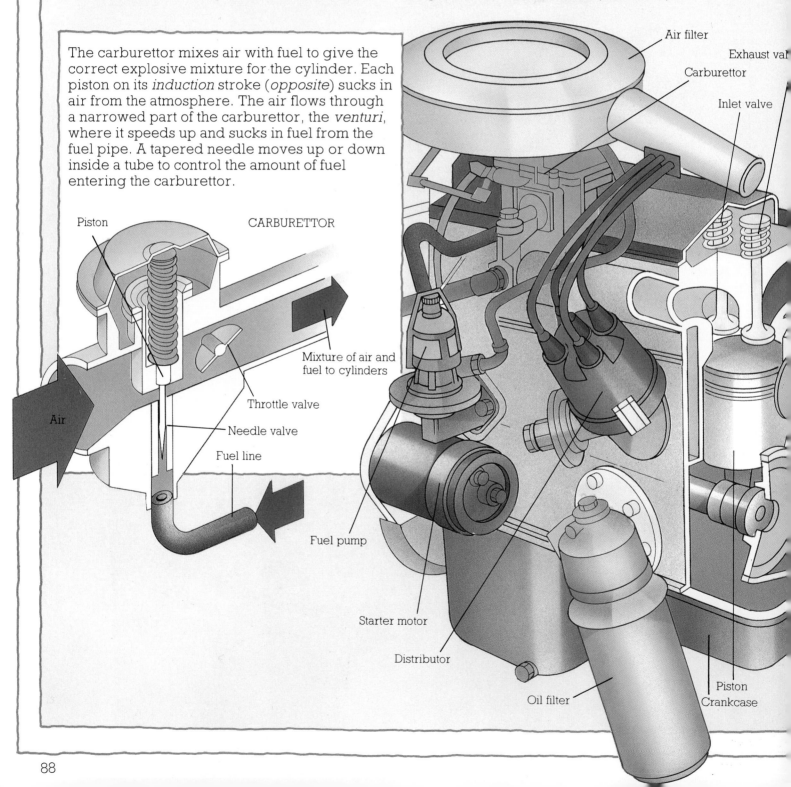

Piston

CARBURETTOR

Mixture of air and fuel to cylinders

Throttle valve

Needle valve

Fuel line

Air

Fuel pump

Starter motor

Distributor

Oil filter

Air filter

Exhaust val

Carburettor

Inlet valve

Piston

Crankcase

After combustion, exhaust gases rushing from the cylinder represent energy going to waste. The turbocharger is a turbine-based device (page 71) spun by these rushing gases. It compresses air and forces extra air/fuel mixture into the cylinders than normal, which increases the power from each combustion 'explosion'

In the diesel type of internal combustion engine the extremely high pressure inside the cylinder raises the temperature of the air/fuel mìxture to exploding point. In a petrol engine, a spark plug makes an electrically-generated spark which 'sets fire' to the mixture. As the engine turns, cams open and close valves in the top of the cylinder. These work in the correct sequence to let in the air/fuel mixture, contain it during combustion, and then let out the waste gases afterwards.

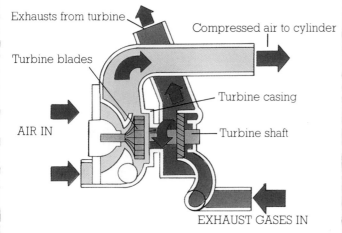

Exhausts from turbine

Compressed air to cylinder

Turbine blades

Turbine casing

AIR IN

Turbine shaft

EXHAUST GASES IN

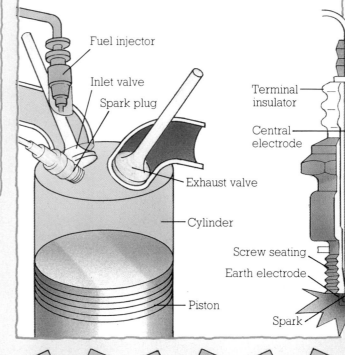

Fuel injector

Inlet valve

Spark plug

Terminal insulator

Central electrode

Exhaust valve

Cylinder

Screw seating

Earth electrode

Piston

Spark

Exhaust manifold

Cooling fan

Fan belt

The family car's petrol engine is four-stroke. Each piston repeatedly goes through a cycle that lasts four strokes: down, up, down, up. First is the down stroke of *induction*, when air/fuel mixture is drawn into the cylinder. Second is *compression*, as the mixture is squeezed, so raising its temperature. Third is *ignition*, when the mixture is exploded by a spark. Fourth is *exhaust*, as waste gases from the explosion are pushed out. Some smaller engines are two-stroke (*right, below*).

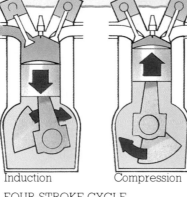

Induction

Compression

Ignition (second turn)

Exhaust (second turn)

FOUR-STROKE CYCLE
TWO-STROKE CYCLE

Induction

Compression

Ignition

Exhaust

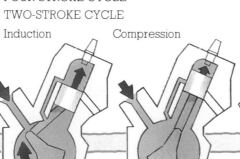
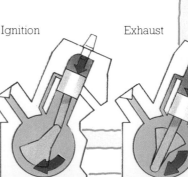

# CLUTCH AND GEARBOX

There are at least four mechanical devices involved in changing the turning motion of the car's engine to its roadwheels: clutch, gearbox, propeller shaft and final drives. Together, these are called the transmission.

All the time the engine is running, the crankshaft is turning – but the car may be standing still in neutral, or cruising along in top gear. The clutch disconnects the engine's spinning crankshaft from the gearbox when changing gear. When the clutch is engaged or 'in' (pedal up), the plates press together and transfer the turning motion to the gearbox. The

clutch is disengaged or put 'out' (pedal pressed) when the two plates are pulled slightly apart. Inside the gearbox, a system of shafts and gear wheels slide to and fro to change gear. In first gear, the engine turns the roadwheels slowly but with much *torque* (turning force). In top gear, for the same engine speed, the roadwheels turn much faster but with less torque.

Some cars have automatic transmission (*bottom*), where the gears change themselves according to the speed of the engine and the turning power needed.

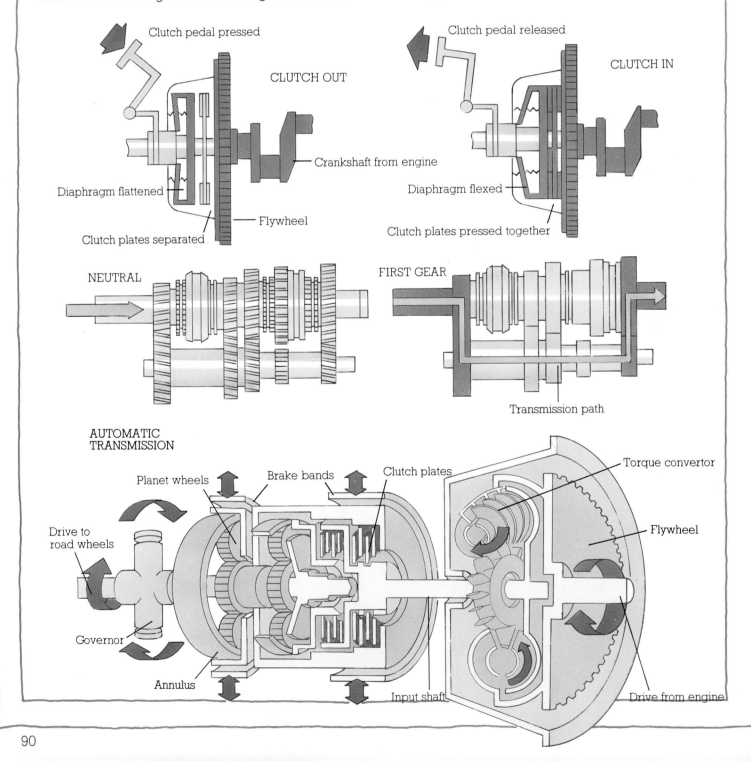

## 5 ENGINE LAYOUTS

A car's stability, handling and manoeuvrability depend partly on how the weight of the various parts is spread between the four roadwheels. Particularly important is the position of the heaviest component, the engine. Also important is whether the engine drives the front or rear wheels, or all four wheels together. A Formula One racing car has a mid-mounted, in-line engine that drives the rear wheels. Several other layouts or *configurations*, are shown here. The mid-engined layout provides good weight distribution. However, in a family car it would take up much of the space that is normally set aside for luggage, in the boot. Four-wheel drive is best for soft, bumpy or otherwise difficult terrain.

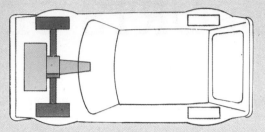

Front wheel drive, transverse engine

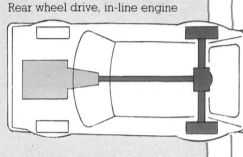

Rear wheel drive, in-line engine

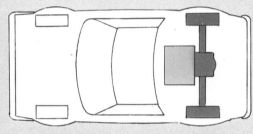

Rear wheel drive, rear-mounted engine

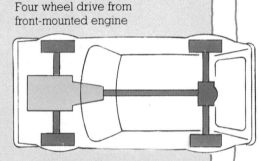

Four wheel drive from front-mounted engine

## 6 DIFFERENTIAL

As a car rounds a corner, the wheels on the outside of the bend travel farther than those on the inside (*far right*). If the wheels are not driven by the engine, each can rotate independently at its own speed. But wheels driven by the engine would skip and skid if they rotated at the same speed. The differential lets the roadwheels turn at different speeds. The pinion on the propeller shaft transmits power to the crown wheel. This turns two *bevel* gears, which mesh with bevel gears on the half-shafts. When the inner roadwheel slows down, the outer one speeds up; the crown wheel turns at the average speed.

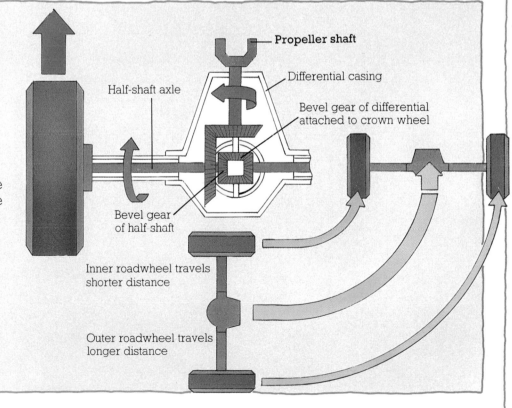

Propeller shaft

Differential casing

Bevel gear of differential attached to crown wheel

Half-shaft axle

Bevel gear of half-shaft

Inner roadwheel travels shorter distance

Outer roadwheel travels longer distance

# THE SPORTS CENTRE

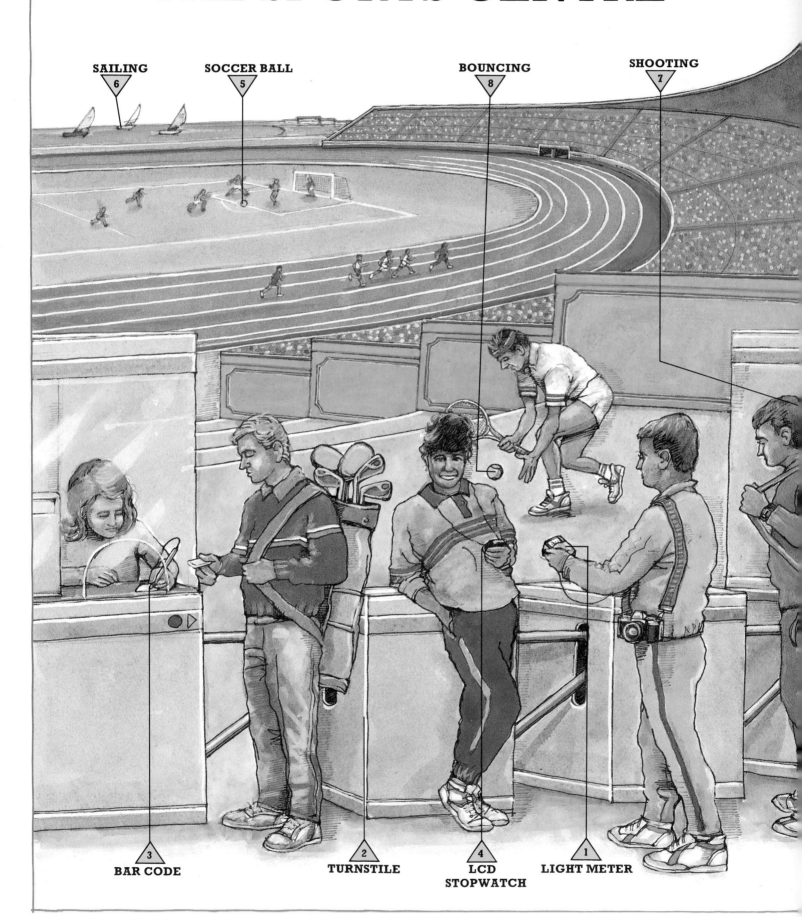

SAILING
6

SOCCER BALL
5

BOUNCING
8

SHOOTING
7

BAR CODE
3

TURNSTILE
2

LCD
STOPWATCH
4

LIGHT METER
1

## 1 LIGHT METER

In outdoor games such as tennis and cricket, players should be able to see the ball clearly! When the sky is overcast, or towards dusk, the light may be too dim for good play. In the light meter, a photo-resistor changes its resistance to electricity according to how much light falls on it. The result is shown by a small needle and dial or a liquid crystal display (LCD).

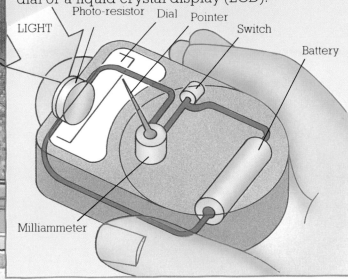

LIGHT
Photo-resistor Dial Pointer
Switch
Battery
Milliammeter

## 2 TURNSTILE

This simple, robust machine is a ratchet. The teeth on the cog wheel slope in one direction. The wheel can turn one way, since the single tooth or 'dog' on the sprung bar is pushed aside smoothly by the sloping part of each tooth on the wheel. But try to turn the wheel the other way, and the dog jams against the first tooth and prevents the wheel rotating.

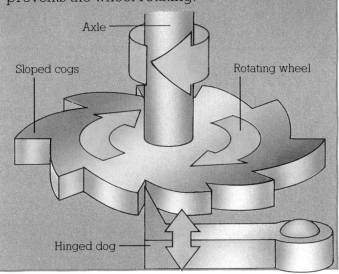

Axle
Sloped cogs
Rotating wheel
Hinged dog

## 3 BAR CODE

Many items are now labelled with a bar code, a series of thick and thin black lines. They carry encoded information – from the membership number of a sports club, to the price and stock number of a packet of washing powder in a supermarket. The code is scanned by a beam, which turns light pulses into electrical signals that are fed into a computer for processing.

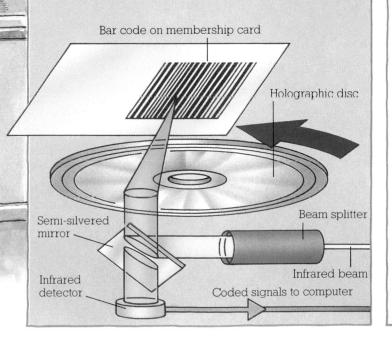

Bar code on membership card
Holographic disc
Semi-silvered mirror
Beam splitter
Infrared detector
Infrared beam
Coded signals to computer

## 4 LCD STOPWATCH

Each segment of a Liquid Crystal Display consists of many liquid crystals sandwiched between two electrodes. The crystals can move or 'flow' like a liquid. When electricity passes between the electrodes, it twists the crystals so that they do not transmit polarized light; that segment then appears black. Place the lenses of two polarized sunglasses together and twist them, for the same effect.

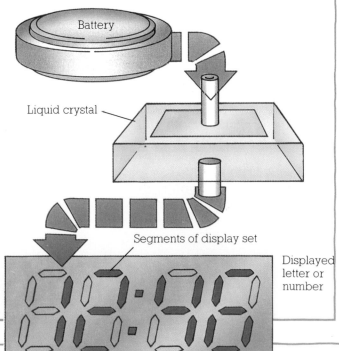

Battery
Liquid crystal
Segments of display set
Displayed letter or number

## 5 SOCCER BALL

An old-fashioned soccer ball has leather panels stitched together to leave a slit-like opening for the inflatable bladder inside. The opening is then laced up like a shoe. However this causes problems because of unequal weight distribution, which makes the ball wobble as it spins. It can also be uncomfortable for a player who heads the ball on the laced-up part! Most balls today have leather panels that are shaped in groups to form parts of a sphere. They are stitched together inside out. Before the last seam is sewn, the ball is turned 'inside in' and the inflatable bladder is inserted. The finished ball is perfectly round and well-balanced.

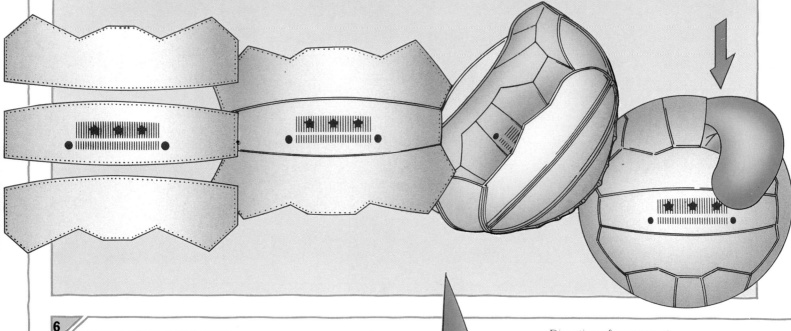

## 6 SAILS AND SAILING

Sail-based sports such as yachting and windsurfing rely on the energy of the wind to push on the broad surface of the sail, which is attached to the craft. Being blown along in the direction of the wind is known as *running* (*near right*). In order to travel across the wind, the craft and sail are set at angles as shown for *reaching* (*far right*). The resistance of the craft to being pushed sideways combines with the direction of the wind on the sail, to make the craft travel forwards. The sailor can move into the wind by *beating*, to the left and right alternately, on a zig-zag course into the wind (*middle right*).

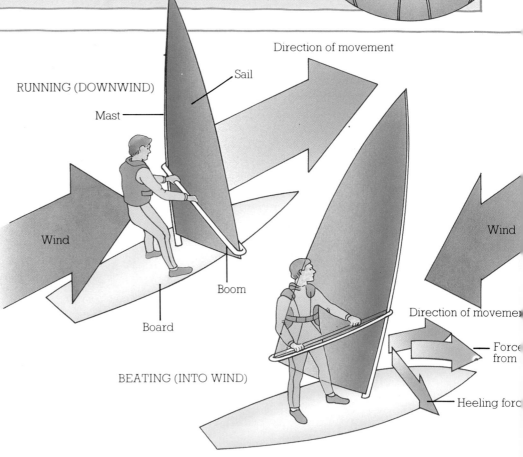

RUNNING (DOWNWIND)
Direction of movement
Sail
Mast
Wind
Boom
Board
BEATING (INTO WIND)
Wind
Direction of moveme
Force from
Heeling forc

## SHOOTING

A basic law of physics says: 'Every action has an equal and opposite reaction'. When the powder in a shell casing explodes, it pushes the bullet one way – out of the barrel. The gun reacts by moving the other way, which is called the recoil.

## 8

## BOUNCING

As a rubber ball falls against the ground, it becomes squashed and stores energy – in a similar, but opposite, way to a stretched elastic band. The ball comes to a sudden halt. The energy is released as the elastic material springs back into shape and propels the ball upward again.

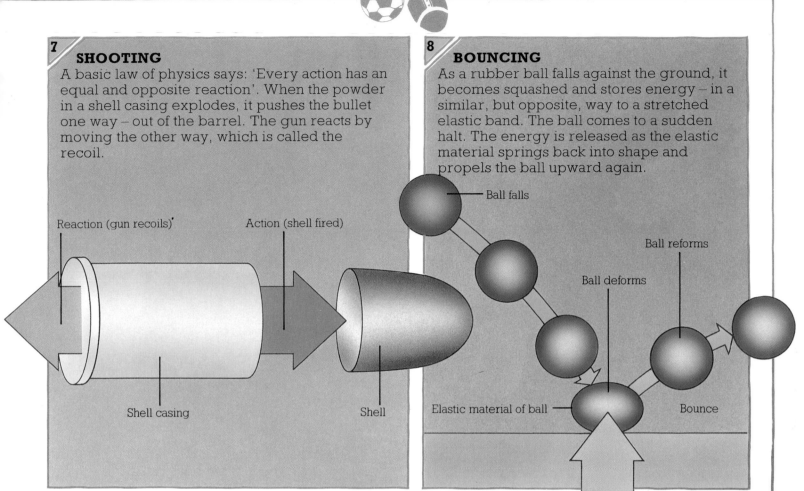

Reaction (gun recoils)

Action (shell fired)

Shell casing

Shell

Ball falls

Ball reforms

Ball deforms

Elastic material of ball

Bounce

REACHING (ACROSS WIND)

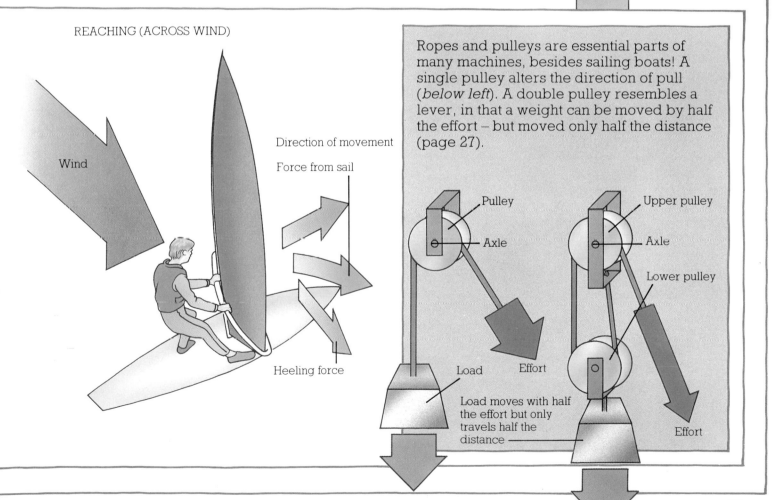

Wind

Direction of movement

Force from sail

Heeling force

Ropes and pulleys are essential parts of many machines, besides sailing boats! A single pulley alters the direction of pull (*below left*). A double pulley resembles a lever, in that a weight can be moved by half the effort – but moved only half the distance (page 27).

Pulley

Axle

Upper pulley

Axle

Lower pulley

Load

Effort

Load moves with half the effort but only travels half the distance

Effort

# PRODUCTION LINE

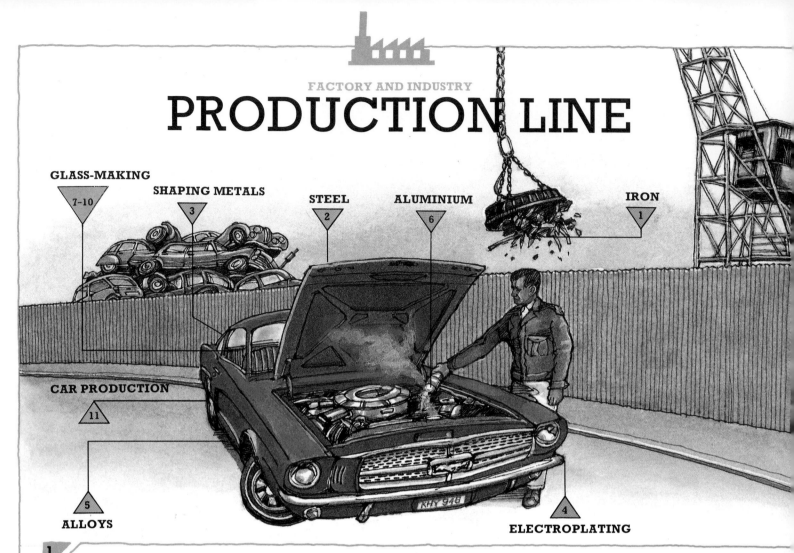

**GLASS-MAKING**
7-10

**SHAPING METALS**
3

**STEEL**
2

**ALUMINIUM**
6

**IRON**
1

**CAR PRODUCTION**
11

**ALLOYS**
5

**ELECTROPLATING**
4

## 1 IRON

Pure metals are rarely found in nature, although lumps of pure iron sometimes reach the Earth in meteorites. Instead, metals are usually found combined chemically with other substances, such as metal ores. Iron was one of the first metals to be purified from its ore, over 3500 years ago. A modern blast furnace makes up to 10,000 tonnes of iron daily. In the furnace, preheated air is blasted through a mixture of iron oxide ore, limestone and a fuel such as coke. As the coke burns it forms the gas carbon monoxide. This combines chemically with the iron oxide to give carbon dioxide and iron, while the limestone 'soaks up' other impurities to create the slag. The resulting iron, still not completely pure, is known as pig iron. It is further refined to wrought iron, cast iron, steel and other forms.

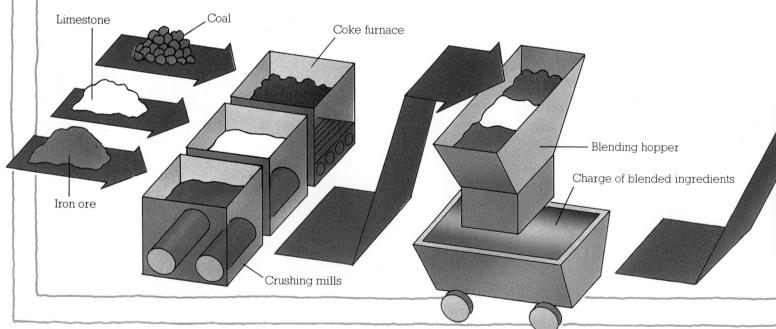

Limestone

Coal

Coke furnace

Blending hopper

Charge of blended ingredients

Iron ore

Crushing mills

## 2 STEEL

Molten iron from the blast furnace is relatively impure, containing five per cent or more of carbon. In the converter it is changed into purer forms known as steels. There are many kinds of steel, made by different processes. In the basic-oxygen process (*right*), molten pig iron is poured onto scrap in a huge vessel. A lance about two metres above the surface blows high-pressure oxygen over the molten metal bath for about 20 minutes. The oxygen combines with the carbon and removes it from the metal. Steels are irons that contain less than 1.7 per cent of carbon. Tiny amounts of other substances may be added such as manganese, nickel and chromium.

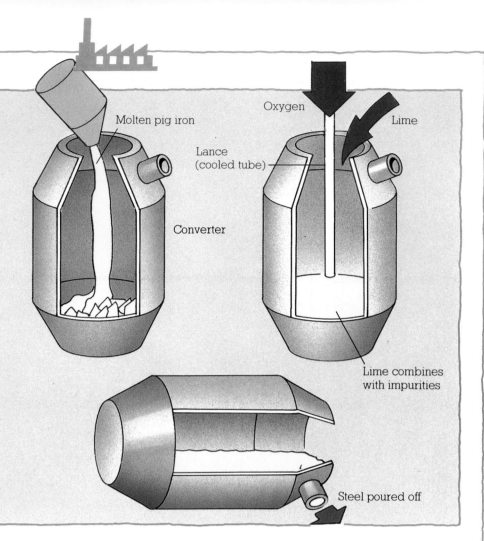

Molten pig iron

Oxygen

Lime

Lance (cooled tube)

Converter

Lime combines with impurities

Steel poured off

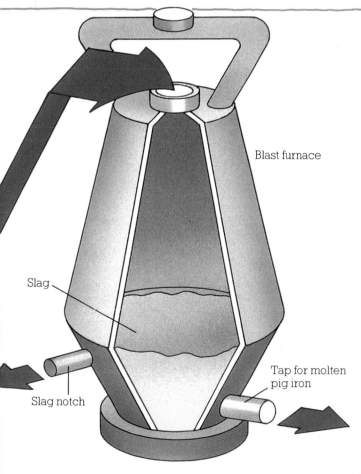

Blast furnace

Slag

Slag notch

Tap for molten pig iron

## 3 SHAPING METALS

We value metals such as iron and steel for their toughness. This same property makes them difficult to shape. If the metal is heated above its melting point, so that it turns into a liquid, it can be moulded or formed in a variety of ways. Iron's melting point is 1535°C. Some metals, like copper, are *ductile*, which means they can be squeezed or drawn out when cold into different shapes (like thin wires), yet still keep their strength.

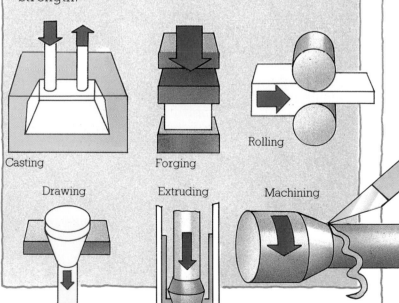

Casting

Forging

Rolling

Drawing

Extruding

Machining

## ELECTROPLATING

When a substance dissolves in a liquid to form a solution, its component parts float freely as electrically-charged particles called *ions*. For example, a solution of common salt, or sodium chloride, forms sodium and chlorine ions. Pass an electric current through the solution between two electrodes, and the ions are attracted to the electrode of the opposite charge, in the way that unlike poles of magnets attract. Electroplating employs an electric current to coat one electrode – the item to be 'plated' – with a substance such as a metal. The metal exists in the form of ions floating about in solution. Metal ions are positively charged, so they gather on the negative electrode, known as the cathode.

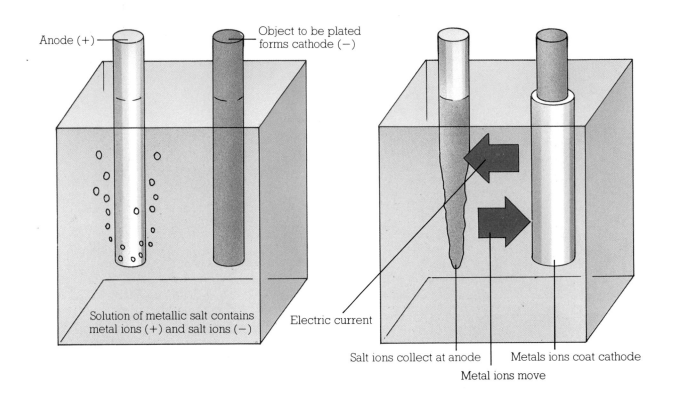

Anode (+)

Object to be plated forms cathode (−)

Solution of metallic salt contains metal ions (+) and salt ions (−)

Electric current

Salt ions collect at anode

Metals ions coat cathode

Metal ions move

## ALLOYS

An alloy is a mixture of metals, or a mixture of a metal and another substance. *Bronze* is an alloy of copper and tin. *Steel* is an alloy of iron and carbon. *Stainless steel* is an alloy of steel with nickel and chromium. One familiar alloy is silver combined with the liquid metal mercury, which forms the amalgam of tooth fillings. Titanium-steel alloys are used for their lightness and strength in planes and spacecraft. Nickel-cobalt 'superalloys' are used in jet-engine turbine blades (page 47) to withstand temperatures of over 1000°C. At the other end of the scale, alloys of metals such as lead, bismuth and cadmium melt at temperatures as low as 50°C, and are used in fire alarms (page 61).

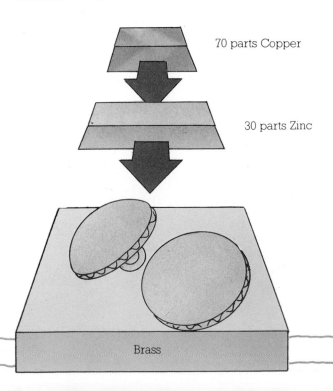

70 parts Copper

30 parts Zinc

Brass

## ALUMINIUM

This extremely light metal is also very abundant – it makes up one-twelfth of the Earth's crust. Its ores are mainly *bauxites*, in which aluminium is combined with oxygen, sand, iron, titanium and other substances. The bauxite is first refined into alumina, a purer form of aluminium oxide, by the Bayer process. The alumina is then separated into aluminium and oxygen by *electrolysis* (*see also electroplating opposite*). This is done at almost 1000°C in a bath of molten cryolite, another substance containing aluminium, as well as sodium and fluorine.

An electric current passes through the alumina between two electrodes – the carbon rods (positive anodes) above, and the carbon linings (negative cathodes) of the reduction pots. The electric current splits the aluminium and oxygen; the positive aluminium gathers around the cathodes and is siphoned off.

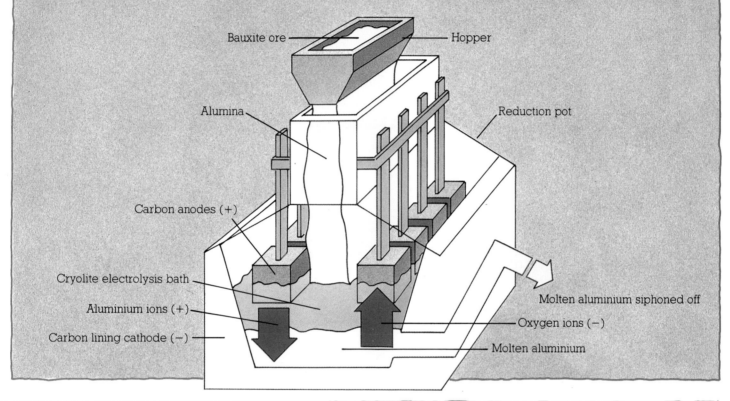

Bauxite ore — Hopper

Alumina

Reduction pot

Carbon anodes (+)

Cryolite electrolysis bath

Aluminium ions (+)

Carbon lining cathode (−)

Molten aluminium siphoned off

Oxygen ions (−)

Molten aluminium

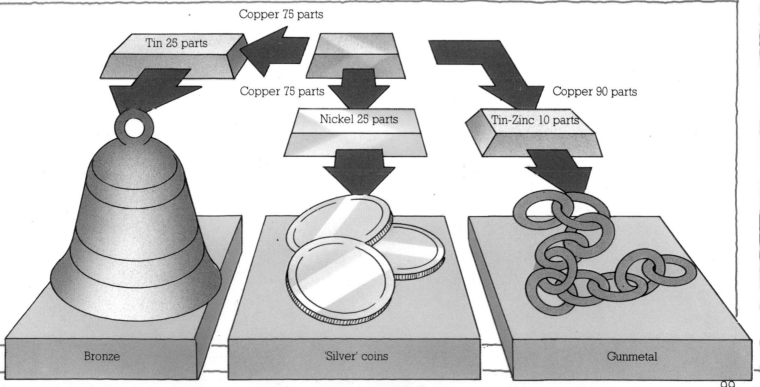

Copper 75 parts

Tin 25 parts

Copper 75 parts

Nickel 25 parts

Copper 90 parts

Tin-Zinc 10 parts

Bronze

'Silver' coins

Gunmetal

**7**

Potash
Limestone
Cullet
**recycled glass**

Regeneration furnace

Bath of molten tin

Sand (silica)

Blending hopper

## GLASS-MAKING

Glass has been made for over 3500 years. It is produced by heating raw materials, mainly sand (silica), soda or potash, and limestone to temperatures of about 1300°C in a furnace. There are small amounts of other additives, such as alumina and magnesia. The float glass process was developed by Alistair Pilkington in the 1950s, to make sheets of flat glass. Molten glass from the furnace is floated over a bath of molten tin metal, and the smooth top of the liquid metal gives the glass an extremely smooth, shiny surface. The sheet glass then cools and hardens in the *annealing lehr*.

Thin layer of molten glass floats on molten tin in oxygen-free environment

Annealing lehr (cooling unit)

**8** **GLASS-BLOWING**

Typical soda glass is made chiefly from silica (72 per cent), soda or sodium oxide (15 per cent) and lime (5 per cent). It softens at around 700°C and can then be blown into a hollow shape, by forcing air into a molten blob or 'gob' of the glass. The glassblower reheats, reblows, twirls and shapes the glass to produce the finished object. Machines make light bulbs from ribbons of glass.

Molten glass from furnace

Air blown into glass

Shaping bench

Hollow sphere

Glass twirled on blow[pipe]

Blowpipe

Pre[

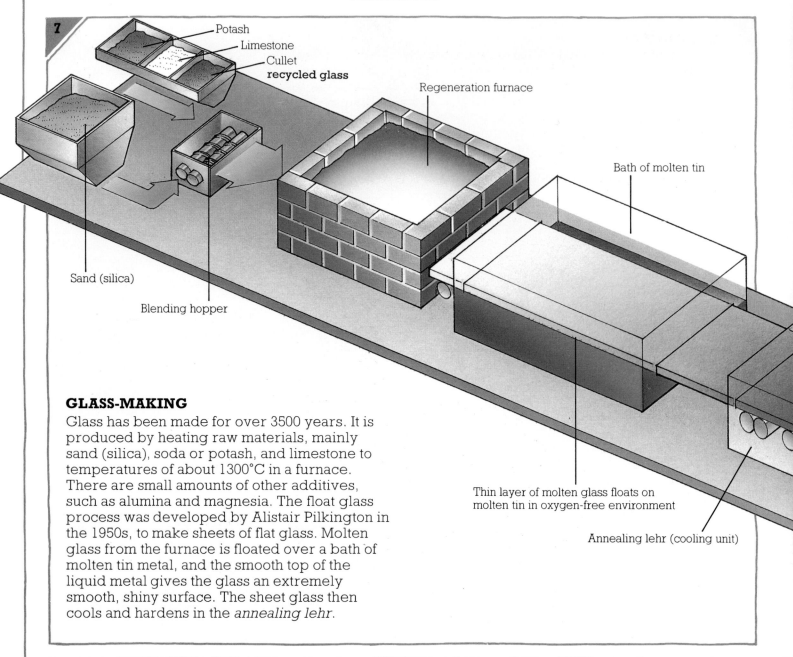

## 9 SAFETY GLASS

Glass can be strengthened enormously by sandwiching a wire mesh between two sheets. This type of glass is used for windows and screens that do not have to be perfectly transparent, but where it is useful to have some sort of view or to let in daylight while remaining very strong.

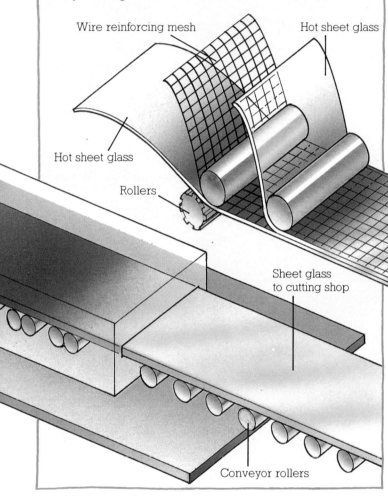

Wire reinforcing mesh

Hot sheet glass

Hot sheet glass

Rollers

Sheet glass to cutting shop

Conveyor rollers

## 10 GLASS CONTAINERS

Bottles, jars and similar glass containers are blown by the thousand on large automatic machines. One method is shown below. In another version a 'gob' of glass is put into a blank mould and pressed into a preliminary tube shape, the *parison*, by a metal plunger. The parison is then put into a bigger blow mould, and blown by compressed air into the finished bottle or jar shape. Glass is used for containers because it is smooth-surfaced, easily cleaned, does not react with most contents – and you can see what's inside.

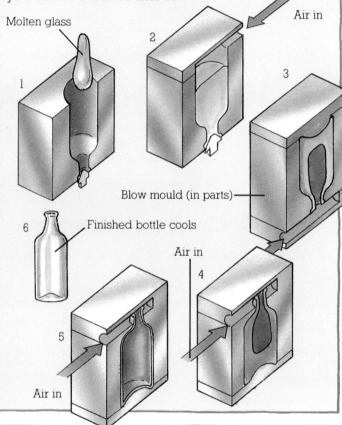

Molten glass

Air in

1

2

3

Blow mould (in parts)

6

Finished bottle cools

Air in

4

5

Air in

s glass flexible

Trimming

Finishing

Cooling

# 11 CAR PRODUCTION

In 1913, Henry Ford began mass-producing his Ford Model T cars using a moving assembly line. His basic process is still used today. The car moves along a track, rails or conveyor and is assembled part by part. A summary of the whole procedure is shown below. In practice, the engines may be made in one factory, while the chassis is produced in another, and the body is pressed and painted in the body shop at another site. These sub-assemblies are then transported to the main production line for final assembly. The work is checked at each stage by quality control staff. Every so often the production line is halted and altered to produce a different version of the basic car, depending on what buyers have ordered or how fashions change. For example, the same body may be fitted with a smaller capacity engine, for better fuel economy.

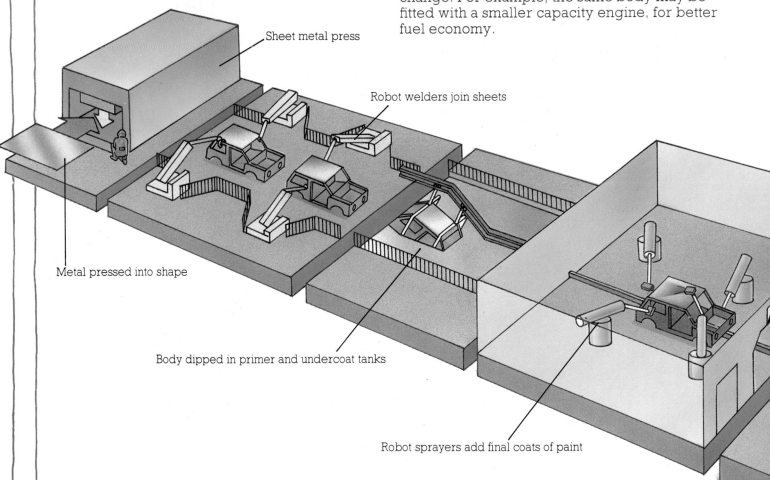

Sheet metal press

Robot welders join sheets

Metal pressed into shape

Body dipped in primer and undercoat tanks

Robot sprayers add final coats of paint

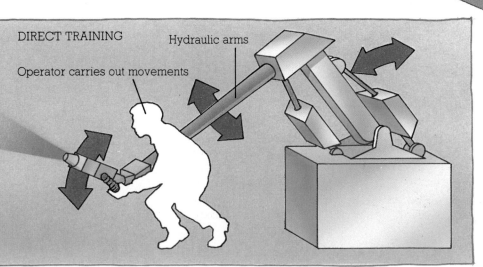

DIRECT TRAINING

The repetitive movements on the production line, fitting the same part time after time, are ideal work for computer-controlled robots. In the direct training method, a skilled worker first 'teaches' the computer the correct movements. These are stored in the computer memory, and copied by the hydraulic robot arm at the desired speed.

Operator carries out movements

Hydraulic arms

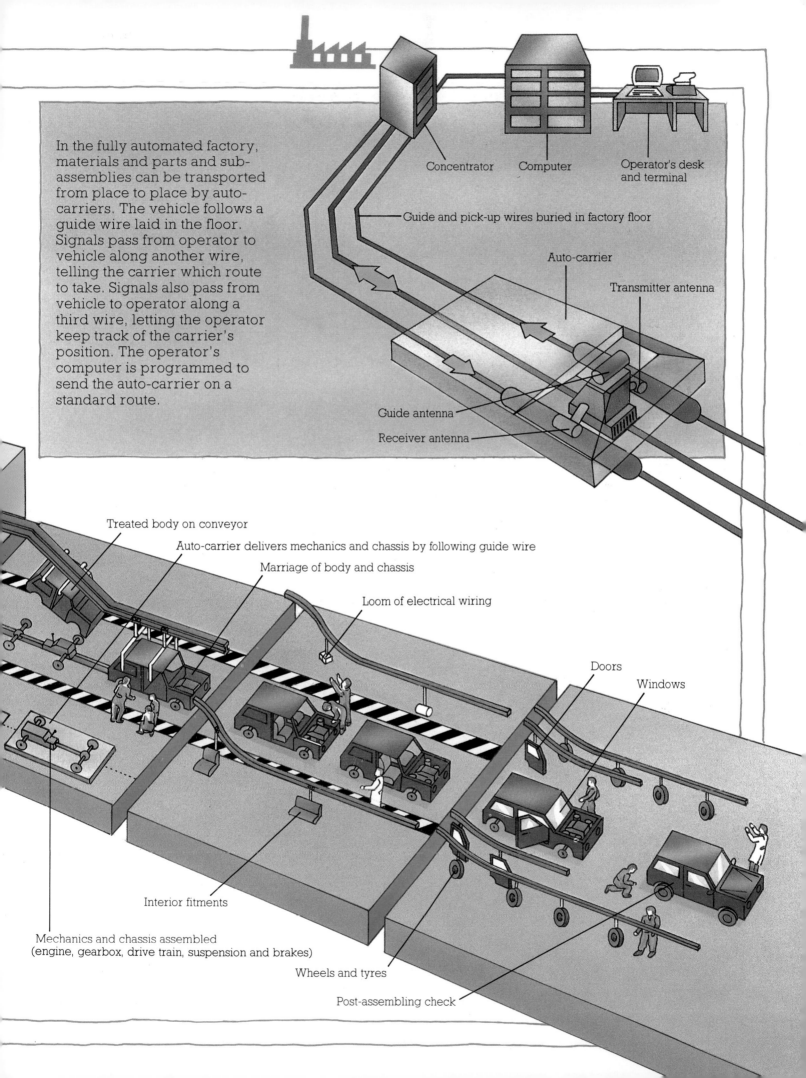

In the fully automated factory, materials and parts and sub-assemblies can be transported from place to place by auto-carriers. The vehicle follows a guide wire laid in the floor. Signals pass from operator to vehicle along another wire, telling the carrier which route to take. Signals also pass from vehicle to operator along a third wire, letting the operator keep track of the carrier's position. The operator's computer is programmed to send the auto-carrier on a standard route.

Concentrator

Computer

Operator's desk and terminal

Guide and pick-up wires buried in factory floor

Auto-carrier

Transmitter antenna

Guide antenna

Receiver antenna

Treated body on conveyor

Auto-carrier delivers mechanics and chassis by following guide wire

Marriage of body and chassis

Loom of electrical wiring

Doors

Windows

Interior fitments

Mechanics and chassis assembled
(engine, gearbox, drive train, suspension and brakes)

Wheels and tyres

Post-assembling check

# TEXTILES

**NATURAL FIBRES** 1 **ARTIFICIAL FIBRES** 3 **WEAVING** 4 **SPINNING** 2

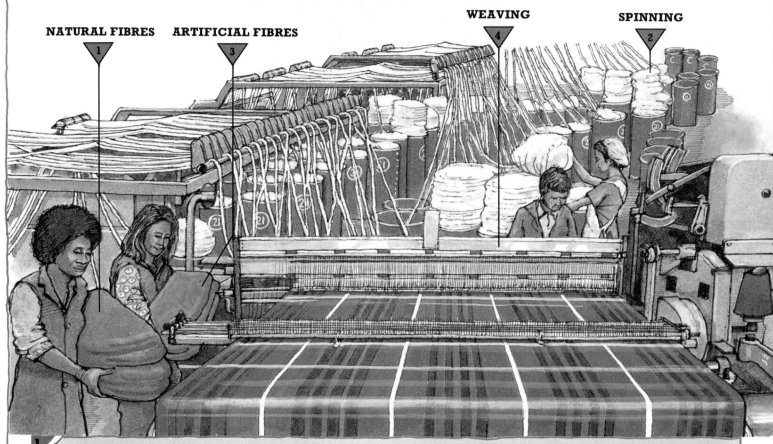

## 1 NATURAL FIBRES

Natural fibres are those produced by animals and plants, such as wool from sheep and goats, and cotton from the fluffy seedheads of cotton plants. Freshly harvested cotton bolls contain the cotton fibres, called *lint*, as well as seeds, leaves and other smaller fibres. In the cotton gin, the fibres are dried and pulled by revolving teeth through small gratings, to remove the seeds and other debris. The fibres are then ready to be spun (*above right*). Silk is another natural fibre. It comes from the 'silkworm' – the caterpillar of the silk moth. As the caterpillar changes into a chrysalis, it spins a cocoon of silken threads around itself. Each cocoon contains up to 1500 metres of extremely thin silk filament.

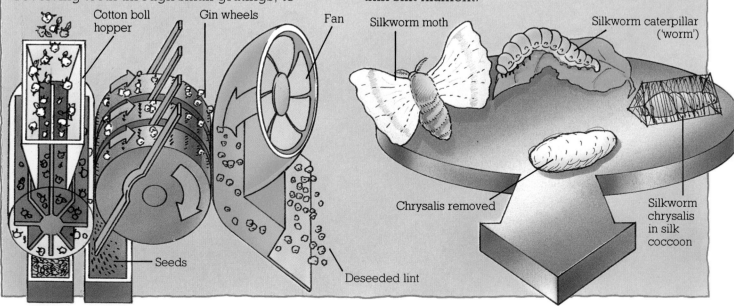

Cotton boll hopper

Gin wheels

Fan

Seeds

Deseeded lint

Silkworm moth

Silkworm caterpillar ('worm')

Chrysalis removed

Silkworm chrysalis in silk coccoon

## 2 SPINNING

There are several stages to the spinning process. The mat of cotton fibres, known as the lap, travels through teasing wires in a carding machine to produce loose bundles of fibres called slivers (*below left*). The slivers are teased and pulled out by rollers rotating at different rates in the roving machine (*below centre*), and wound onto reels or bobbins. The slivers are then thinned even further and spun into cotton yarn that is wound on another bobbin, ready for weaving or knitting into cotton cloth.

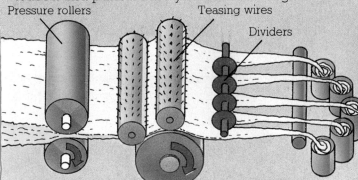

Pressure rollers
Teasing wires
Dividers

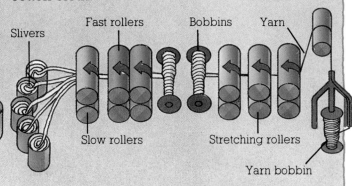

Slivers
Fast rollers
Bobbins
Yarn
Slow rollers
Stretching rollers
Yarn bobbin

## 3 ARTIFICIAL FIBRES

Chemicals are used to make artificial or synthetic fibres, such as nylon, polyester and acrylic. A common type, nylon 66, is made from hexamethylene diamine and adipic acid. The molecules *polymerize*, which means they link together in enormously long chains that give the material its strength and flexibility. In one technique, the raw chemicals are melted, extruded into long filaments, cooled and spun together.

Nylon polymer chips
Steam
Cooling air
Heater
Spinneret
Cooled fibre

## 4 WEAVING

In a woven fabric the yarns run in a criss-cross fashion, alternately over and under each other. The warp yarns are the ones already arranged in place along the weaving loom. Their ends are wound onto the warp beam. The weft or filler yarn is then passed to and fro between the alternating sets of warps, which are moved up and down on harness beams. Each harness beam moves every other warp yarn. The weft yarn unwinds from the shuttle.

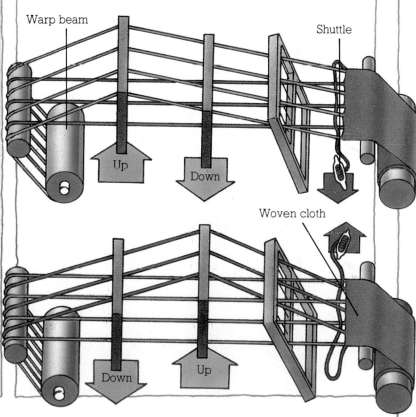

Warp beam
Shuttle
Up
Down
Woven cloth
Down
Up

# THE REFINERY

## REFINING NATURAL GAS

## REFINING NATURAL GAS

Natural gas collects in pockets within the Earth's crust and is obtained by drilling, in a similar way as for oil (page 62). It is about nine-tenths methane, a hydrocarbon (combination of hydrogen and carbon) with the chemical formula $CH_4$. But there are usually other hydrocarbon gases mixed with it, such as ethane ($C_2H_6$), propane ($C_3H_8$), and butane ($C_4H_{10}$). Each of these is suitable as a fuel or raw material in its own right. At the refinery, the gases are separated by *fractionation*. Each gas has a different boiling point, and fractionation relies on changes in temperature and pressure to tap off each gas in turn. Liquefied petroleum gas is made from crude petroleum (*opposite*) or by refining from natural gas. It contains greater proportions of propane and butane than natural gas, and it turns into a liquid more easily, making it more suitable for transport by tanker.

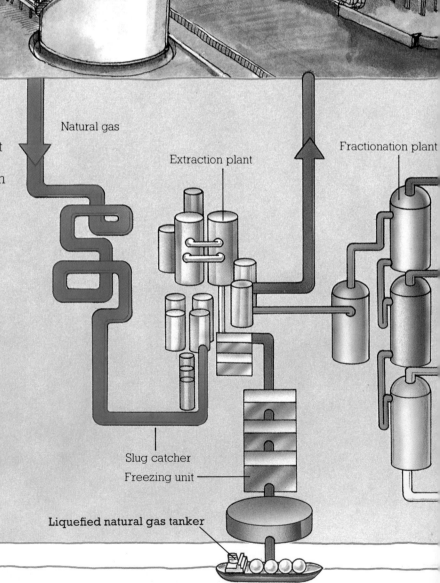

Natural gas

Extraction plant

Fractionation plant

Slug catcher

Freezing unit

Liquefied natural gas tanker

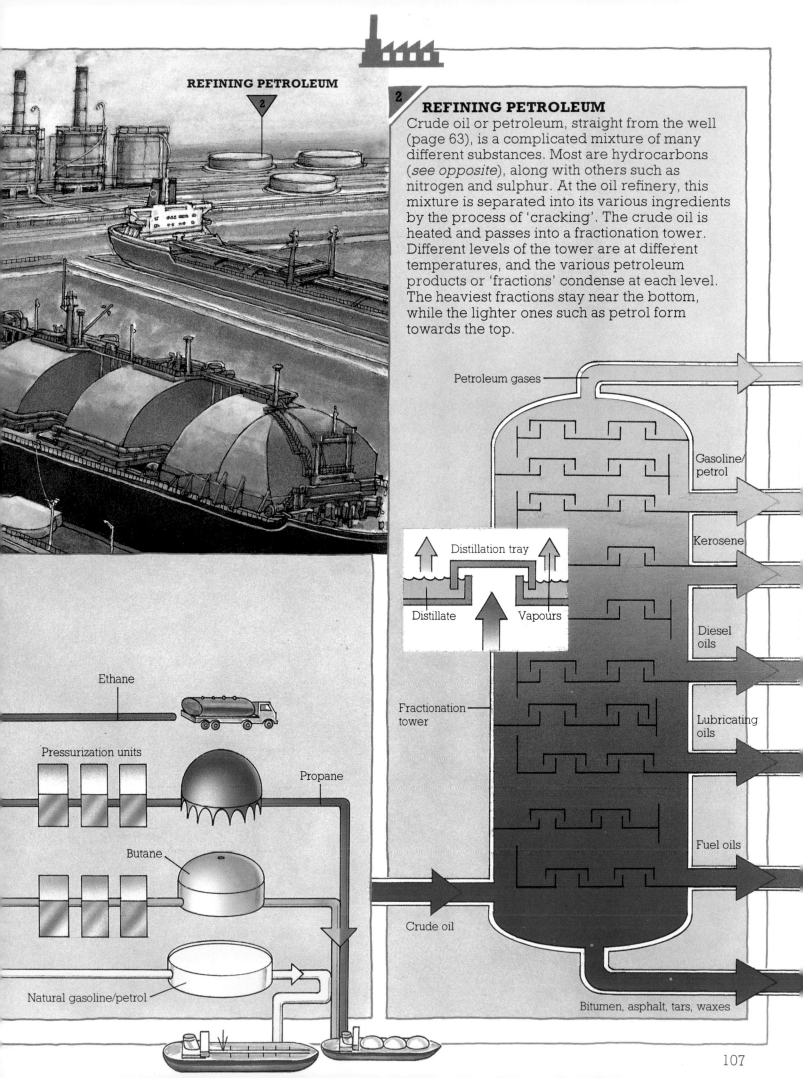

## 2 REFINING PETROLEUM

Crude oil or petroleum, straight from the well (page 63), is a complicated mixture of many different substances. Most are hydrocarbons (*see opposite*), along with others such as nitrogen and sulphur. At the oil refinery, this mixture is separated into its various ingredients by the process of 'cracking'. The crude oil is heated and passes into a fractionation tower. Different levels of the tower are at different temperatures, and the various petroleum products or 'fractions' condense at each level. The heaviest fractions stay near the bottom, while the lighter ones such as petrol form towards the top.

Petroleum gases

Gasoline/ petrol

Kerosene

Distillation tray

Distillate        Vapours

Diesel oils

Fractionation tower

Lubricating oils

Fuel oils

Crude oil

Bitumen, asphalt, tars, waxes

Ethane

Pressurization units

Propane

Butane

Natural gasoline/petrol

# INSIDE YOUR BODY

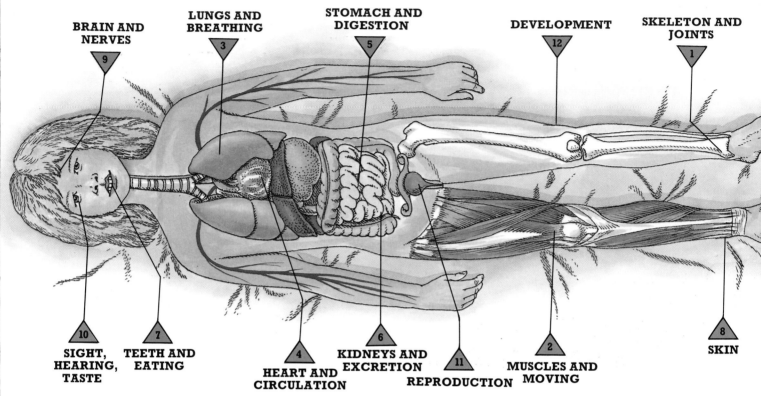

**BRAIN AND NERVES** 9

**LUNGS AND BREATHING** 3

**STOMACH AND DIGESTION** 5

**DEVELOPMENT** 12

**SKELETON AND JOINTS** 1

**SIGHT, HEARING, TASTE** 10

**TEETH AND EATING** 7

**HEART AND CIRCULATION** 4

**KIDNEYS AND EXCRETION** 6

**REPRODUCTION** 11

**MUSCLES AND MOVING** 2

**SKIN** 8

## 1 SKELETON AND JOINTS

The human body has a framework of about 208 rigid bones, which together make up its skeleton. Each bone is hard and strong, composed chiefly of minerals such as calcium and phosphate, and the tough protein known as collagen. Where bones meet, there are joints. Some joints, like those between the skull bones, are fixed and do not allow movement. Other joints let the bones move in relation to each other. The largest single bone is the femur (the thigh bone), and the biggest single joint is the knee. The smallest joints are between the smallest bones, in the ear (page 112).

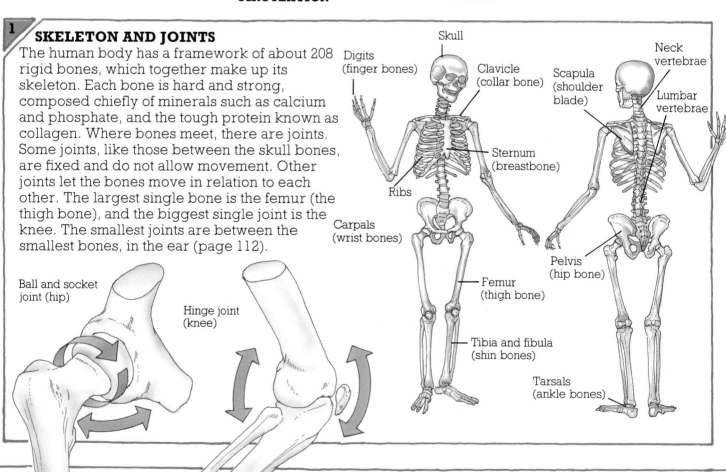

Ball and socket joint (hip)

Hinge joint (knee)

Skull

Digits (finger bones)

Clavicle (collar bone)

Neck vertebrae

Scapula (shoulder blade)

Lumbar vertebrae

Sternum (breastbone)

Ribs

Carpals (wrist bones)

Pelvis (hip bone)

Femur (thigh bone)

Tibia and fibula (shin bones)

Tarsals (ankle bones)

## 2  MUSCLES AND MOVING

There are over 600 skeletal muscles in the body. They move the skeleton, and they are under conscious control, so you can 'will' them to move when you wish. Many other muscles are in the digestive system (page 110), heart and other internal organs, but these work mainly automatically. A muscle can pull, but not push. So most skeletal muscles are arranged in pairs. One pulls the bone one way, and the other pulls it back.

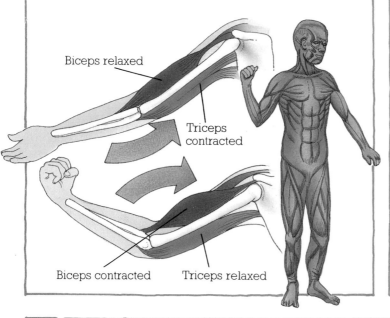

Biceps relaxed

Triceps contracted

Biceps contracted

Triceps relaxed

## 3  LUNGS AND BREATHING

The lungs, trachea (windpipe), throat and nose make up the body's respiratory, or breathing system. To breathe in, a series of muscles lifts up the ribs, while the diaphragm muscle becomes flat and pulls the bases of the lungs down. This makes the lungs bigger, and they suck in air. To breathe out, the various muscles relax. The elastic lung tissue springs back, returning the lungs to their smaller size and pushing out the air.

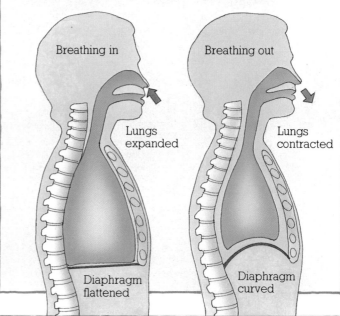

Breathing in

Breathing out

Lungs expanded

Lungs contracted

Diaphragm flattened

Diaphragm curved

## 4  HEART AND CIRCULATION

In the lungs, blood absorbs oxygen from the air. The blood then flows to the heart, which pumps it around the body, to deliver its oxygen to all body parts. In one heartbeat, blood is first sucked into the two upper chambers, the atria (1). It then flows through non-return valves into the lower chambers, the ventricles (2). These squeeze powerfully to push the blood out through the blood vessels, closing the valves to the atria (3). As the ventricles expand again, valves into the main vessels close to prevent blood flowing back into them (4).

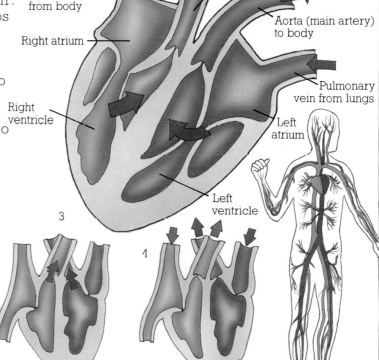

Venae cavae (main veins) from body

Pulmonary artery to lungs

Right atrium

Aorta (main artery) to body

Right ventricle

Pulmonary vein from lungs

Left atrium

Left ventricle

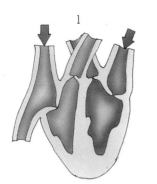

1

2

3

4

## 5 STOMACH AND DIGESTION

Like any mechanism, the body needs fuel. It obtains this from food. Digestion is the process of breaking down food into pieces small enough to be absorbed, through the wall of the small intestine into the blood. The teeth and the stomach chew and mash the food physically, while the stomach and the pancreas make powerful digestive juices that attack the food chemically. Food moves through the digestive system by the muscle-powered process of peristalsis. Leftover bits, together with rubbed-off parts of the stomach and intestines, are stored in the rectum before disposal.

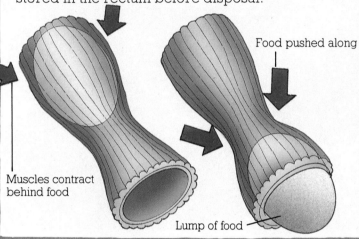

Food pushed along

Muscles contract behind food

Lump of food

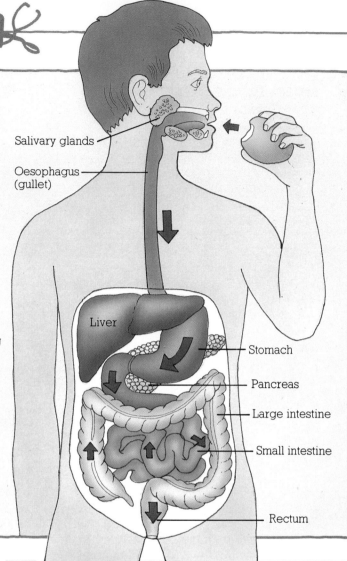

Salivary glands

Oesophagus (gullet)

Liver

Stomach

Pancreas

Large intestine

Small intestine

Rectum

## 6 KIDNEYS AND EXCRETION

The hundreds of chemical processes inside the body make various unwanted substances. The blood collects these. As it flows through the kidneys, more than a million microscopic filtering units in each kidney 'clean' the blood. The wastes form a fluid, urine. This trickles down tubes, or ureters, and is stored in the bladder.

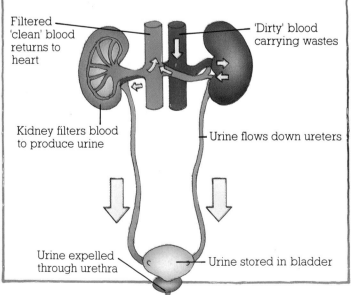

Filtered 'clean' blood returns to heart

'Dirty' blood carrying wastes

Kidney filters blood to produce urine

Urine flows down ureters

Urine expelled through urethra

Urine stored in bladder

## 7 TEETH AND EATING

The whitish enamel of a tooth is the hardest substance in the body. Inside, the tooth's living centre contains blood vessels and nerves. Its roots are fixed into the jaw bone by slightly flexible ligaments, which absorb some of the shocks and jars of biting. A child has a set of 20 teeth, and an adult has 32. The teeth at the front (incisors) are chisel-shaped for biting; those at the back (molars) are flattened for crushing.

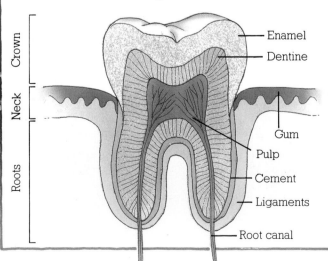

Crown

Neck

Roots

Enamel

Dentine

Gum

Pulp

Cement

Ligaments

Root canal

## 8 SKIN

Under a microscope, skin reveals two main layers. The outer layer is the epidermis, the inner one is the dermis. The epidermis continually replaces itself, as its surface is rubbed off and worn away by the body's movements and friction. At the base of the epidermis, cells are continually multiplying. They pass up through the various layers within the epidermis, becoming flatter and harder, and they eventually die. They reach the surface after about four weeks, where they are soon rubbed off. The dermis contains blood vessels, tough fibres of the protein collagen, and nerve endings of various kinds that detect changes in temperature, light touch, heavier pressure, and pain.

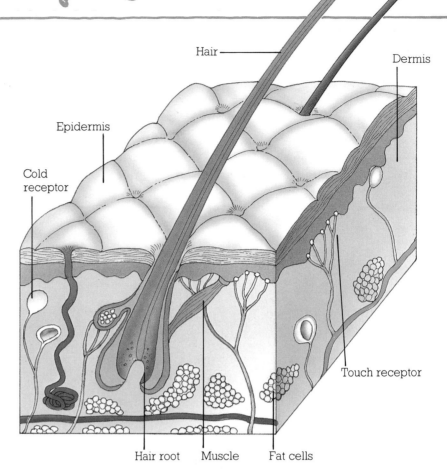

Hair — Dermis — Epidermis — Cold receptor — Touch receptor — Hair root — Muscle — Fat cells

## 9 BRAIN AND NERVES

The brain is made up of about ten billion nerve cells, or neurones, connected into one vast network. Nerve signals flash around the network in the form of tiny pulses of electricity. Nerves link the brain to all parts of the body. They carry signals to the brain from the sense organs (eyes, ears, nose), and signals from the brain to muscles. Most 'thinking' and 'remembering' takes place in the two large wrinkled lobes, the cerebral hemispheres. The corpus callosum connects the right and left halves of the brain. The pituitary gland, just below the main part of the brain, is the controller of the body's system of chemical messengers, known as the hormonal or endocrine system.

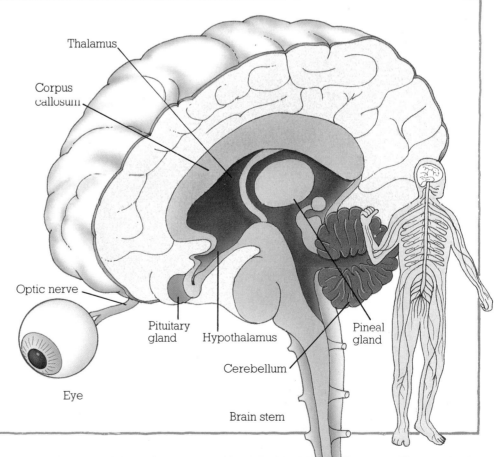

Thalamus — Corpus callosum — Optic nerve — Eye — Pituitary gland — Hypothalamus — Cerebellum — Pineal gland — Brain stem

## 10 SIGHT, HEARING, TASTE

Skin (page 111) is the body's biggest sense organ. But there are four other main senses: sight, hearing, taste and smell. In the eye, a lens focuses light rays onto a thin layer, the retina, which contains more than 130 million light-sensitive cells. These turn the patterns of light rays into coded nerve signals, which travel to the brain along the optic nerve. The ear changes airborne vibrations – sound waves – into vibrations that pass along three tiny bones, the hammer, anvil and stirrup. When the vibrations reach the fluid of the inner ear, they

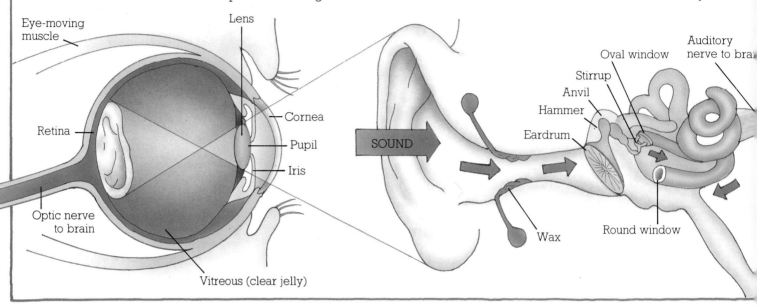

Eye-moving muscle

Lens

Retina

Cornea

Pupil

Iris

Optic nerve to brain

Vitreous (clear jelly)

SOUND

Oval window

Auditory nerve to bra[...]

Stirrup

Anvil

Hammer

Eardrum

Wax

Round window

## 12 DEVELOPMENT

All people begin life as a fertilized egg. The egg, in the woman, is fertilized by the sperm from a man. The egg splits into two and then four, then eight new cells. This continues until there are many millions of cells. Five days after fertilization some cells grow outwards from the developing *embryo* and into the wall of the uterus. This forms the placenta which passes food and oxygen to the embryo. Different cells in the embryo develop into different organs such as the heart and muscles. After nine months the baby is fully formed and is born.

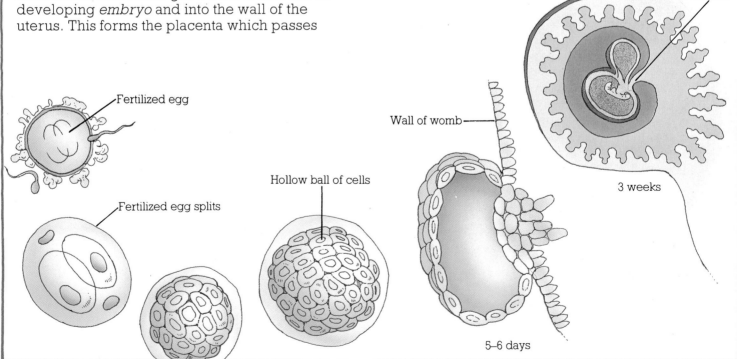

Fertilized egg

Fertilized egg splits

Hollow ball of cells

Wall of womb

Placenta

3 weeks

5–6 days

rock tiny hairs attached to nerve cells, producing nerve signals that go to the brain. In the tongue, taste buds detect the flavour substances in food and drink, converting the chemical reactions into nerve signals – which once again pass to the brain.

Surface of tongue

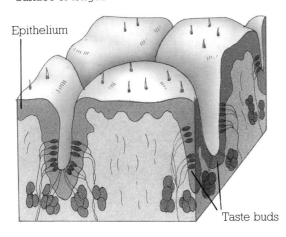

Epithelium

Taste buds

## REPRODUCTION

All animals, including humans, begin life as an egg. The human egg is only one-tenth of a millimetre across, and it comes from the woman's ovary. The man's testes make millions of microscopic, tadpole-shaped sperm cells. During sexual intercourse, sperm from the man's penis swim along the woman's vagina and through the womb, to the egg waiting in the oviduct.

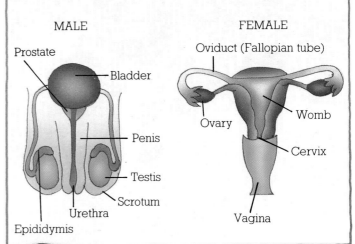

MALE

Prostate
Bladder
Penis
Testis
Scrotum
Urethra
Epididymis

FEMALE

Oviduct (Fallopian tube)
Womb
Ovary
Cervix
Vagina

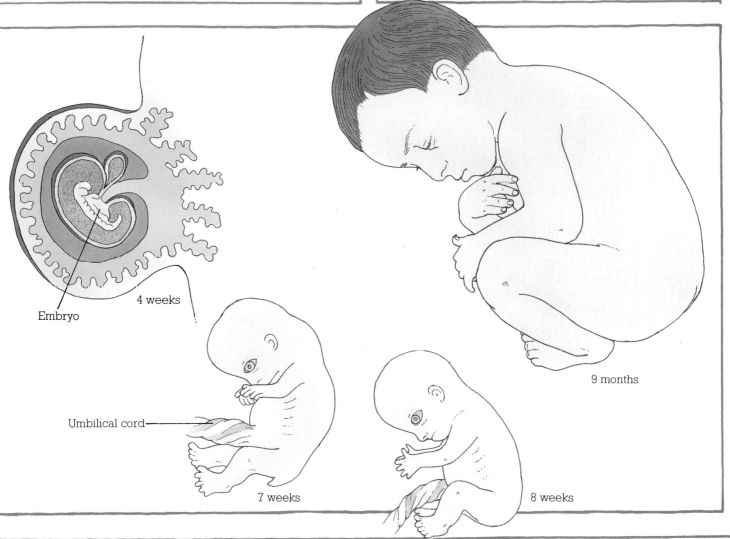

Embryo

4 weeks

Umbilical cord

7 weeks

8 weeks

9 months

# THE DOCTOR'S SURGERY

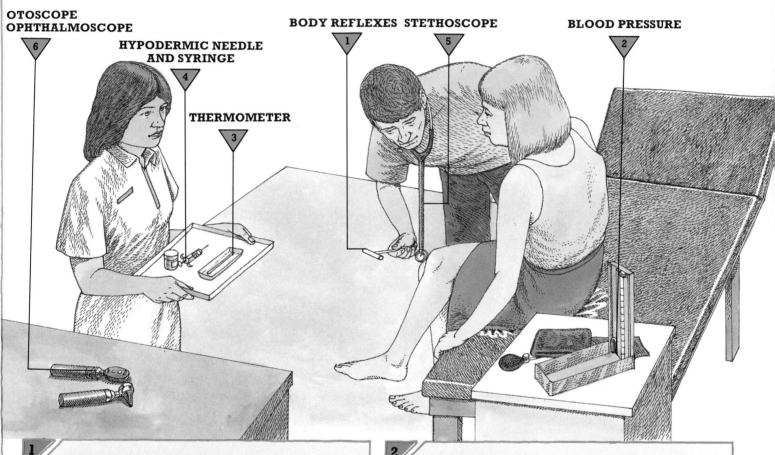

**OTOSCOPE**
**OPHTHALMOSCOPE**
6

**HYPODERMIC NEEDLE
AND SYRINGE**
4

**THERMOMETER**
3

**BODY REFLEXES**
1

**STETHOSCOPE**
5

**BLOOD PRESSURE**
2

---

1 **BODY REFLEXES**

The brain controls many of the body's actions, but not all of them. A reflex is a sudden, automatic reaction in which nerve messages travel to the spinal cord, pass around a reflex loop, and go out to muscles, without involving the brain. The knee-jerk reflex is a convenient way to check nerves and muscles.

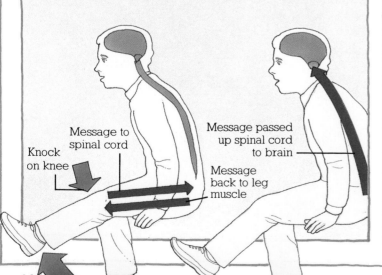

Knock on knee

Message to spinal cord

Message passed up spinal cord to brain

Message back to leg muscle

---

2 **BLOOD PRESSURE**

Blood pressure is checked with a sphygmomanometer. The cuff is inflated until its air pressure is sufficient to stop blood flowing (temporarily) through an artery in the arm. The doctor listens for blood flow through the stethoscope (*see opposite*). The air pressure pushes liquid mercury around the U-shaped tube.

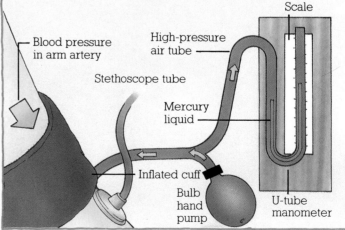

Scale

Blood pressure in arm artery

High-pressure air tube

Stethoscope tube

Mercury liquid

Inflated cuff

Bulb hand pump

U-tube manometer

## 3 THERMOMETER

Most substances expand when heated, and mercury is no exception. Body heat makes it expand from the bulb up into the stem. The notch stops the mercury in the stem from shrinking back into the bulb, so allowing time to take the reading on the scale.

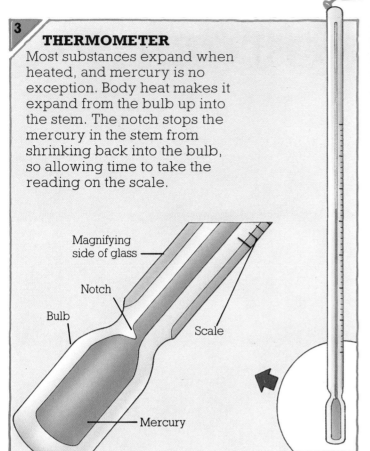

Magnifying side of glass

Notch

Bulb

Scale

Mercury

## 4 HYPODERMIC NEEDLE AND SYRINGE

Vaccines, drugs and other substances can be injected into the body using a hollow needle. *Hypodermic* means 'below the skin'. The vaccine is sucked out of its bottle through a self-sealing rubber stopper. Air bubbles must then be removed, or they could cause an airlock and prevent blood flow if they got into a blood vessel.

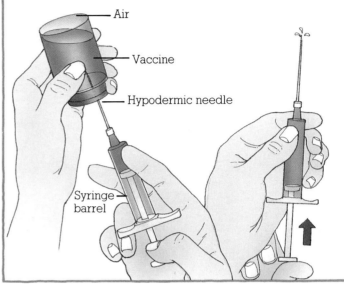

Air

Vaccine

Hypodermic needle

Syringe barrel

## 5 STETHOSCOPE

This listening device has a thin, flexible diaphragm that vibrates as it picks up sound waves or vibrations. The diaphragm's vibrations create sound waves that funnel up a hollow tube to the earpieces. The stethoscope amplifies sounds from the beating heart, breathing lungs, creaking joints, blood swishing through blood vessels, and food gurgling through intestines.

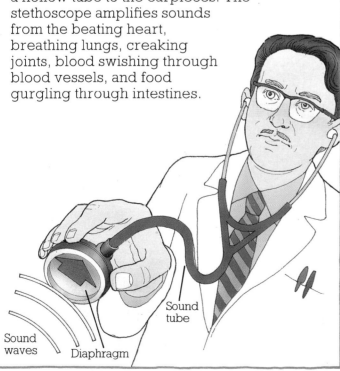

Sound waves

Diaphragm

Sound tube

## 6 OTOSCOPE AND OPHTHALMOSCOPE

Inside the eye is a convenient place for examining the body's blood vessels, which give an indication of general health. Small vessels show up on the retina, the light-sensitive layer at the back of the eyeball. The ophthalmoscope shines a beam of light into the eye, to illuminate the retina. When looking into the ear with an otoscope, the doctor can see through the partly-transparent eardrum to the tiny bones beyond (page 112).

OTOSCOPE

OPHTHALMOSCOPE

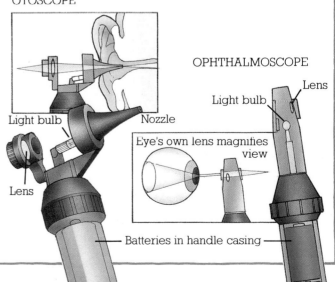

Light bulb

Nozzle

Lens

Lens

Light bulb

Eye's own lens magnifies view

Batteries in handle casing

# THE OPERATING THEATRE

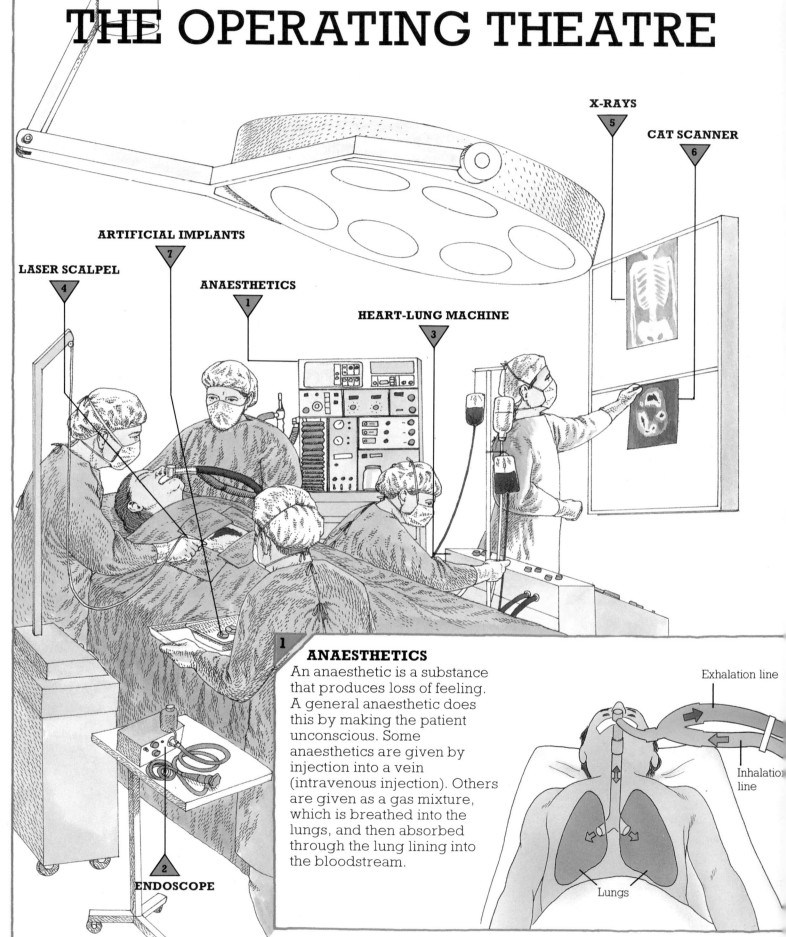

**X-RAYS**
5

**CAT SCANNER**
6

**ARTIFICIAL IMPLANTS**
7

**LASER SCALPEL**
4

**ANAESTHETICS**
1

**HEART-LUNG MACHINE**
3

1 **ANAESTHETICS**

An anaesthetic is a substance that produces loss of feeling. A general anaesthetic does this by making the patient unconscious. Some anaesthetics are given by injection into a vein (intravenous injection). Others are given as a gas mixture, which is breathed into the lungs, and then absorbed through the lung lining into the bloodstream.

Exhalation line

Inhalation line

Lungs

2 **ENDOSCOPE**

## 2 ENDOSCOPE

Endoscopes are inserted into the body through an opening (such as the mouth) or through a small cut. Modern versions use a bundle of thin, flexible optical fibres (page 75) that can be 'steered' through the body, with a light to illuminate the view, and tiny pincers to take a sample, or 'biopsy' for later analysis. The bronchoscope looks into the lungs, the gastroscope into the stomach, and the cystoscope into the bladder.

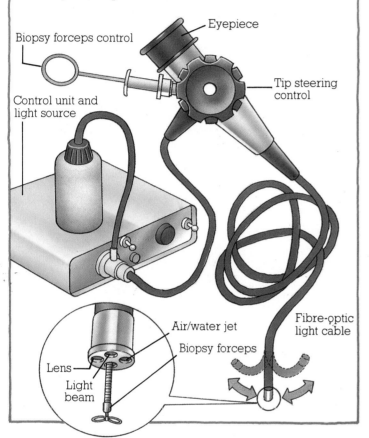

Biopsy forceps control

Eyepiece

Control unit and light source

Tip steering control

Air/water jet

Biopsy forceps

Fibre-optic light cable

Lens

Light beam

Biopsy forceps

## 3 HEART-LUNG MACHINE

The technical name for this device is the cardiopulmonary bypass machine, since it takes over the jobs of both heart and lungs. Blood returning along veins, from the body's organs to the heart, is led out of the body along a tube to a gas-exchange unit. Here carbon dioxide is removed from the blood and oxygen is added – thus doing the lungs' job. The blood then flows through a rotary pump – which does the heart's job – and back into the main arteries. The CP machine is used when surgeons need to operate on the heart, for example, when replacing a diseased heart valve with an artificial one (page 119).

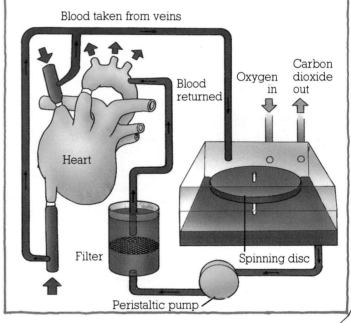

Blood taken from veins

Blood returned

Oxygen in

Carbon dioxide out

Heart

Filter

Spinning disc

Peristaltic pump

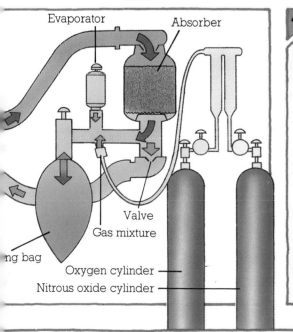

Evaporator

Absorber

Valve

Gas mixture

ng bag

Oxygen cylinder

Nitrous oxide cylinder

## 4 LASER SCALPEL

Laser light is a concentrated form of energy (page 135). It can burn through the body's tissues, in a similar fashion to the metal scalpel blade that cuts through them. But the laser scalpel can be controlled very accurately, producing a thinner, neater cut. Because it is hot it singes and seals the small blood vessels on either side of the cut. This means that there is less bleeding than with a metal scalpel.

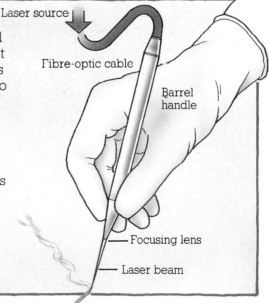

Laser source

Fibre-optic cable

Barrel handle

Focusing lens

Laser beam

## 5  X-RAYS

X-rays are part of the electromagnetic spectrum that includes light rays and radio waves. They pass easily through the body's muscles, intestines and other soft parts. But they cannot travel through the hard parts, such as bones, cartilages and teeth. In a medical X-ray picture, or radiograph, X-rays from a gas-discharge tube shine through the body onto a fluorescent screen and photographic plate. Where rays can pass through, they produce a dark area. Dense parts like bones and metal jewellery show up white.

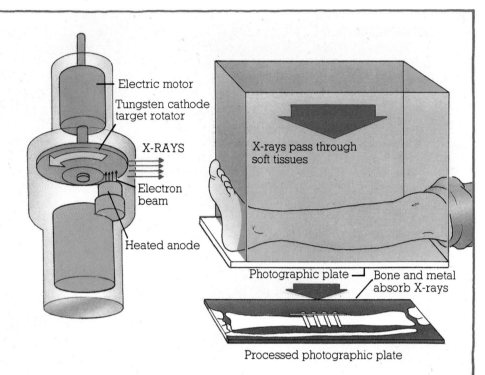

Electric motor

Tungsten cathode target rotator

X-RAYS

Electron beam

Heated anode

X-rays pass through soft tissues

Photographic plate — Bone and metal absorb X-rays

Processed photographic plate

## 6  CAT SCANNER

Computerized Axial Tomography involves passing very weak X-rays through the body. The patient lies inside a large rotating drum containing the X-ray source and recording camera. These move around and along the body, taking several pictures from different angles. The pictures are then combined by computer to show a 'slice' through the body. Like an ordinary X-ray, dense parts of the body show up lighter. The CAT scanner can distinguish between different soft tissues, such as muscles and nerves.

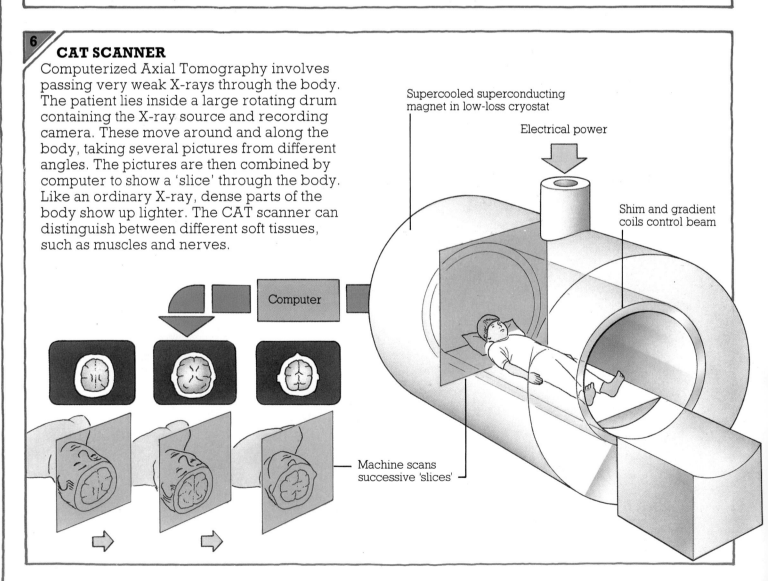

Supercooled superconducting magnet in low-loss cryostat

Electrical power

Shim and gradient coils control beam

Computer

Machine scans successive 'slices'

118

## ARTIFICIAL IMPLANTS

Many diseased or worn-out parts of the body can now be replaced with artificial substitutes. Medical scientists are continually researching into better, longer-lasting materials. In addition, these materials should be biologically inert – they should not cause blood to clot on their surfaces, and they should not provoke the body into reacting against them, as though they were 'invaders' like germs. Plastics such as teflon, and metals such as stainless steel are often used. As electronic devices become smaller and more sophisticated, they are being used to help parts of the body that rely on electrical nerve messages. For example, the cochlear implant receives sound waves, converts them into electrical signals, and feeds these directly to the cochlea, the part of the ear which normally turns vibrations into nerve messages.

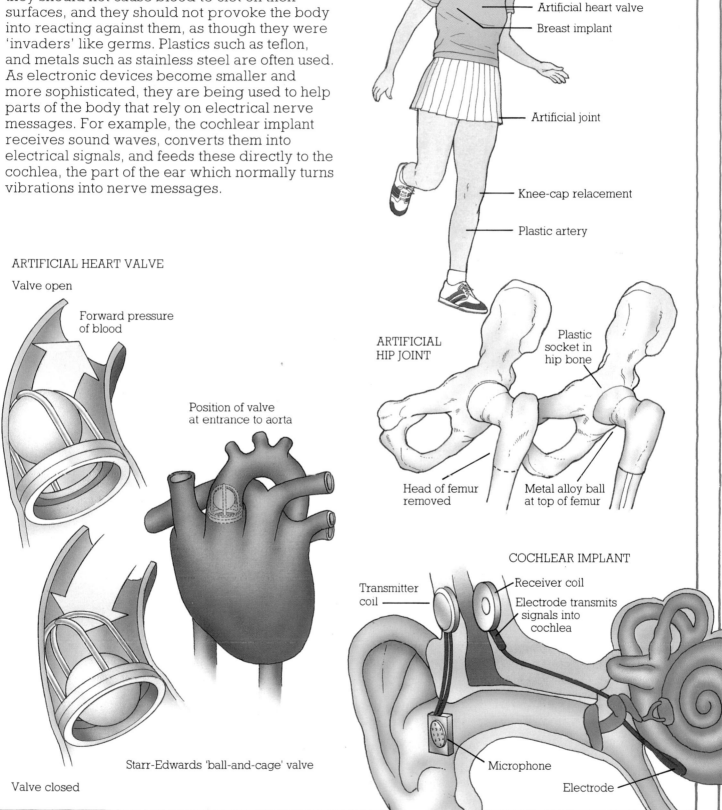

Skull plate
Cosmetic false eye
Cochlear implant in ear
False teeth
Artificial larynx
Cardiac pacemaker
Artificial heart valve
Breast implant
Artificial joint
Knee-cap relacement
Plastic artery

ARTIFICIAL HEART VALVE

Valve open

Forward pressure of blood

Position of valve at entrance to aorta

Starr-Edwards 'ball-and-cage' valve

Valve closed

ARTIFICIAL HIP JOINT

Plastic socket in hip bone

Head of femur removed

Metal alloy ball at top of femur

COCHLEAR IMPLANT

Transmitter coil

Receiver coil

Electrode transmits signals into cochlea

Microphone

Electrode

# HARVEST TIME

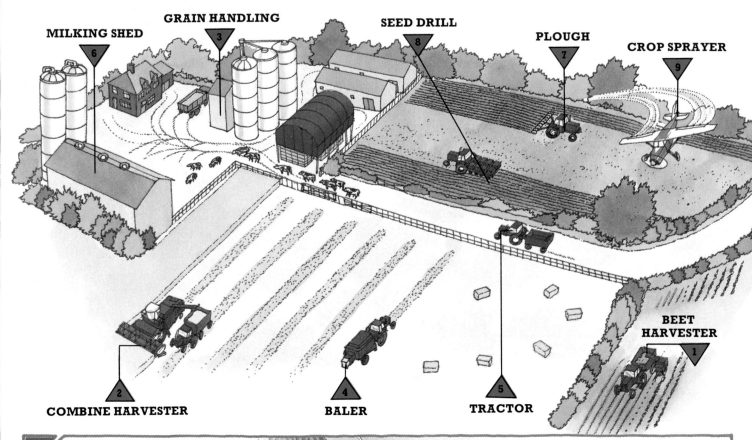

**MILKING SHED** 6

**GRAIN HANDLING** 3

**SEED DRILL** 8

**PLOUGH** 7

**CROP SPRAYER** 9

**COMBINE HARVESTER** 2

**BALER** 4

**TRACTOR** 5

**BEET HARVESTER** 1

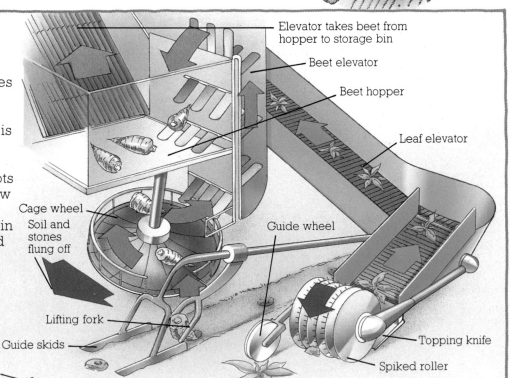

**1**

## BEET HARVESTER

Like the combine harvester above, the beet harvester 'combines' several processes in one machine. In this case, the beet plant's leaves are removed, and the beet root is lifted from the ground by a mechanical fork. In the rotating cage wheel, the roots are shaken and spun to throw off stones and soil. The cleaned roots are collected in a hopper, and often emptied straight into a trailer being pulled alongside the harvester.

Elevator takes beet from hopper to storage bin

Beet elevator

Beet hopper

Leaf elevator

Cage wheel

Soil and stones flung off

Guide wheel

Lifting fork

Guide skids

Topped beet in ground

Topping knife

Spiked roller

## 2 COMBINE HARVESTER

The crop is cut by the revolving wheel and cutter bar (1), pushed into the machine by the feeder (2), and taken by the transfer auger (3) to the main grain auger (4). The thresher separates the grain from the windrow, via distribution augers (5). A fan (6) blasts air through a series of sieves (7) to blow away the chaff. Unsorted grain is sent round again by the return cross auger (8). The threshed grain travels along the grain auger (9) and distribution auger (10) to the storage tank (11). The entire machine is powered by a diesel engine (12) and controlled by the driver in the cab (13).

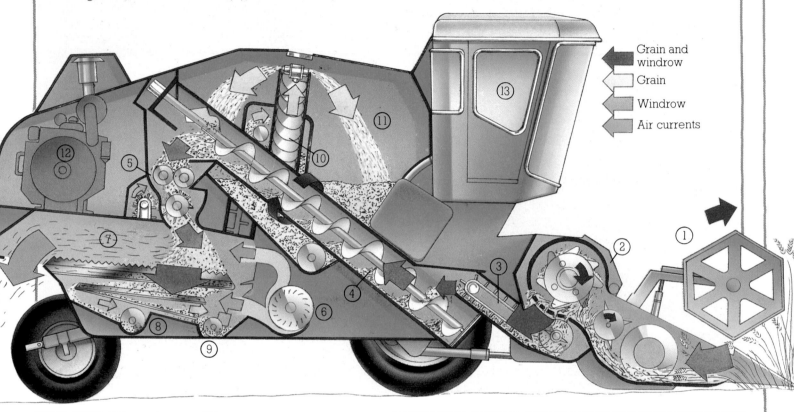

Grain and windrow

Grain

Windrow

Air currents

## 3 GRAIN HANDLING

Grain is ground into flour, which is an ingredient of many foods such as breads, pastries and cakes. The 'grains' are actually small seeds, which would otherwise grow into new plants. After the grain has been harvested (*see above*) it must be prevented from germinating (starting to grow) or going mouldy, otherwise it would be of no use to the miller. The seeds are kept extremely dry, and in some cases in a special mixture of gases, before they are taken to the grinding mill.

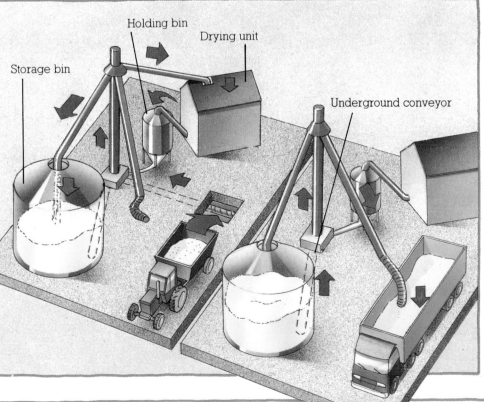

Holding bin

Drying unit

Storage bin

Underground conveyor

### 4 BALER

Hay is cut, dried grass, and makes a nutritious food for farm animals. Straw is the leftover stems of grain plants – cereals such as wheat, oats, barley and rye. The baler collects hay or straw, presses it into neat blocks, and ties these with twine. Straw has many uses, from animal bedding to making mats and stuffing mattresses!

3 Hay is tied and ejected as a bale

1 Crop is separated and packed into charee chamber

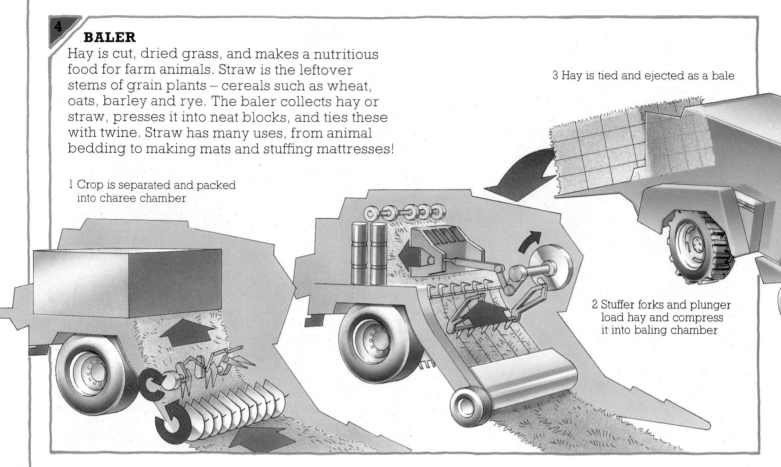

2 Stuffer forks and plunger load hay and compress it into baling chamber

### 6 MILKING SHED

Mechanical milking sheds are regularly inspected by health experts, to ensure the cleanest possible conditions. The milk is sucked from the cow's udder by a vacuum system, in the same way that a calf would suck the milk from its mother. The pulsator unit produces vibrations which massage the teat and encourage milk flow.

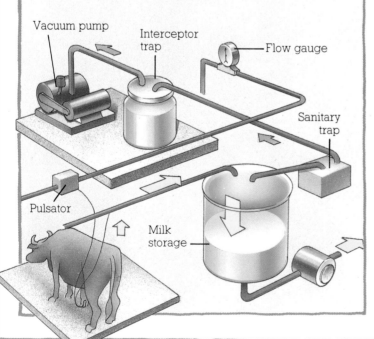

Vacuum pump

Interceptor trap

Flow gauge

Sanitary trap

Pulsator

Milk storage

### 7 PLOUGH

Today's plough has changed little from medieval times, although the pulling power is now usually a diesel-engined tractor! The blade cuts into the soil and the mouldboard turns it over, ready for the new crop.

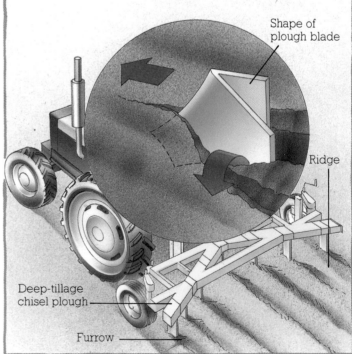

Shape of plough blade

Ridge

Deep-tillage chisel plough

Furrow

## TRACTOR

The farm tractor is powered by a large diesel engine (page 89). A tractor is able to pull or push implements, such as ploughs and harrows. A large tractor can pull a 21-blade plough and cover 60 hectares in one day.

In addition, there are take-off drive shafts which are set in motion using the extra gear lever in the cab. The take-off shafts drive other machines, such as separators or circular saws.

TRACTOR

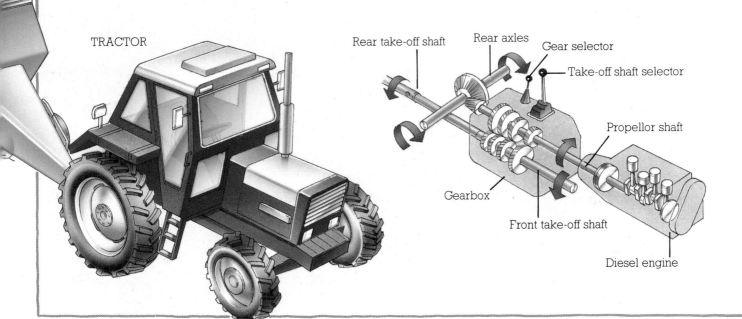

Rear take-off shaft

Rear axles

Gear selector

Take-off shaft selector

Propellor shaft

Gearbox

Front take-off shaft

Diesel engine

## SEED DRILL

Jethro Tull's invention of the horse-drawn mechanized seed drill, in about 1701, brought great changes to agriculture. Rather than simply throwing seeds onto the soil, or planting them by hand, the drill inserted each seed to the correct depth in the soil, and covered it over. Planting seeds in neat rows also paved the way for mechanical harvesters.

4-ROW SEED DRILL

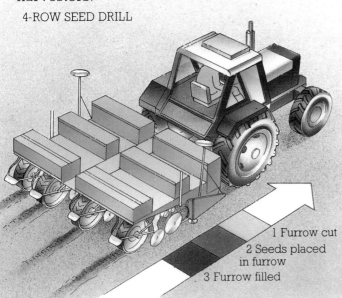

1 Furrow cut
2 Seeds placed in furrow
3 Furrow filled

## CROP SPRAYER

Herbicides kill weeds and other unwanted plants. Fungicides kill mildews, rusts and other unwanted fungi. Pesticides kill beetles, aphids and other unwanted animals. All of these can be sprayed onto crops from the air, without damaging the growing plants.

Low-altitude spray run

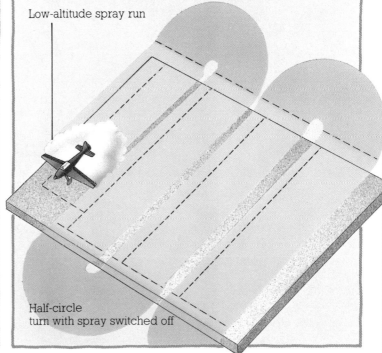

Half-circle turn with spray switched off

# THE NATURAL WORLD

BIRDS
**6**

FISHES
**3**

PLANTS
**1**

MAMMALS
**7**

NATURAL CYCLES
**8**

REPTILES
**5**

STINGS AND POISONS
**9**

INSECTS AND ARACHNIDS
**2**

ECOLOGY
**10**

AMPHIBIANS
**4**

## 1. PLANTS

The living world can be studied in the same way as a machine, to see how the parts fit together and how they 'work'. This is the science of ecology (page 129). Plants are vital since they feed animals. A plant absorbs minerals from the soil through its roots. It traps the energy in sunlight using its leaves. The minerals and energy are combined with carbon dioxide from the air, to form new plant tissues during growth. The flower contains egg cells that are fertilized by pollen from another flower, and they develop into seeds. The seeds are spread by wind, water or animals, and grow into new plants.

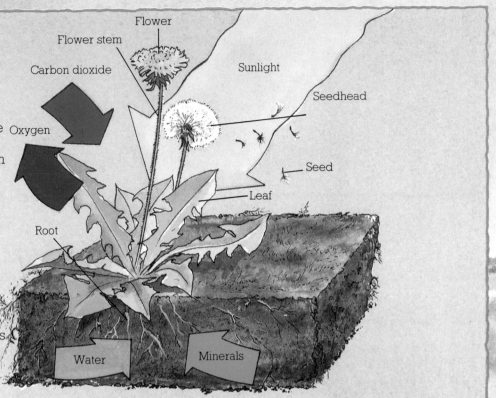

Flower
Flower stem
Carbon dioxide
Oxygen
Sunlight
Seedhead
Seed
Leaf
Root
Water
Minerals

## 2. INSECTS AND ARACHNIDS

These small animals are among the most numerous on Earth. All insects, including butterflies, beetles, grasshoppers, ants, bees and flies, have six legs. Arachnids have eight legs and they include spiders, scorpions, mites and ticks. Both types have a hard outer casing, or exoskeleton, which protects the soft parts inside. As the creature grows, the old casing is shed regularly and replaced by a new, larger one.

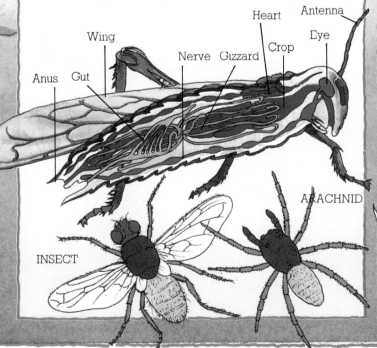

Heart
Antenna
Wing
Eye
Nerve   Gizzard   Crop
Anus   Gut
ARACHNID
INSECT

## 3. FISHES

Like other animals, a fish needs to take in oxygen and get rid of carbon dioxide. It 'breathes' the oxygen dissolved in water. The oxygen passes through the very thin coverings of the gill filaments into the blood just beneath. As the fish swims forwards, a current of water flows over its gills. This ensures continuing supplies of oxygen, and the water carries away unwanted carbon dioxide.

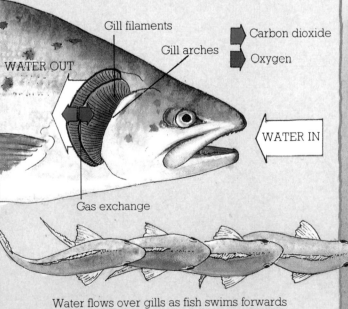

Gill filaments
Gill arches
Carbon dioxide
Oxygen
WATER OUT
WATER IN
Gas exchange

Water flows over gills as fish swims forwards

**4**

## AMPHIBIANS

Most amphibians have thin, moist skin that soon dries out, so they live in damp places or near water. They must return to water to lay their jelly-coated eggs, or spawn. The eggs hatch into young, called tadpoles, which live in water for the first few weeks and breathe using gills. As they grow, their gills disappear and they begin to breathe with lungs. Their body gradually changes to the adult form, a process called *metamorphosis*.

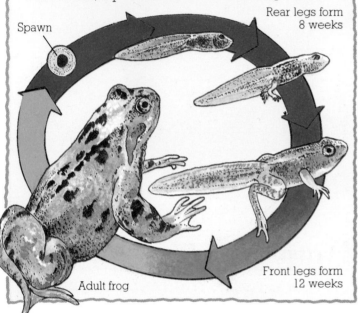

Spawn

Rear legs form
8 weeks

Adult frog

Front legs form
12 weeks

**5**

## REPTILES

Unlike the amphibian egg, the reptile egg is enclosed in a tough, waterproof shell. Reptiles have scaly, waterproof skin. This means they can live entirely on land, unlike amphibians. Reptiles are not 'warm-blooded' like birds and mammals, but they can keep their bodies relatively warm by basking in the Sun when cold, or cooling off in the shade when hot.

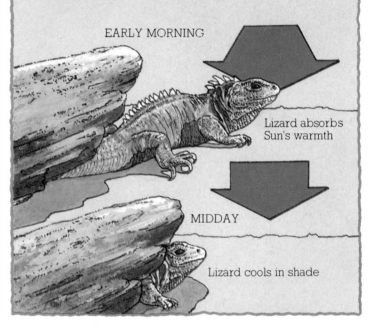

EARLY MORNING

Lizard absorbs
Sun's warmth

MIDDAY

Lizard cools in shade

**6**

## BIRDS

Birds are the only animals with feathers. The feathers help to keep body warmth in, and they also overlap to form a broad, airtight wing surface for flight. A bird spends much time preening its feathers, getting rid of dirt and spreading waterproofing oils, to keep them in good condition. Like reptiles, birds lay shelled eggs. When the chicks first hatch they have no feathers, or only very small ones. They are cared for by their parents until they can fly.

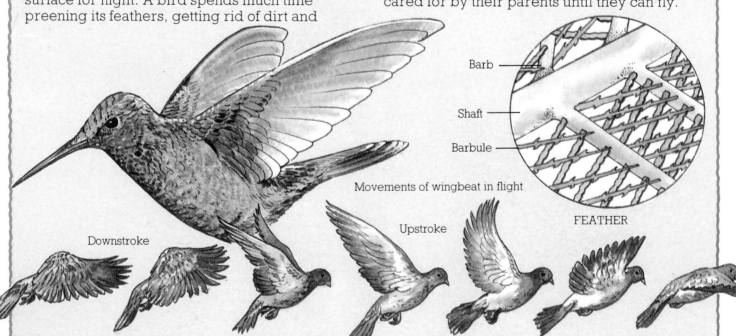

Barb

Shaft

Barbule

Movements of wingbeat in flight

FEATHER

Downstroke

Upstroke

## 7 MAMMALS

A mammal is a warm-blooded animal with fur, that feeds its young on milk. Marsupial mammals have pouches, where the young live during most of their growth and development. Marsupial mammals include kangaroos, koalas and opossums. The young of placental mammals develop in the womb, inside the mother's body.

Placental mother lacks pouch

Marsupial baby feeds and shelters in pouch

## 8 NATURAL CYCLES

Nature wastes nothing. Plants obtain their minerals and nutrients from the soil. They are eaten by herbivorous animals, such as cows, sheep, horses and rodents. Carnivores eat other animals; those which eat insects are called insectivores. As plants and animals die, their remains rot back into the soil again. Or they may become food for detritivores, such as dung beetles and maggots. Natural recycling is an important part of ecology (page 129).

Animals communicate with each other in many ways. Wolves use facial expressions, body posture and tail position to convey their moods and intentions.

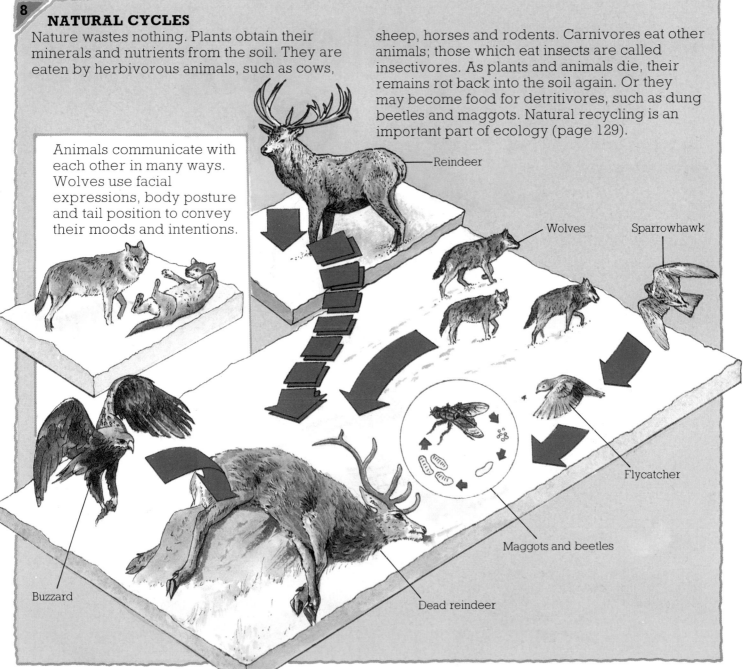

Reindeer

Wolves

Sparrowhawk

Flycatcher

Maggots and beetles

Buzzard

Dead reindeer

## STINGS AND POISONS

Various plants and animals have poisonous stings or bites. In plants the stings are for defence, to prevent animals eating them. The spines of cacti and the thorns of rosebushes and brambles do a similar job. Some animals have a poisonous bite or sting for defence, such as scorpions and bees. Others use their poison to catch and subdue their prey. Among these are jellyfishes, coneshells, spiders, certain fishes such as the weever and stonefish, and venomous snakes. The fangs of a snake work like a hypodermic needle (page 115), to inject the poison into the victim.

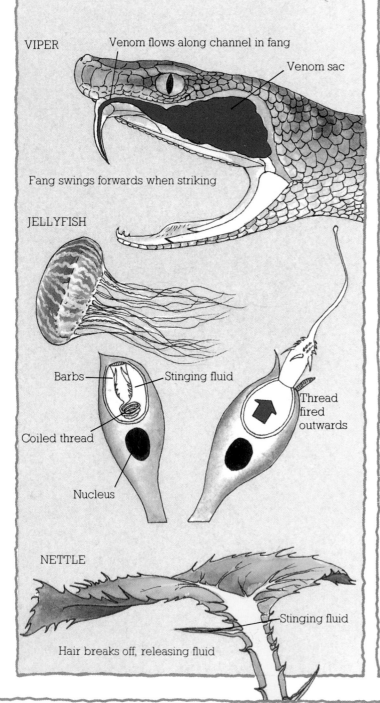

VIPER

Venom flows along channel in fang

Venom sac

Fang swings forwards when striking

JELLYFISH

Barbs — Stinging fluid

Coiled thread

Thread fired outwards

Nucleus

NETTLE

Stinging fluid

Hair breaks off, releasing fluid

## 10

## ECOLOGY

This is the study of how animals and plants live together: who eats what, who shelters where, and how minerals and nutrients are recycled in the living world. Shown here are only a few of the animals that live in and around a river. Each is adapted to a certain way of life. The *niche* of an animal or plant describes its position in the web of nature – including its requirements for warmth, moisture, light or shade, food, shelter, nesting sites, and other factors.

Male stickleback guarding eggs in nest among reeds

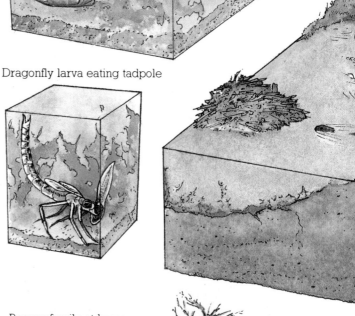

Dragonfly larva eating tadpole

Beaver family at home in lodge, in lake

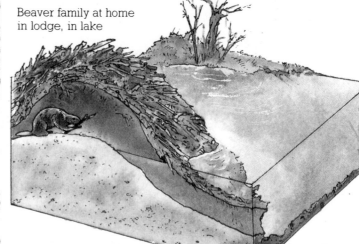

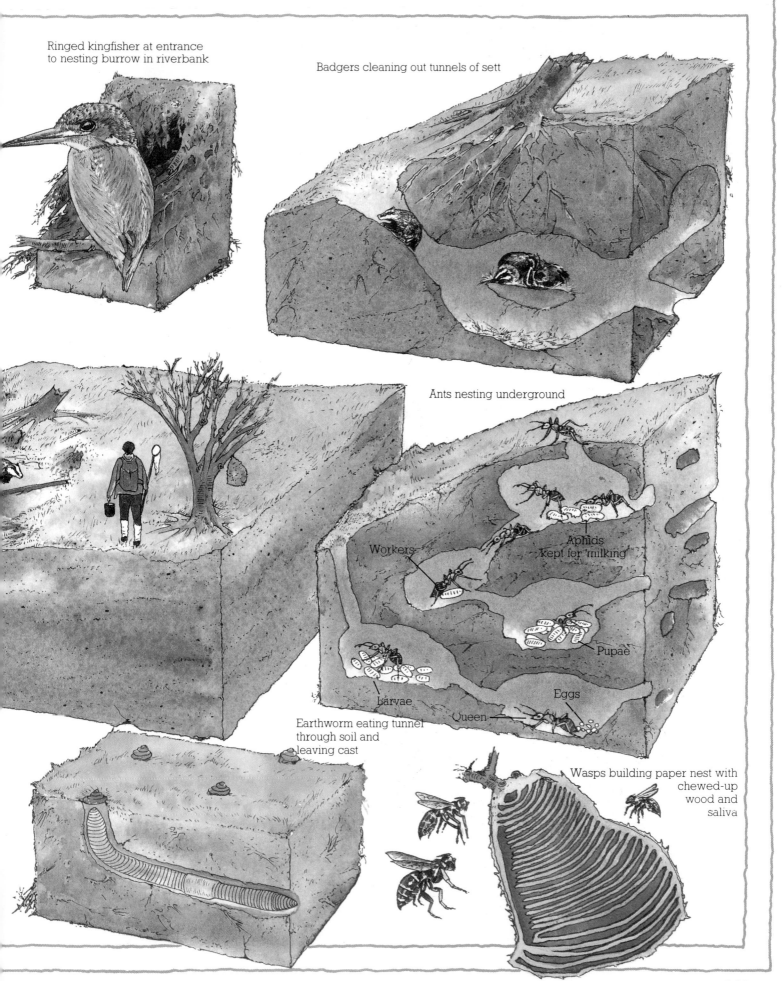

Ringed kingfisher at entrance to nesting burrow in riverbank

Badgers cleaning out tunnels of sett

Ants nesting underground

Workers

Aphids kept for 'milking'

Pupae

Larvae

Eggs

Queen

Earthworm eating tunnel through soil and leaving cast

Wasps building paper nest with chewed-up wood and saliva

# ENTERTAINMENT

**PIANO**

**HI-FI MUSIC SYSTEM**

**VIDEO CAMERA AND PLAYER**

**TELEVISION**

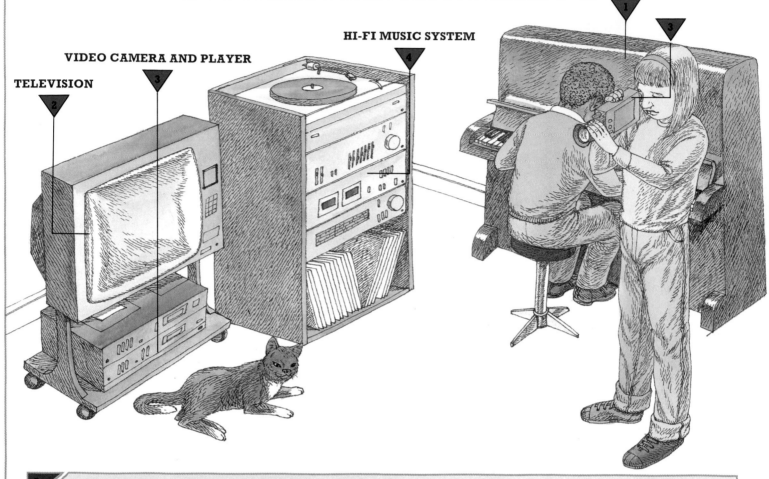

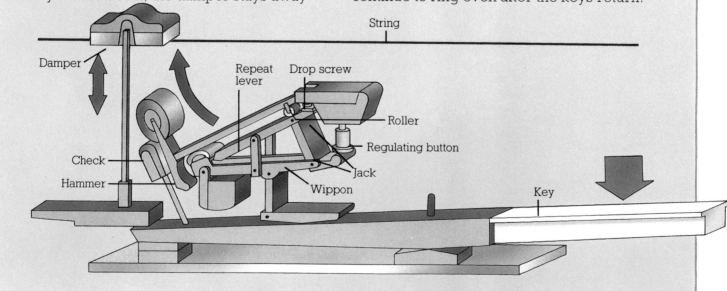

## PIANO

Each piano key works as a simple lever that sets in motion a series of levers, catches and springs. The result is that the damper lifts from the string as the hammer strikes it. As long as the key is held down, the damper stays away from the string. When the key is allowed to return, the damper comes back into contact with the string and stops its vibrations. A foot pedal moves all the dampers so that the strings continue to ring even after the keys return.

String

Damper

Repeat lever

Drop screw

Roller

Regulating button

Check

Jack

Hammer

Wippon

Key

## TELEVISION

The colour television has three *electron guns*: red, green and blue. These 'shoot' beams of electrons at the screen. The direction of the beams is controlled by electrically charged plates or deflector coils. These make the beams sweep across the screen to form a line, then move down the screen, sweeping line by line, to build up the picture. There are 25 or 30 complete pictures each second. The electron beams strike the screen, where each beam causes a corresponding colour of phosphor strip to glow and give off light. When all three guns aim at the same place, each produces tiny spots of its own colour. From a distance, the eye merges these spots of primary colour and sees 'white'. If no electrons strike the screen, the eye sees it as 'black'. The *chrominance* signals control the relative brightness of each colour, while the *luminance* signal controls the overall brightness of all three colours.

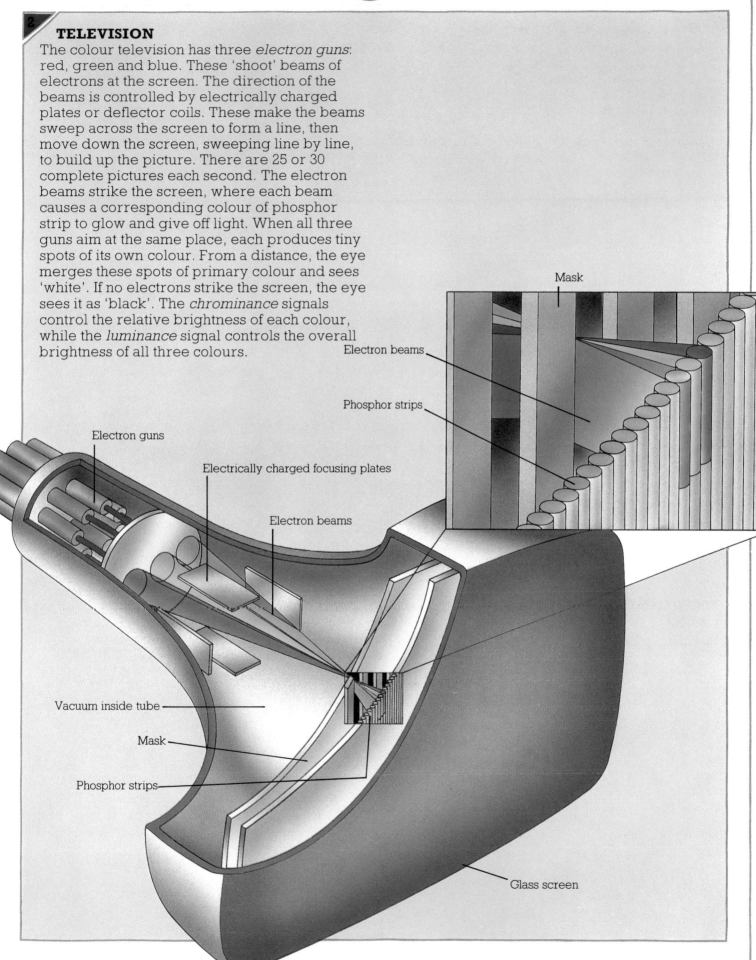

Mask

Electron beams

Phosphor strips

Electron guns

Electrically charged focusing plates

Electron beams

Vacuum inside tube

Mask

Phosphor strips

Glass screen

## VIDEO CAMERA AND PLAYER

A video camera does not use light to create a chemical change in photographic film, as in the ordinary camera (page 77). Instead, the light is focused onto a target plate that has a layer of *photoconductive* material. This is a material that conducts varying amounts of electricity, according to the amount and colour of light that shines onto it. The photoconductive material is scanned point-by-point across the plate by electronic circuitry, and the image on it is coded into a stream of electrical signals. These are recorded as tiny magnetized patches on magnetic tape – dozens of images each second. The tape is contained in a plastic case called a videocassette. When the tape is played, the record-playback heads pick up the coded patches of magnetism and convert them into electrical signals, which are fed to the television set. Sound is also recorded, in a narrow strip at the top of the tape.

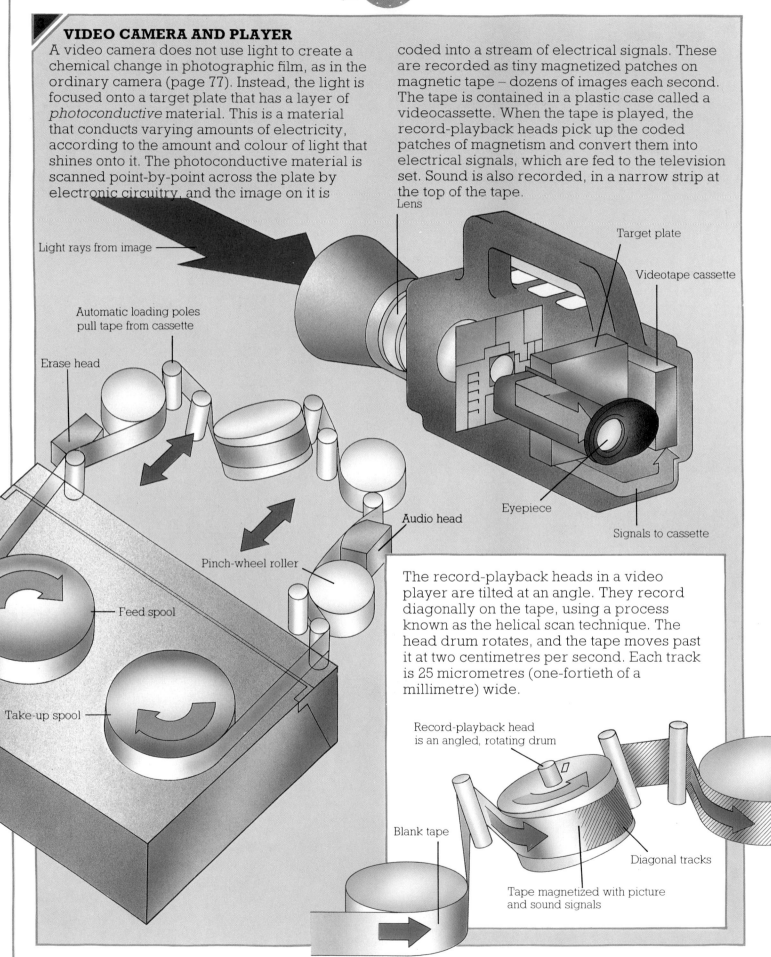

Light rays from image

Lens

Target plate

Videotape cassette

Automatic loading poles pull tape from cassette

Erase head

Audio head

Pinch-wheel roller

Feed spool

Take-up spool

Eyepiece

Signals to cassette

The record-playback heads in a video player are tilted at an angle. They record diagonally on the tape, using a process known as the helical scan technique. The head drum rotates, and the tape moves past it at two centimetres per second. Each track is 25 micrometres (one-fortieth of a millimetre) wide.

Record-playback head is an angled, rotating drum

Blank tape

Diagonal tracks

Tape magnetized with picture and sound signals

## HI-FI MUSIC SYSTEM

A typical home hi-fi (high-fidelity) system consists of inputs, an amplifier and a control unit, and outputs. The inputs detect coded signals in a variety of forms, turn them into electrical signals, and feed them to the amplifier. For example, the radio tuner detects signals broadcast as radio waves, using its aerial. In the vinyl disc 'record player', the signals are coded as bumps and waves in a V-shaped groove. In a compact disc player, they are in the form of microscopic bumps and pits which are read by a laser beam. In an audio cassette, the signals are tiny patches of magnetism on the tape. The signals are altered by the tone controls, made stronger in the amplifier, and then fed to the outputs – usually loudspeakers or headphones.

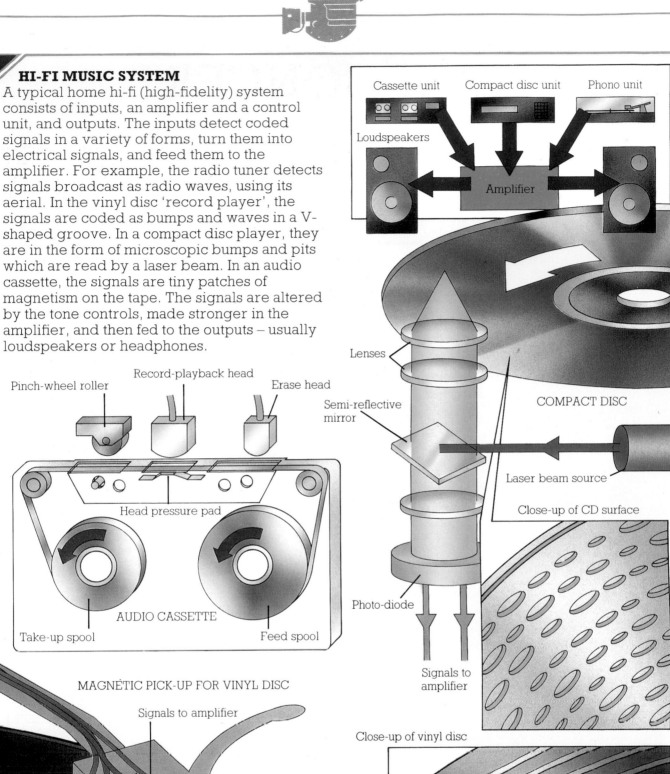

Cassette unit    Compact disc unit    Phono unit
Loudspeakers
Amplifier

Lenses
Semi-reflective mirror

COMPACT DISC

Laser beam source

Close-up of CD surface

Photo-diode

Signals to amplifier

Pinch-wheel roller    Record-playback head    Erase head

Head pressure pad

AUDIO CASSETTE

Take-up spool    Feed spool

MAGNETIC PICK-UP FOR VINYL DISC

Signals to amplifier

Close-up of vinyl disc

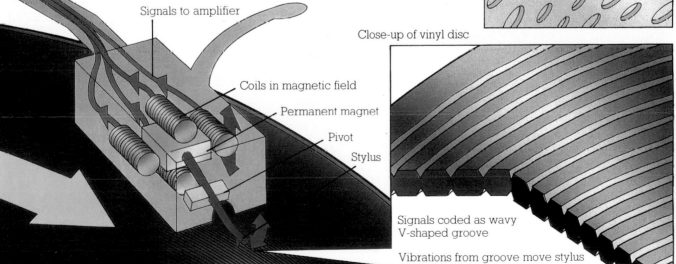

Coils in magnetic field
Permanent magnet
Pivot
Stylus

Signals coded as wavy V-shaped groove

Vibrations from groove move stylus

# ROCK CONCERT

**LOUDSPEAKER** — 3

**ELECTRIC GUITAR** — 10

**LASER BEAM** — 4

**DRUM** — 9

**VIOLIN** — 7

**FLUTE** — 5

**TRUMPET** — 6

**HOLOGRAM** — 1

**MICROPHONE** — 2

**SAXOPHONE** — 8

## 1 HOLOGRAM

A hologram exists on a flat sheet, like an ordinary photograph. But, when viewed in certain conditions, the image is three-dimensional and has 'depth'. A hologram is recorded on special holography photographic film. One part of a laser beam, the object beam, shines on the object to be photographed and is reflected by the object onto the plate. The other part, the reference beam, is split off by a partially-reflecting mirror and shines directly onto the plate. The plate records the pattern made by the two beams interfering with each other. When the hologram is illuminated by a reference laser beam, the exact pattern of the object beam is recreated.

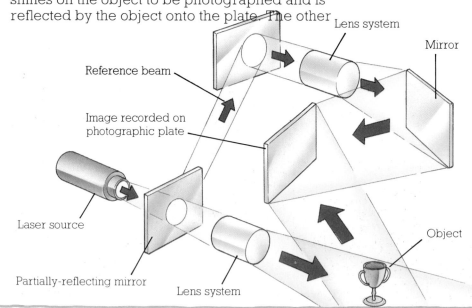

Reference beam

Image recorded on photographic plate

Laser source

Partially-reflecting mirror

Lens system

Lens system

Mirror

Object

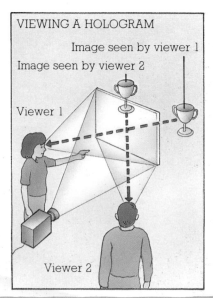

VIEWING A HOLOGRAM

Image seen by viewer 1

Image seen by viewer 2

Viewer 1

Viewer 2

## 2 MICROPHONE

A moving-coil microphone uses the principle of *inductance*. Sound waves vibrate the diaphragm, which is linked to a small coil of wire. As the coil moves in a magnetic field, small amounts of electricity are induced in its wiring, and these are fed to the amplifier.

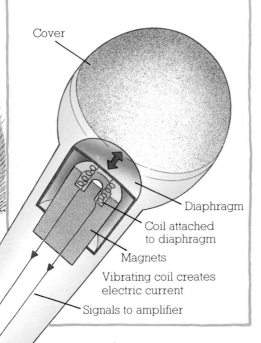

Cover

Diaphragm

Coil attached to diaphragm

Magnets

Vibrating coil creates electric current

Signals to amplifier

## 3 LOUDSPEAKER

The speaker works in the opposite way to the microphone (*left*). Varying amounts of electricity from the amplifier travel through the coil attached to the loudspeaker cone. This coil is in the field of a strong permanent magnet, and so it vibrates as the electrical signals change. The vibrations move the cone, which vibrates the air and so creates sound waves.

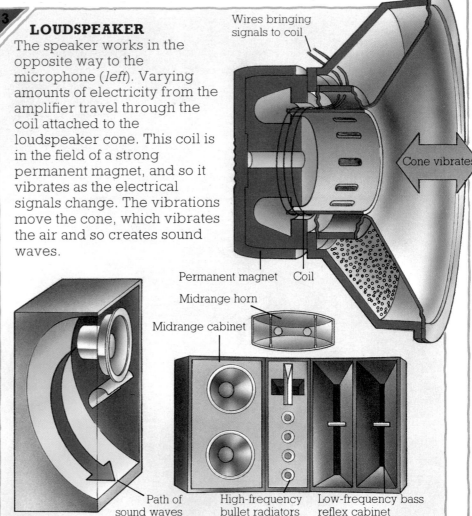

Wires bringing signals to coil

Cone vibrates

Permanent magnet

Coil

Midrange horn

Midrange cabinet

Path of sound waves

High-frequency bullet radiators

Low-frequency bass reflex cabinet

## 4 LASER BEAM

High-voltage electricity passes through a glass tube containing a mixture of gases, such as helium and neon. The electricity stimulates the gas atoms to give off tiny 'packets' of light, called photons. These stimulate other atoms to emit photons. Mirrors reflect most of the light back into the gas for further amplification. A partially silvered mirror at one end allows out a narrow, parallel beam of intensely bright, pure, single-colour light – the laser beam. 'Laser' stands for Light Amplification by Stimulated Emission of Radiation.

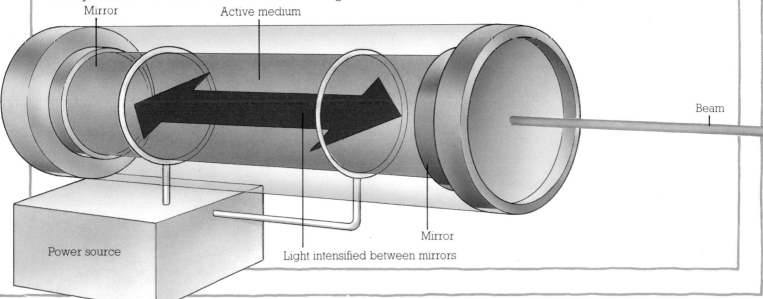

Mirror

Active medium

Beam

Mirror

Light intensified between mirrors

Power source

## 5 FLUTE

A certain volume and shape of air vibrates or 'resonates' at its natural frequency, to produce a musical note. You can demonstrate this by blowing across the top of an empty bottle. The air inside resonates to give a humming note. Half-fill the bottle with water and blow again – less air means a higher note. A flute works in a similar way. The player blows across the hole in the mouthpiece. The keys open holes in the flute body, which change the size and shape of air vibrated, thereby altering the note produced.

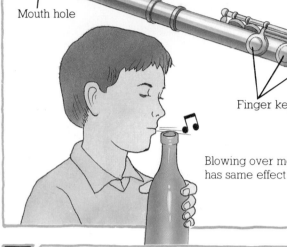

Mouthpiece

Mouth hole

Finger keys

Standard 13-hole cylindrical body

Foot joint

Blowing over mouth of empty bottle has same effect

## 6 TRUMPET

Like the flute, the trumpet relies on the resonating quality of a volume of air. The player uses his or her lips to produce a 'buzzing' in the mouthpiece, which vibrates the column of air inside the instrument. The brass bore is really one long tube 130 centimetres in length, curved and folded into a more compact size and shape. Each key opens a valve that alters the distance the air travels, so changing the note slightly.

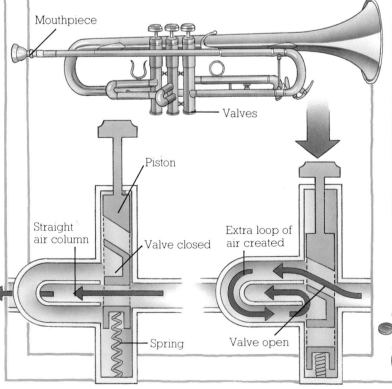

Mouthpiece

Valves

Piston

Straight air column

Valve closed

Extra loop of air created

Spring

Valve open

## 7 VIOLIN

As the violinist draws the bow across the strings, these vibrate and set in motion vibrations in the surrounding air. In turn, these vibrations make the violin's belly soundboard vibrate, which amplifies the note. The very best violins such as those made by Stradivarius are made from specially selected woods and assembled with supreme craftsmanship.

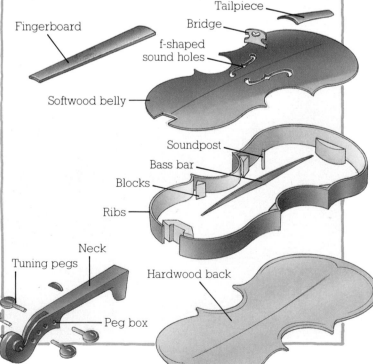

Tailpiece

Bridge

f-shaped sound holes

Fingerboard

Softwood belly

Soundpost

Bass bar

Blocks

Ribs

Neck

Tuning pegs

Hardwood back

Peg box

## 8 SAXOPHONE

This instrument was invented by Adolphe Sax in the 1840s. It has a reed in the mouthpiece, which vibrates as air is blown over it. The vibrations create sound waves that resonate the body and bell. As in a flute or oboe, keys change the amount of air which vibrates, and so alter the notes.

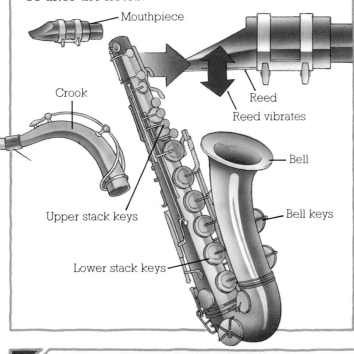

Mouthpiece

Crook

Reed

Reed vibrates

Bell

Upper stack keys

Bell keys

Lower stack keys

## 9 DRUM

The drum is one of the simplest musical instruments. Yet a good drummer can obtain varied sounds by altering the tension (tightness) of the drum head, hitting it in different places, and using various strikers such as ordinary drum sticks, wire or bristle brushes, or felt-padded hammer-head sticks.

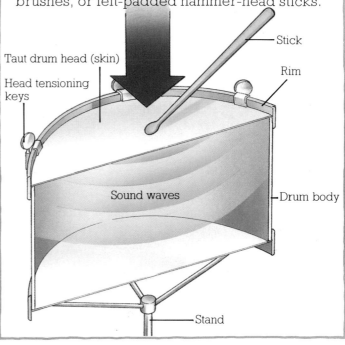

Taut drum head (skin)

Head tensioning keys

Stick

Rim

Sound waves

Drum body

Stand

## 10 ELECTRIC GUITAR

A guitar is a stringed instrument that works in the same basic way as a violin. The string vibrates to give a note according to its length. As the fingers press just behind the frets, shortening the vibrating part of the string, the note becomes higher. In an acoustic guitar, the strings produce sound waves which are amplified by the resonating guitar body.

In an electric guitar, the metal strings vibrate in the magnetic field of the pick-ups. The vibrations alter the amounts of electricity in the wire coils of the pick-ups, creating electrical signals that travel along the lead to the amplifier.

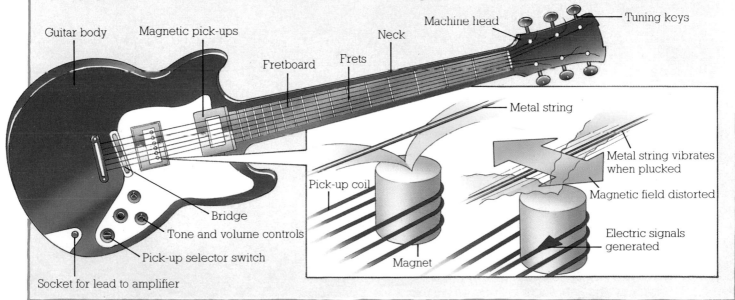

Guitar body

Magnetic pick-ups

Neck

Machine head

Tuning keys

Fretboard

Frets

Metal string

Metal string vibrates when plucked

Magnetic field distorted

Pick-up coil

Bridge

Tone and volume controls

Pick-up selector switch

Electric signals generated

Socket for lead to amplifier

Magnet

# THE FILM SET

**CINE CAMERA** ▼2

**CINERAMA** ▼1

**SPECIAL EFFECTS** ▼5

**CINE PROJECTOR** ▼7

**LIGHTING** ▼6

▲3 **CINE FILM**

▲4 **EDITING**

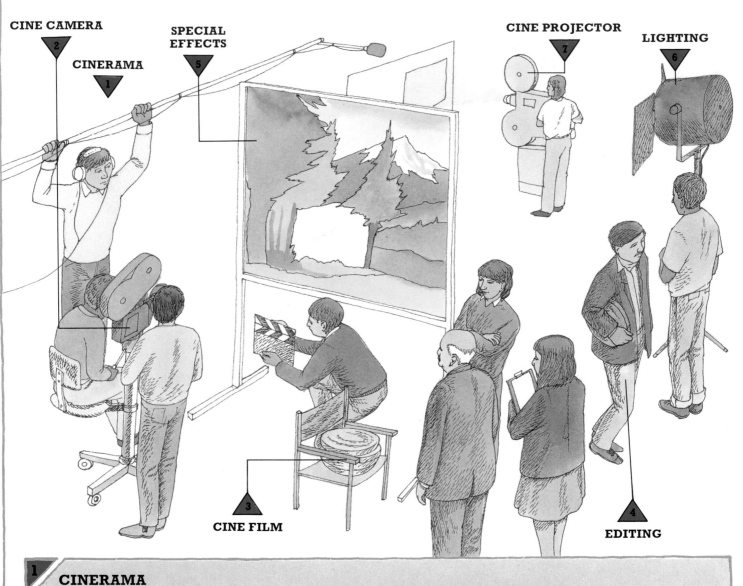

**1** **CINERAMA**

A single cine projector shining onto a large, flat screen cannot show clearly the objects near the edge of the screen. Neither can viewers sitting to one side see the other side of the screen clearly. But with the curved Cinerama screen, three co-ordinated cameras show different parts of the scene at exactly the same time and the picture 'wraps around' the viewer.

Screen

Multiple loudspeakers for 'Surroundsound'

Three synchronized 35mm projectors

Object | Curved screen

Viewer

## 2 CINE CAMERA

Inside a cine camera, a revolving mirror shutter directs the light along two alternative paths, more than 20 times each second. One path is into the viewfinder (*below left*). The other is onto the film, through the film gate (*below right*). Each exposure records the scene as a separate picture on the roll of film, as the film is pulled past the film gate by the motor and sprocket drive (*below*).

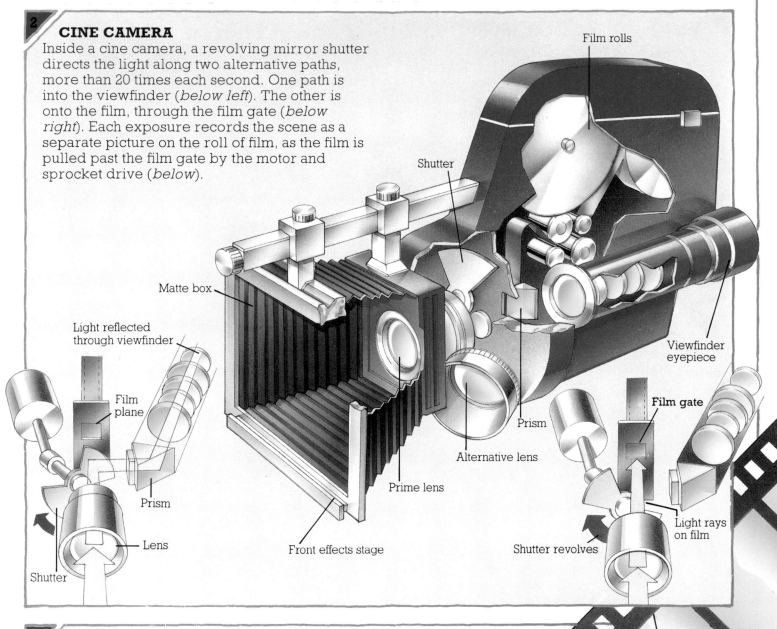

Film rolls

Shutter

Matte box

Light reflected through viewfinder

Film plane

Prism

Lens

Shutter

Viewfinder eyepiece

Prism

Alternative lens

Prime lens

Front effects stage

**Film gate**

Light rays on film

Shutter revolves

## 3 CINE FILM

Cinematic (movie) film is wound onto a reel in a lightproof cartridge or magazine. This clips onto the camera (*above*) so that the film travels past the film gate. The teeth on the drive sprockets fit into the rows of holes along each side of the film, and the drive motor is linked to the revolving mirror shutter. The film has three light-sensitive layers, and each layer reacts to light of a certain colour.

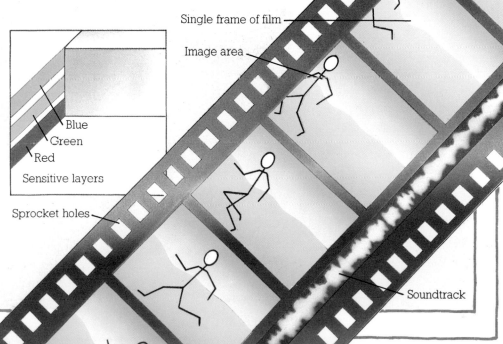

Single frame of film

Image area

Blue
Green
Red

Sensitive layers

Sprocket holes

Soundtrack

## 4 EDITING

Few movies are recorded from start to finish on one film roll, in one camera. When editing, the film-maker chooses which individual pictures, or frames, of film should follow each other. The frames are cut up and joined together ('spliced') into the new sequence using glue.

Unwanted frame identified

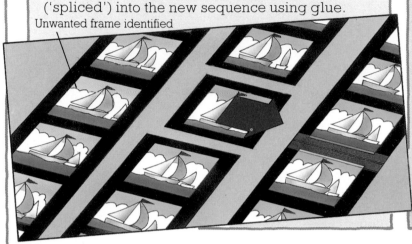

## 5 SPECIAL EFFECTS

Film-makers use many kinds of special effects to create scenes that do not exist in real life. One method is to film people through a hole in a fake 'background' of painted scenery, called a matte. The people might look as though they are in a huge restaurant, whereas in fact they are at one table, and the rest of the view is painted onto the matte. Another method is to film a person against a blue background, using either camera filters or film that cannot record the blue colour. Another camera records a different background. The two views are blended together before being shown to the viewer. This technique is often used for television weather reports, to show the weather map on one camera combined with the weather presenter on another.

## 6 LIGHTING

There are many different kinds of light sources, such as the fluorescent tube (page 17) and the laser (page 135).

The light bulb is also called the incandescent lamp. It is made of a thin coil of special resistance wire containing the metal tungsten, which can withstand very high temperatures. The wire glows brightly, at a temperature of more than 2500°C, when electricity flows along it. A special gas mixture inside the glass, or a vacuum of no gas at all, prevents the wire from burning out too quickly. Very powerful incandescent lamps are used to light film sets, so that the cameras can pick up all the details of the actors, objects and scenery. These lamps are rated at many thousands of watts of electricity, compared to the typical home light bulb of about 60, 100 or 150 watts.

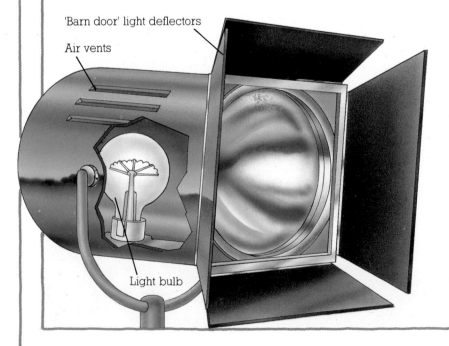

'Barn door' light deflectors

Air vents

Light bulb

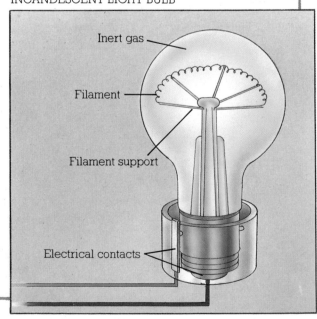

INCANDESCENT LIGHT BULB

Inert gas

Filament

Filament support

Electrical contacts

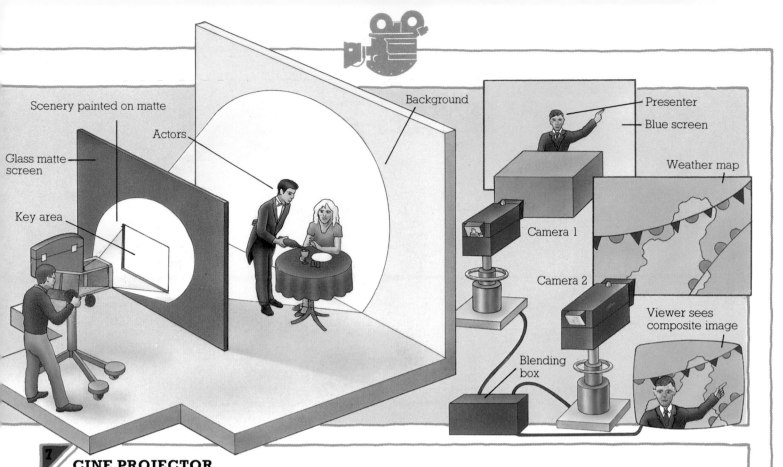

Scenery painted on matte

Actors

Background

Presenter

Blue screen

Glass matte screen

Key area

Weather map

Camera 1

Camera 2

Blending box

Viewer sees composite image

## CINE PROJECTOR

The source of light in a typical cine projector is the continuous and intensely bright 'spark' of a carbon arc lamp. The spark leaps between two carbon rods. As the carbon burns away, electrical motor drives move the rods along slowly to replace it. Heat shields protect the film from the high-temperature arc. The light shines through the film in the film guide, then through a system of lenses and across the cinema onto the screen. The soundtrack is picked up either by an optical reader, if it was recorded in the form of light patterns, or by a magnetic pick-up if it was recorded on magnetic tape.

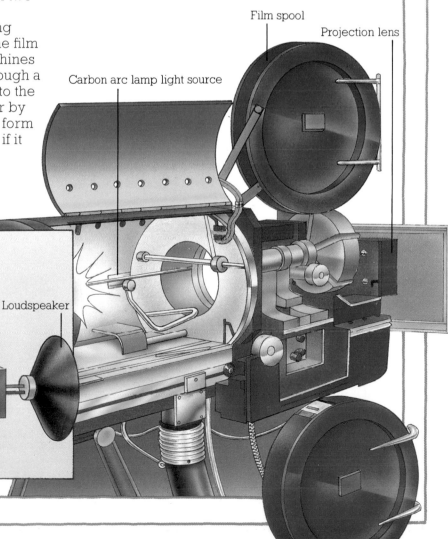

Film spool

Projection lens

Carbon arc lamp light source

Sprockets

Sound drum

Loudspeaker

Amplifier

# THEME PARK

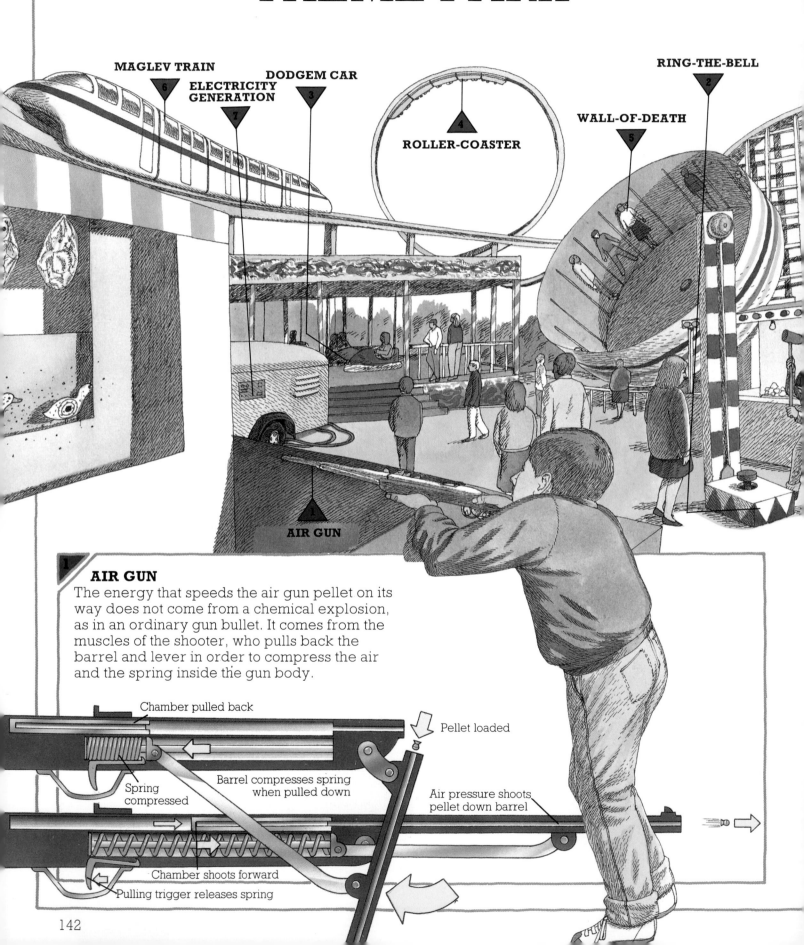

**MAGLEV TRAIN** 6

**ELECTRICITY GENERATION** 7

**DODGEM CAR** 3

**ROLLER-COASTER** 4

**RING-THE-BELL** 2

**WALL-OF-DEATH** 5

**AIR GUN** 1

## 1 AIR GUN

The energy that speeds the air gun pellet on its way does not come from a chemical explosion, as in an ordinary gun bullet. It comes from the muscles of the shooter, who pulls back the barrel and lever in order to compress the air and the spring inside the gun body.

Chamber pulled back

Pellet loaded

Spring compressed

Barrel compresses spring when pulled down

Air pressure shoots pellet down barrel

Chamber shoots forward

Pulling trigger releases spring

## RING-THE-BELL

Like the air gun (*opposite*), energy to work this device comes from the competitor's muscles. A simple lever combines with the physical principle that every action has a reaction (page 95). The hammer crashes down on one end of the lever, lifting the other end, which knocks the clapper upwards. Friction and the force of gravity between the clapper and the rail quickly slow the clapper, so that most hits do not ring the bell at the top.

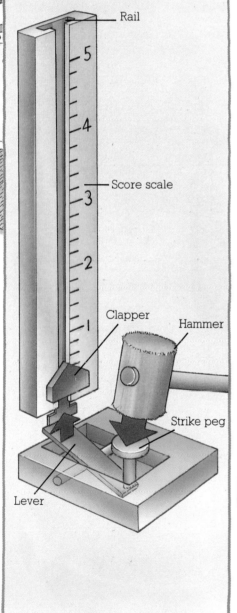

Rail

5
4
3
2
1

Score scale

Clapper

Hammer

Strike peg

Lever

## DODGEM CAR

The sliding contact, contact arm, car motor and metal front wheel form part of an electrical circuit, between the metal screen in the roof and the metal floor of the dodgem rink. People standing on the floor are too far away from the roof screen to be in danger of completing the circuit themselves – and being electrocuted. The motor is mounted on the front wheel and turns with it, to avoid the need for complex as in a car (page 87). As the dodgem car moves, the sliding contact rubs along the roof screen. Sparks fly between the contact and screen when there are small gaps.

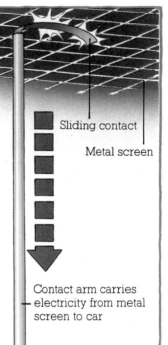

Sliding contact

Metal screen

Contact arm carries electricity from metal screen to car

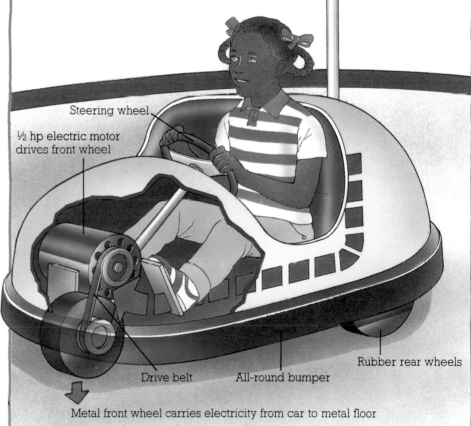

Steering wheel

½ hp electric motor drives front wheel

Drive belt

All-round bumper

Rubber rear wheels

Metal front wheel carries electricity from car to metal floor

## ROLLER-COASTER

The laws of physics state that a moving object will continue in a straight line unless acted on by an outside force, to change its speed or direction. As the riders in a roller-coaster loop the loop, they are moving in a circle and are therefore changing direction from a straight line. The force causing this to happen is the *centripetal* force, which acts towards the centre of the circle, continually pushing the riders inwards. The reaction to centripetal force is felt when the riders are pressed into their seats.

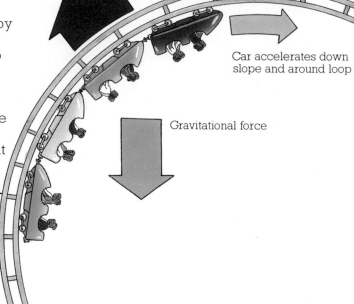

Reaction to centripetal force

Car accelerates down slope and around loop

Gravitational force

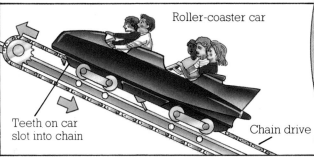

Roller-coaster car

Teeth on car slot into chain

Chain drive

## WALL-OF-DEATH

The 'Wall-of-Death' works in a similar way to the roller-coaster. The motion in this case is in a horizontal circle rather than a vertical one. The centripetal force acts to make the riders go round in a circle, rather than along in a straight line. As a reaction to this force, they press against the revolving drum wall, and stay there – even when the floor is lowered from under their feet! The old term of '*centrifugal* force' is no longer used to explain these types of movements.

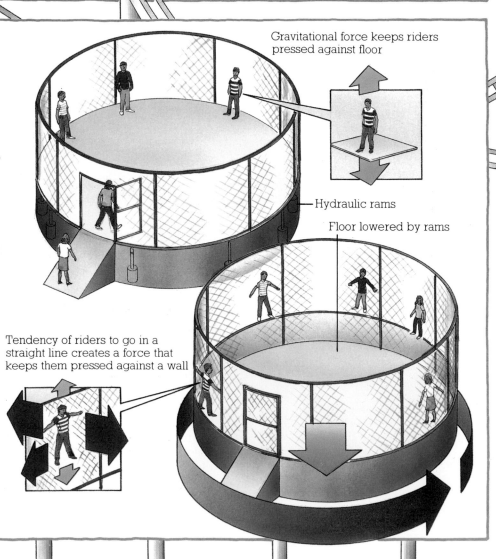

Gravitational force keeps riders pressed against floor

Hydraulic rams

Floor lowered by rams

Tendency of riders to go in a straight line creates a force that keeps them pressed against a wall

## MAGLEV TRAIN

A magnet has two poles, North and South. Like poles repel (push apart). Unlike poles attract (pull together). The Maglev train uses this principle. Electromagnets in the train base and the single rail create very powerful magnetic fields. Their poles are arranged so that the train and rail repel each other. The upper repelling force lifts, or levitates, the train so it runs in 'mid-air'. The lower repelling force keeps the train steady as it travels along.

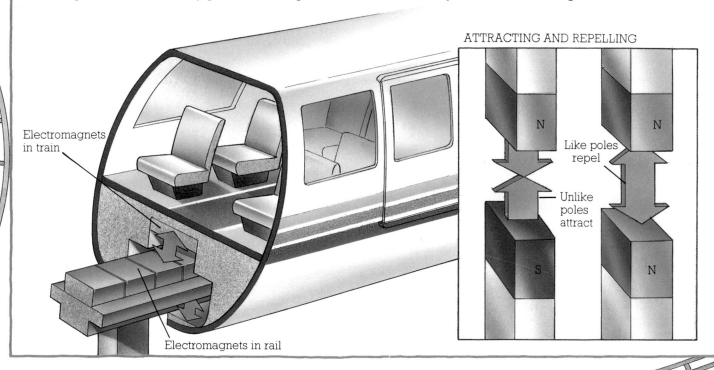

Electromagnets in train

Electromagnets in rail

ATTRACTING AND REPELLING

Like poles repel

Unlike poles attract

## ELECTRICITY GENERATION

When a wire moves in a magnetic field, an electric current is induced (page 139) in the wire. In the direct-current (DC) generator, wire coils spin between two strong permanent magnets. The electricity induced in the coils reverses its direction as each part of the coil moves from the North to South poles of the magnets, but gaps in the *commutator* mean that a steady direct current is produced. In the alternating-current (AC) generator, each end of the wire coil has a separate brush, so that the current reverses – alternates – with each turn.

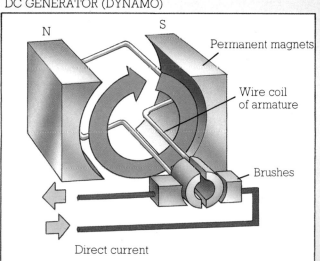

DC GENERATOR (DYNAMO)

N    S

Permanent magnets

Wire coil of armature

Brushes

Direct current

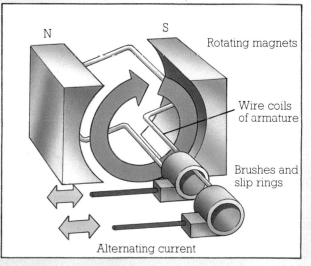

AC GENERATOR (ALTERNATOR)

N    S

Rotating magnets

Wire coils of armature

Brushes and slip rings

Alternating current

# GLOSSARY

*Note: The following descriptions aim to explain, in a simple way, the terms as they are used in this book. Some of the terms have more restricted scientific meanings or wider everyday usages. Consult a good dictionary for these.*

**Aerofoil** The specially curved shape of an aircraft wing, when viewed from the side, that produces lift as air flows past it.

**Amp (ampere)** A unit of measurement for electrical current – the rate of flow of electricity (see also Volt, Watt).

**Amplifier** An electronic device that makes an electrical signal more powerful or stronger.

**Anchor** A heavy weight, sometimes designed to stick in soil or mud, which stops an object such as a ship from drifting away.

**Annealing** involves heating and then cooling a substance under closely-controlled conditions, to make it strong and tough without being too brittle.

**Annealing lehr** A tunnel-shaped oven for annealing glass.

**Anode** In an electrical circuit, the positive electrode (see also Cathode and Electrode).

**Arc** In electricity, when the electricity 'leaps' between a small gap in the circuit, usually producing light, noise and heat as a spark.

**Archimedes screw** A long ramp wrapped around a central shaft, like a corkscrew. As it turns it pushes material along its length.

**Atom** The smallest particle of a substance that still has the chemical properties of that substance (see also Electron, Neutron, Proton).

**Balance** When an object is supported at, or below its centre of gravity, so that gravity does not pull more on one side and tip it over.

**Barometer** An instrument for measuring air pressure, used in meteorology and in some types of altimeter ('height-meter') in aircraft.

*Battery*

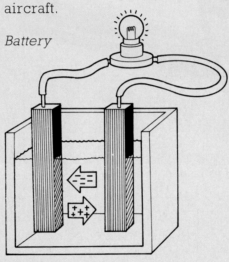

**Battery** The common name for an electrical cell, which makes electricity by chemical reactions. A true 'battery' is really a number of cells joined together.

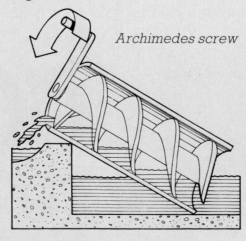

*Archimedes screw*

**Bevel gears** Gear wheels whose teeth are sloping or at an angle, rather than at right angles to the wheel's flat surface.

**Bimetallic strip** Two pieces of metal joined so that they bend with changes in temperature, because the two metals expand at different rates.

**Bulb** A light bulb is a hollow glass globe containing a wire filament, that glows brightly as electricity passes through it.

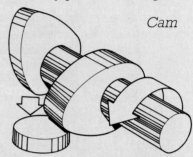

*Cam*

**Cam** A 'lump' on an axle or shaft. As it rotates, the cam presses on or moves another part of the machine.

**Camber** The 'slope' or 'banking' on an object. A cambered road surface allows the rain to drain away and gives better cornering on bends.

**Cantilever** Part of a structure, such as a bridge, that projects outwards from its support as an 'overhang', and so helps to support the structure.

**Cathode** In an electrical circuit, the negative electrode (see also Anode and Electrode).

**Centre of gravity** The point at which all an object's weight can be thought to be concentrated, so that it balances if supported below this point.

**Centrifugal force** A force which is often thought to act on an object going in a circle (see Centripetal force).

**Centripetal force** The force which acts to keep an object moving in a circle. Twirl a ball on a string and the 'pull' in the string represents the centripetal force.

**Chrominance** The part of a television signal that controls the relative brightness of the three colours: red, green and blue.

**Circuit** In electricity, a series of conductors joined into a loop, around which the electricity flows.

**Conductor** A substance that allows electricity to pass through it easily. Most metals are good conductors (see also Resistance).

**Cold-blooded** See Warm-blooded.

**Condenser** A device for condensing a substance, changing it from gas to liquid.

**Cracking** In an oil refinery, separating the crude oil into its many ingredients by heating and then condensing at different temperatures.

**Crank and crankshaft** A device for changing a rotary (turning) motion to an oscillating (to-and-fro) one, or vice versa. The shaft has one or more bars, called cranks, fixed to it at an angle. These are usually linked to other bars by pivots. As the shaft turns round, the ends of the bars travel backwards and forwards (see also Oscillation).

**Damping** To even out or 'cushion' bumps and vibrations.

**Diaphragm** A disc or sheet of flexible material which, for example, bends to operate a valve or suck in a fluid.

**Drill** A length of hard material (the drill bit) such as steel, with a sharpened end, turned by a

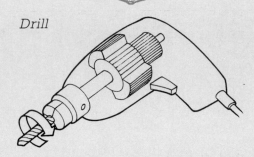

*Drill*

machine such as an electric motor. It gouges out a circular hole as it twists around.

**Electricity** A type of energy involving electrons or similar particles with an electrical charge. In an electrical circuit, electrons flow from the negative terminal of the battery to the positive one (see Electron).

**Electric motor** A machine that changes electrical energy into the energy of spinning motion.

**Electrode** In an electrical circuit, the part that either collects (anode) or emits (cathode) the moving electrons which form the electric current.

**Electrolysis** Producing a chemical reaction using electricity. Usually it refers to splitting a substance into its constituent parts by dissolving it and then passing electricity through the solution.

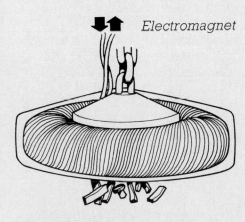

*Electromagnet*

**Electromagnet** A magnet which is magnetized only when electricity passes through the wire coil around it.

**Electron** One type of particle

that makes up atoms. The electron has a negative charge and orbits the central part of the atom, the nucleus (see also Atom, Neutron, Proton).

**Electrostatic** When electrical charges are at rest, on or in an object, rather than flowing through a wire as an electric current.

**Element (heater)** Special wire that resists the flow of electricity, becoming hot in the process.

**Escapement** In a clock, the mechanism that allows the stored energy in the spring to 'escape' in small, regular amounts.

**Feedback** Information coming back into a system about the way it is changing. A thermostat, that shuts down the central heating system when the temperature rises above a certain level, is one example (see Thermostat).

**Fertilization** In reproduction, when a male cell (sperm) joins with a female cell (egg), ready to grow into a new individual.

**Filter** A fine net, meshwork or similar that removes solid impurities from a fluid, or separates larger particles from smaller ones.

**Foundations** The secure and stable base to a structure, such as a skyscraper or bridge, that stops it sinking into the earth or toppling over.

**Four stroke** An internal combustion engine driven by pistons that have a complete power cycle every four strokes: down, up, down, up.

**Friction** When two surfaces 'rub' together as they move past each other. It often produces heat, and can be minimized by lubricating oil.

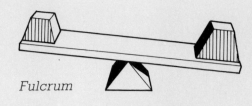

*Fulcrum*

**Fulcrum** The pivot point of a lever.

**Furnace** A very hot chamber or oven.

**Gear** A wheel with V-shaped teeth, cogs or notches around its edge, which meshes with a similar wheel or interlocks with the row of holes in a chain.

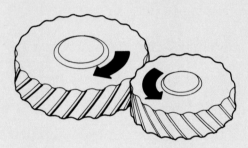

*Two interlocking gear wheels*

**Generator** A machine that produces electricity from another form of energy, such as moving water (hydroelectricity) or the chemical energy in a fuel like petrol.

**Gene** A set of instructions, in the form of a chemical code (DNA), which controls the building or working of part of the body.

**Germination** When a seed has the right conditions of moisture, light, temperature and so on, and starts to grow.

**Gravity** The force of attraction between objects. Usually used for the attraction of the Earth on objects near its surface, pulling them down towards its centre.

**Gyroscope** A spinning wheel with a heavy rim, on a set of pivots, which tends to resist change in position (see Inertia).

**Heat-exchanger** A device for transferring heat from one substance to another, for example, when hot exhaust gases pre-warm the cool air coming into a combustion engine.

**Hormone** A type of 'chemical messenger' in the body, made by a gland, which travels around in the blood and controls the way certain organs work.

**Hydraulics** In a hydraulic machine, fluid – usually special hydraulic oil – is used to transmit pressure along pipes from one part to another.

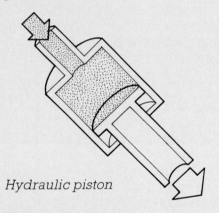

*Hydraulic piston*

**Hydroelectricity** Electricity generated from the energy of moving water.

**Hydrophone** A type of microphone designed to pick up sounds under water.

**Inductance** When a magnetic field and nearby conducting wire move relative to each other, creating an electric current in the wire.

**Inertia** The tendency of objects to stay still or keep moving as they are, resisting any change in position or motion.

**Internal combustion engine** A machine that changes the chemical energy in fuel, such as petrol, into the energy of a turning shaft, by small 'explosions' (combustions) in an enclosed space, the cylinder.

**Insect** An animal with six legs, a three-part body, and a hard outer casing called an exoskeleton.

**Jack** A lifting machine that raises a heavy load by small amounts, using a smaller effort moving a much greater total distance.

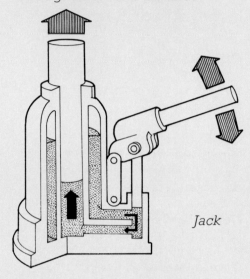

*Jack*

**Jet** A fast-moving stream of fluid, such as water or air. A jet engine produces a fast-moving stream of hot gases from its exhaust.

**Key** A specially-shaped object, usually metal, that fits into and opens a lock.

*Key and lock*

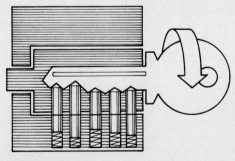

**Laser** A powerful pure-colour beam of light produced from a gas or crystal, by the process of **L**ight **A**mplification by the **S**timulated **E**mission of **R**adiation.

**Lens** A specially shaped piece of glass, usually with curved surfaces, that brings light rays together (convergence) or spreads them apart (divergence).

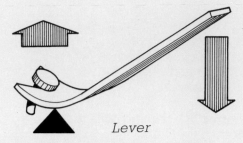

*Lever*

**Lever** In its simplest form, a rigid bar that pivots on its fulcrum or 'hinge'. Press down on one side, and the other side moves up.

**Light** A form of energy, as electromagnetic waves, that we can see with our eyes.

**Luminance** The part of a television signal which controls the overall brightness of the image.

**Magnet** A piece of material, usually iron-based metal, that has a magnetic field around it and can attract or repel other magnets (see also Electromagnet).

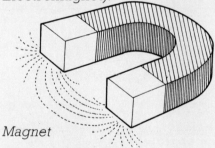

*Magnet*

**Magnetic field** Lines of magnetic force around a magnet, that tend to attract or repel other magnets and attract magnetic objects (see also Inductance).

**Matte** A frame or border used to blank out part of a scene or show painted scenery, when making films or TV programmes.

**Nerve** A 'thread' of living tissue inside an animal, that carries electrical nerve signals in the way that a wire conducts electricity.

**Neutron** One type of particle

that makes up atoms. The neutron has no charge and is in the central part of the atom, the nucleus (see also Atom, Electron, Neutron).

**Niche** In ecology, the 'position' of a living thing in the natural world, including its requirements for food, light, warmth and shelter.

**Nut** In engineering, a flat-sided object with a helical groove in a hole in its centre, that is twisted onto a bolt.

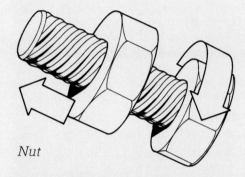

*Nut*

**Oscillation** Moving to-and-fro or backwards-and-forwards.

**Otoscope** A light-and-lens device used by a doctor to examine the inside of the ear.

**Oxidation** Simply, when a substance combines chemically with oxygen (see also Reduction). The full scientific definition involves loss of electrons.

**Peristalsis** Wave-like muscular squeezing of a tube inside an animal, such as the gut, which pushes along the contents.

**Pig iron** Fairly impure iron straight from the furnace, which still contains relatively large amounts of carbon and other impurities.

**Pinion** A small gearwheel that meshes with a larger one (see also Rack).

**Piston** A (usually) cylindrical object that moves up and down

inside a hollow cylinder, as in a car engine.

*Piston*

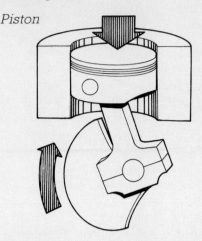

**Plough** A curved blade pulled through the soil, that churns it up and turns it over.

**Pollen** Tiny grains containing male cells, made by the male parts of a flower, which fertilize the female parts to form seeds (see Fertilization).

**Polarization** When the up-and-down motions of waves all happen in the same direction. Without polarization, the ups and downs occur at any angle (sideways, diagonally and so on).

**Pressure** The force acting on a certain area. The same total force pressing on a surface of 10 square metres, would have 10 times the pressure if it pressed on one square metre.

**Primary colours** A set of three colours from which all other colours of the spectrum can be obtained, by mixing. For light rays they are usually red, green and blue. For printing inks they are yellow, magenta and cyan.

**Prism** A piece of transparent material, usually glass or clear plastic, that changes the direction of light rays by reflection or refraction. Some prisms are used to separate white light into the different colours of the spectrum.

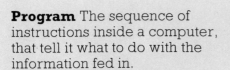

**Program** The sequence of instructions inside a computer, that tell it what to do with the information fed in.

**Propeller** Angled blades on a central shaft, that 'screw' through a gas or liquid and propel themselves along.

**Proton** One type of particle that makes up atoms. The proton has a positive charge and is in the central part of the atom, the nucleus (see also Atom, Electron, Neutron).

**Quartz crystal** A crystal made of quartz (silicon dioxide), which vibrates at a certain frequency when electricity passes through it. The vibrations can be used to control an electronic time-keeping circuit.

**Radar RA**dio **D**etection **A**nd **R**anging. Navigation or detecting objects using radio waves and/or their reflections (see also Sonar).

**Rack and pinion** The rack is a row of teeth on a bar, that mesh with the teeth on a pinion (small gear wheel). As the pinion turns, the bar slides along.

**Ratchet** A point on a bar that presses against sloped teeth on a wheel. The wheel can turn one way, when the 'ramp' on each tooth lifts the point, but the point jams against the teeth and stops the wheel turning the other way.

**Receiver** A device that detects waves or signals, such as a radio receiver that picks up radio waves.

**Rectifier** A device that allows electricity to pass in one direction only. It converts alternating current to direct current.

**Reduction** Simply, when an oxygen-containing substance loses its oxygen (see also Oxidation). The full scientific definition involves gaining electrons.

**Reflection** When rays 'bounce off' an object, as when light rays reflect from a mirror or sound waves bounce off a wall to give an echo.

**Reflex** An automatic response by the body, which happens before the brain realizes, such as pulling your finger away from a hot object.

**Refraction** When rays of light bend at the place where they go from one substance into another, such as from air into the glass of a lens.

**Resistance** When a material resists the flow of electricity. Electrical insulators such as plastics have very high resistance (see also Conductor).

**Resonance** When an object vibrates at its own natural frequency, as when a wineglass vibrates and eventually shatters from the sound waves of a certain musical note.

**Robot** A machine that can carry out a fairly complex task, usually in the manner of a person, such as spraying a car body with paint. Modern robots are usually computer-controlled.

**Satellite** An object that goes around (orbits) another, usually larger, object. The Moon is a natural satellite of the Earth. Hundreds of artificial satellites orbit the Earth.

**Siphon** When a continuous stream of fluid flows around an upside-down U tube from a higher to a lower level. Fluid in the down tube 'pulls' more fluid up and around the U bend.

**Skeleton** The hard, stiff 'framework' of an animal or structure. In humans, it is formed of bones. In an insect it consists of the hard outer shell or exoskeleton.

**Sonar SO**und and **NA**vigation **R**anging. Navigating or detecting objects using sound waves and/or their reflections (see also Radar).

**Sound waves** Patterns of vibrating molecules which travel through the air, and which we hear as sounds.

**Spindle** A thin central axle or shaft in a wheel, bobbin, etc.

**Spring** A coiled device, usually made of metal or special plastic. It can be squeezed or stretched, but always tries to return to its normal length.

*Spring*

**Suspension bridge** A bridge in which the deck hangs (is suspended from) main cables strung between supporting towers.

**Switch** A device that opens or closes a gap in an electrical circuit, to stop the electricity or allow it to flow.

**Theodolite** An instrument that measures angles, used in surveying.

**Thermostat** A 'switch' that turns on or off a heating or cooling system, to keep the temperature roughly constant.

**Thrust** A propelling force, as

when hot gases rush from the back of a jet engine and cause the engine to react by being pushed forwards.

**Torque** When a force acts in a circular direction, to turn or twist.

**Transformer** An electrical device that increases or decreases the voltage, with a corresponding fall or rise in the current (see Amp, Volt).

**Transmitter** A device that sends out waves or signals, such as a radio transmitter that emits radio waves.

**Turbine** Angled blades mounted on a central shaft, like a fan. Fluid (such as water or hot gases) moving past the blades makes them spin.

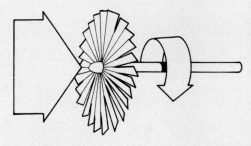

*Turbine*

**Turbofan** A type of jet engine that has a very large fan-like turbine at the front.

**Two-stroke** An internal combustion engine driven by pistons that have a complete power cycle every two strokes: up, down.

**Universal joint** Two U-shaped joints pivoted together so that one shaft can transmit its turning motion to another shaft which is at an angle to it.

**Valve** A device that lets a substance flow one way but not the other (non-return valve), or that controls the rate of flow of a substance, such as water or air.

**Volt** A unit of measurement for the potential difference of electricity, which can be thought of as its 'pushing strength' around the circuit (see also Amp, Watt).

**Warm-blooded** When an animal makes heat inside its body, by chemical reactions, to keep its temperature above that of the surroundings. Cold-blooded animals do not make their own heat and must absorb it from the surroundings.

**Warp** In weaving, the yarns that are stretched along the length of the loom, and between which the weft (filler) yarn passes on the shuttle.

**Watt** A unit of measurement of power. In an electrical system it is equal to Volts multiplied by Amps (see also Amp, Volt).

**Wedge** Two sloping ramps placed back-to-back. A wedge forces apart two surfaces when pushed between them.

**Weft** In weaving, the filler yarn carried by the shuttle, that threads its way between alternating sets of warp yarns.

**Weld** A joint made by melting two substances (usually metals), and allowing them to run together before they cool and solidify.

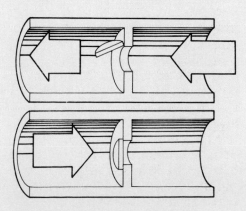

*Valve open (top) and Closed (above)*

**Wheel** A disc-shaped object mounted on a central shaft or axle. The wheel is either fixed to the axle or is free to spin on it.

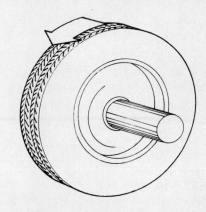

**X-ray** Rays that are part of the electromagnetic spectrum (which includes radio and light rays). They are given off when a suitable substance is bombarded with electrons (see Electron).

**Zip** A fastening device in which two rows of teeth-and-sockets are brought together so that they interlock.

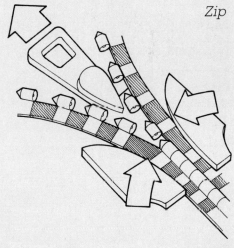

*Zip*

# INDEX